# Contents

# Illustrations

## Maps

# Foreword by Geoffrey Duke, OBE

HOW DO YOU write a foreword for a history book? The facts, the figures, they all speak for themselves and there is no way in which you or I can improve, embellish or change what has happened in the past. The fact that this book is about the history of the Isle of Man TT races, in which I must admit to having more than a passing interest, makes my task a little easier.

To me the Isle of Man Tourist Trophy races always have been and always will be the greatest challenge to any road-racing motorcyclist. The Mountain course demands more of the machine and the rider than probably any other racing circuit in the world. For this reason and this reason alone, I am proud to have competed in the TT races and can honestly say that winning on the Island meant ten times more to me than winning any other International Grand Prix.

In those good old, bad old days, success on the Island meant that as a rider you were established, you had passed your road-racing apprenticeship and, with a works' contract in your pocket, you could ride the world's Grand Prix circuits in confidence. If you could master and succeed on the 37¾-mile Mountain Circuit, then the rest came easy!

The Isle of Man is, of course, more than a road-racing circuit; it is a marvellous community which, for a number of weeks in the year, lives, eats and sleeps (if they're not too close to the circuit for early morning practice) motorcycling. For almost 70 years, the Manx people have made us motor-cyclists welcome, providing facilities which make the TT races one of the best-organised events in the Grand Prix calendar.

Many riders and motorcycle manufacturers have become household names because of their achievements on the Isle of Man and it would be so easy for me to start reminiscing about the past, but this would be wrong because this is what Charles Deane's book is about, the history of the TT. Personally, I look to the future of the TT races, the new riders, the new 'aces' who will make history and proudly say: 'I won a TT and it was the greatest race I've ever won!'.

In no way does success come easily in the Isle of Man races. Each and every event brings its own share of joy and sorrow, happiness and despair, failure and triumph! Too many words have been spoken by so few people about the dangers of the TT circuit and, although I am greatly saddened by the loss of any life, we must all accept that speed sports of any kind are dangerous. Just living itself can be dangerous if you decide to go skin diving, pot holing, rock climbing, parachuting or take part in any other sport which makes a man be a man and feel that he has achieved something in life.

That is what motorcycling to me is all about, living, reaching for the almost unattainable and, when succeeding, enjoying the acclaim, the rewards and most of all the self-satisfaction. If people who have had considerable success in racing on the Island suddenly believe that the circuit has become too dangerous for them, then like me they should be honest with themselves, admit that any kind of racing is dangerous and give it up!

There will always be young men to take up the challenge of running faster, swimming further, flying higher and riding harder to break the records set in previous years. But then, that is what history is all about and in the following pages you will be able to read about the achievements of man, the development of the motorcycle and the challenge of the Mountain.

Geoff Duke

# CHAPTER ONE

# The way to Mona's Isle

FIVE MINUTES to go! The mournful echoes of the warning siren above the pits in Glencrutchery Road silences the murmuring crowds in the grandstand. The air becomes electric, full of nervous tension as riders, stomachs brimming full of violently flapping butterflies, fiddle with fuel taps, ignition switches or make last-minute adjustments to riding gear; anything which will relieve the mind-bending thoughts of the task ahead – fighting a motorcycle at speeds often in excess of 140 mph over the toughest road racing circuit in the world, the Isle of Man Tourist Trophy Mountain Course.

The minute boards displayed in front of the competitors build tension to fever pitch; four . . . three . . . two . . . the starter, stopwatches and flag in hand, mounts his rostrum. Mechanics, frantically making last-minute checks or sparking plug swops, are ushered away from their riders' machines by course marshals.

One minute to go . . . a pin could be heard dropping to the ground a hundred yards away as the first pair of riders shuffle with their motorcycles up to the start line. Thirty seconds to the start . . . riders are putting goggles down or securing visors; a quick check to see that the fuel is on, machine is in first gear, back on compression. Ten seconds to go . . . the starter's flag rises . . . both riders, clutch lever in, push hard against the restraining front brakes of their motorcycles.

The starter's flag drops, brakes release, silence for a brief second, then the patter of racing boots on the granite-chip road as both men attempt to heave their silent raceware to life. Pushing as though their very lives depend upon it, the riders release the clutches on their mounts and the engines spin, cough, then fire . . . fire into a 10,000 rpm ear-shattering crackle through open exhausts that causes the quietly feeding seagulls in Nobles Park to take to the air. The riders leap side-saddle on to their mounts and hurtle off towards Bray Hill. Within a matter of seconds they are tucked down behind the fairings in a 140-mph plunge down the hill past open-mouthed, awe-struck spectators.

Meanwhile, the second pair of riders has moved up to the start line to repeat the process. So it goes on until 100 or more competitors have roared off down Glencrutchery Road in the hope of winning a place in TT history, or at least a replica to prove they have competed in the greatest motorcycle road races in the world.

This is the scene as we see it today after nearly 70 years of TT history in which the names of Fowler, Collier, Davies, Dixon, Wood, Twemlow, Bennett, Tyrell-Smith, Guthrie, Simpson, Frith, Daniell, Duke, Doran, Anderson, Graham, Lomas, McIntyre, Ubbiali, Surtees, Hartle, Provini, Hocking, Hailwood, Read, Redman, Ivy, Deubel, Agostini and many more are carved with pride.

Yet the difference between today's high-speed heroes, Peter Williams, Mick Grant, Charlie Williams, Jack Findlay and so on, in their skin-tight racing leathers and 'space' helmets, is as chalk to cheese when compared with the curious-looking bunch of individuals that gathered with their motorcycles outside the schoolhouse at St John's on a wet, blustery day in May 1907. No racing leathers or safety helmets for them; just a heavy jersey, riding breeches, a pair of boots and a cloth cap turned back to front, held on by a pair of goggles.

Their 'racing' machines were little more than power-assisted pedal cycles, having no such refinements as multi-speed gearboxes or even adequate braking systems. Their scoreboard was literally the blackboard borrowed from the schoolhouse and, because the machines of the day were somewhat unreliable, the rider also had to be an efficient mechanic able to carry out his own running repairs on the circuit. Consequently, apart from carrying an adequate toolkit on the motorcycle, the competitors left the start line bedecked with tyres and tubes wrapped around their bodies to cope with the many punctures inflicted by the rutted, flint-strewn tracks which made up the old St John's Circuit.

But for all the hardships endured by the riders of those days, including the long slog up from Ballacraine to Kirkmichael, which was usually pedal-assisted for a good part of the way due to the slipping of the drive belt, they had one thing very much in common with the riders of today – a love for motorcycles leaning almost towards fanaticism.

It was this fanaticism which brought the pioneers of the TT to the Isle of Man. They were living in a society in England where public prejudice and persecution by the police led them to seek a place where they could test motorcycles and compete with friends and rivals from the infant motorcycle industry, which was beginning to find its feet in the industrialised nations of the western world.

A 20-mph speed limit imposed on all English roads in 1903 made it impossible for the British manufacturers to race-prove their products, so they turned to the Continent where a newly formed Fédération Internationale des Clubs was organising International Cup races. These competitions were open to any nation who wished to enter a team of three riders and machines, with the first event being staged near Paris.

Not unnaturally, it was a Frenchman who won the first of these races, mainly because the Continental manufacturers were at that time ahead of the British both in the design and reliability of their motorcycles.

The second International Cup race was held in France in 1905. This time the Austrian team won and, with the regulations specifying that the winning nation be the hosts for the following event, the international motorcycle race scene moved to Putzau in Austria in 1906. On home ground the Austrian Puch motorcycles proved victorious, but there was a huge outcry from other competing nations because it was claimed that the two leading Puch machines and riders had received outside assistance from the Puch factory during the race. Apparently, just to make sure their riders were in with every chance of winning, they had arranged that a sidecar outfit full of spares should be around the circuit at strategic points to help if needed.

'Can't be done . . . not cricket, old boy!', cried the British. 'We protest!' 'Mon Dieu . . . pas possible!', exclaimed the French. 'Nous protestons!' And after much recrimination, it turned out that the appeals were never heard, the International Cup races were discontinued and the poor old Fédération Internationale des Clubs was disbanded. This was a bitter blow for international motorcycle competition that was to be righted later with the formation of the Fédération Internationale Motocycliste (FIM).

Fortunately for motorcycling in England, there happened to be a tiny little speck of green sitting in the middle of the Irish Sea known as the Isle of Man. In spite of being part of the British Isles, it

had (and still has) its own Government, namely the House of Keys or Tynwald. The Governor at the time was a fairly astute chap by the name of Lord Raglan and, in 1904, seeing the impasse faced by the British motor industry at that particular time, due to the severity of the road traffic laws, he invited the Royal Automobile Club to stage trials for the Gordon Bennett Cup car races on the Isle of Man. Naturally enough, the RAC leapt at the idea and, to prove their good faith and, of course, on the grounds of safety, the House of Keys rushed a bill through their parliament making it possible to close public roads for the purpose of car racing. That was something which had been defeated without question when put to the British Parliament.

The RAC was able to use a circuit approximately 52 miles long which covered practically all of the roads negotiable by car on the Isle of Man and went from Douglas to Port Erin, Peel, Jurby, St Judes, Ramsey and from there over the mountain to Hillberry and back to Douglas.

Nowadays, the roads which make up the TT Mountain Circuit are among the best metalled roads in the world, giving superb adhesion through their granite-chip surface in wet or dry conditions. In those days, the roads were little more than cart tracks, with loose, dry and dusty surfaces or wet, slippery mud depending upon the weather. In fact, the course should be likened more to a special-stage rally than to a road-racing circuit.

Nevertheless, the Auto-Cycle Club, forerunner of the Auto-Cycle Union, which had decided to send a team to the 1905 International Cup race in France, also had the foresight to seek permission from the Isle of Man authorities to map a 'closed roads' circuit there. This was so they could hold eliminating trials for the 1905 International Cup race and in case they might become involved in playing host to the Continental teams, should our riders win the race.

In no more time than it took Mike Hailwood to get from the start to the bottom of Bray Hill, plans were being made to map out the proposed motorcycle 'race' circuit. The course began at Tynwald Green, St John's, and proceeded along the Peel Road (or track as it was then) to Ballacraine. There it joined today's TT circuit to turn left towards Laurel Bank and through Glen Helen. Then came the hard, pedal-pushing part past Sarah's Cottage and up Creg Willey's Hill and on to the Cronk-y-Voddy straight. The course continued along the present circuit past the 11th Milestone, Handley's Cottage, Barregarrow, Rhencullen and into Kirkmichael, where it turned left away from Ramsey to

head back along the coast road to Peel. There it
turned left once again on to the home straight for
St John's.

The course measured a very trying 15 miles, 1,430
yards. The pedal-assisted, single-speed motorcycles
of those days would never have completed the even
more difficult route 'over the Mountain' used by
the car racers.

Although the entries in 1905 were rather sparse,
the A-CC eliminating trial proved successful with
the winner being J. S. Campbell on a 6 hp Ariel-
JAP; second was Harry Collier, brother of the
famous Charles Collier, on a 6 hp Matchless-JAP,
and third was C. B. Franklin riding a 6 hp JAP. It
is interesting to note that, after his success on the
St John's course with his Matchless, the following
year it was Harry Collier who finished third to the
two Puch riders at Putzau in Austria in the International Cup race.

And here, as most authors would say, is where
the plot thickens, because, while Harry Collier was
returning from Austria by train with his brother,
Charles, they came into discussion with Freddie
Straight, the secretary of the A-CC, and the
England-based Frenchman Marquis de Mouzilly
St Mars.

Naturally enough the conversation centred
around the bust-up that had taken place in Austria
and the hopes for staging a similar event to the
International Cup races on the roads of England.
Obviously, following the refusal by the British
Parliament to allow closed roads for racing on the
mainland, all seemed lost. But the Marquis, being
more than faintly interested in motorcycle sport
and the development of the machines, promised to
provide a trophy for the race should ever a suitable
course be found.

The race had to be for touring motorcycles on
proper roads, not for super-special, one-off racing
machines on billiard-table smooth tracks. Only in
this way could the manufacturers develop their
roadster motorcycles for the public along the right
lines, unlike some of the monsters which were being
built at the time for out-and-out speed in a straight
line or in a speed bowl.

On arriving back in England, the idea which had
been discussed on the long train journey from
Austria between the Marquis, Freddie Straight and
the Collier brothers started to develop. Then, at an
A-CC dinner in January 1907, during an after-
dinner toast to motorcycling by journalist Etienne
Boileau, mention was once again made of the race
to beat all races for ordinary production touring
motorcycles.

It had to be a long-distance event; none of those
short track, high-speed races which were won by
motorcycles bearing no relation to those used on
the roads. Ordinary touring motorcycles should
compete against each other on roads used by
ordinary members of the public!

But where? Where in Britain was it possible for
ordinary roads to be used for racing?

It was obvious to all. Right under their very noses
was the answer to their problem – Manxland,
Mona's Isle, the Isle of Man; call it what you will
but this was the chosen land for all that was
eventually to prove great for the British motorcycle
industry.

Freddie Straight wasted no time in compiling the
regulations necessary for a race for motorcycles
similar to those sold to the public. It was quite easy
really; all he had to do was specify more or less
exactly what *was* being sold to the motorcycle
enthusiasts of the time. It could be a single- or twin-
cylinder machine (different race classes, of course),
with no capacity or weight limit, but a very strict
rationing of fuel which would allow a minimum of
75 miles-per-gallon for the twins and 90 miles-per-
gallon for the single-cylinder motorcycles. This in
itself ensured that giant racing engines would
automatically be out of the running.

It was also necessary to have efficient silencers
fitted to the motorcycles, plus an ordinary touring
saddle, mudguards and at least 2-inch tyres.
Naturally, with the rather fragile and temperamental machines of that era, pedal assistance was
still allowed under the regulations.

It was decided to hold the first of these new
'touring' machine races in May 1907 and, with the
approval of the helpful Manx Government, the
A-CC chose to use the existing St John's course,
which had proved so satisfactory in the previous
motorcycle trials held on the Island.

The next question was to set the number of laps
which competitors had to complete to finish the
race. If they were too few, the race wouldn't prove
the reliability or stamina of machines nor help in
finding their weaknesses. If they were too many,
then it was quite likely that neither the machines
nor riders would complete the race because, apart
from the mechanical failings of the bikes due to the
severity of the rough and bumpy course, the riders
themselves would suffer considerable physical
punishment because of the lack of suspension on
those pioneer machines.

Freddie Straight solved the problem by making
the race ten laps with each competitor making a
ten-minute compulsory rest stop after completing

11

five laps. This was a wise decision under the circumstances as it allowed for a quick little and often necessary bit of fettling to both man and machine.

As promised, the Marquis de Mouzilly St Mars duly presented a trophy for the race, similar in design to the Montagu Trophy used in the tourist car races. It was a magnificent silver figure of Mercury, the mythological messenger of the Roman gods, atop a winged wheel. This trophy, which is that nowadays presented to the winner of the Senior TT, was to be awarded to the winner of the single-cylinder class in the race, while a second award presented by Dr Hele-Shaw was to be made to the victor in the twin-cylinder category. There were also cash awards for the first three riders to finish, with £25 for the winner, £15 for second and £10 for third. Compared with the £1,000 received by present-day winners, this sum of money appears quite meagre, but, when you consider that for a little over twice that amount you could buy the machines they were riding in those days, in the competitors' eyes it was money well worth winning.

Finally came the choice of the title for the race. Should it be the Marquis de Mouzilly St Mars Trophy Race or the International Auto-Cycle Club Trophy Race? No, it was a race for touring motorcycles over ordinary public highways and therefore, like the RAC had decided for their car events, it would be called the Tourist Trophy Race!

And so it came to be. Because of the foresight of the Manx Government, a little bit of rule-bending by Puch in the International Cup races in Austria, a friendly chat on the train between a group of motorcycle enthusiasts and the downright stupidity of the British Government of the day, the Isle of Man Tourist Trophy races were born.

On May 28th 1907, outside the schoolhouse at St John's, 25 gallants prepared to push or pedal off in pairs, at one-minute intervals, on their bone-shaking motorcycles to prove to themselves and to the world that the motorcycle was here to stay. An amused if somewhat disinterested crowd gathered to watch these crazy motorcyclists chugging away

into the gloom of a dull, wet and dismal day, wondering if any would achieve the impossible claim of motorcycling 158 miles in an afternoon.

Not surprisingly, only ten machines actually attained their goal, but, as the physically shattered riders were almost literally lifted from their motorcycles at the end of this historic event, they were exalted by their achievement. Like winning a marathon at the Olympic Games, like landing on the moon for the first time, like swimming the English Channel, they wanted more.

They were full of the stories of their escapades around the circuit because, apart from mending punctures and repairing belt drives, which were the rule rather than the exception, they told of racing through a wall of flame which had enveloped one of the machines competing in the race. This was a particularly hair-raising tale brought in by the eventual twin-cylinder class winner 'Rem' Fowler.

The competitors' enthusiasm for the Tourist Trophy race was welcomed by the Manx Government who promised continued support for the event, having the sense to see it as a bright, new and very 'modern' additional holiday attraction on the Island. Meanwhile, the imaginative British motorcycle manufacturers, frustrated by the unimaginative 'go-slow' British Government, knew that at last they had found a haven where motorcycling would be accepted and they could now develop machines to beat the world!

The names Norton, Triumph and Matchless were among the winners of the first, historic Tourist Trophy race. Charlie Collier riding his single-cylinder Matchless won at an average speed of 38.22 mph. He took 4 hours, 8 minutes and 8 seconds and was over 11 minutes ahead of Jack Marshall on his Triumph single-cylinder motorcycle. Then came Rem Fowler on the twin-cylinder Norton, followed by Freddie Hulbert on his single-cylinder Triumph! These were great riders on incredible machines which were also to make their mark later on the world's motorcycle market through the lessons learned the hard way on the Isle of Man TT circuits.

# CHAPTER TWO

# The TT's winning ways

COCK-A-HOOP with the success of the first-ever Tourist Trophy race around the 'short' St John's course, Freddie Straight, secretary of the A-CC, returned to the mainland with his mind full of ideas on how to improve the following year's event. There was no doubt that the basic formula was right, but what if Jack Marshall had had pedals on his single-speed Triumph as had Charlie Collier on his Matchless? In all probability he might have won the race instead of Collier.

Judging by some of the narrow escapes of competitors in the event it would also be wise to have efficient marshals around the course to help keep people off the circuit and remove any animals found straying on the 'roads'. Fuel consumption, too, was a little on the generous side according to some members of the A-CC Tourist Trophy Committee and so, with some deliberation, the regulations for the 1908 event were published.

The question of marshals removing stray animals from the circuit and asking people to keep off what were, after all, their own public roads seemed a tricky one, but the visionary Manx Government quickly came up with a solution to the problem – the marshals would be made special constables!

The Governor himself, Lord Raglan, 'swore in' the marshals, giving them the power of a member of the police force on and around the circuit when the roads were closed for racing. So began one of the many TT traditions which still remain to this very day.

Minimum fuel consumption was raised to 100 mpg for the single-cylinder machines and 80 mpg for the twins. The bone of contention regarding pedal assistance was also resolved by eliminating pedals completely. The result proved the point in the TT race of that year, with Jack Marshall on his Triumph reversing the 1907 decision by beating Charlie Collier and his Matchless by almost four minutes, in spite of having to stop to mend a puncture and change an exhaust valve!

The race distance of 158 miles was completed in 3 hours 54 minutes and 50 seconds at an average speed of 40.49 mph, the first time the 40-mph

barrier had been broken! Third rider to finish in the single-cylinder class was, believe it or not, a captain in the Royal Navy, Sir R. K. Arbuthnot, who had taken leave especially to compete in the TT with his Triumph.

In spite of the superiority in cubic capacity of the twin-cylinder motorcycles over the single-cylinder machines, they were unable to surpass the achievements of the all-conquering Matchless and Triumph motorcycles in the first two Tourist Trophy events. But the writing was on the wall; during the brief decade in which motorcycles had appeared on the roads, tremendous strides were being made in their development.

Initially, the twins were considered to be unreliable and much less efficient than the singles and that, of course, did prove to be the case in the first two races. However, with further alterations to the regulations for the 1909 TT, which limited the singles to 500 cc and the twins to 750 cc, together with the lifting of all fuel restrictions, the pendulum swung in the favour of the rapidly improving twin-cylinder motorcycles; particularly as they were now to compete in one race for the one premier award.

The Collier brothers were among the first to realise the advantages to be gained from racing the twin-cylinder bikes. Therefore, abandoning their allegiance to their trusty single-cylinder Matchless, which had proved so successful in the first two events, they chugged their way into TT history at an incredible 49 mph taking 3 hours, 13 minutes, and 37 seconds to complete the 158-mile course.

This time it was Harry Collier who was to take the honours by beating the American V-twin Indian, ridden by G. L. Evans, across the line by just under four minutes. Third was the first of the single-cylinder machines, a Triumph ridden by W. F. Newsome.

As a point of interest, it was around this period that the genius Alfred Scott was developing his two-stroke motorcycle. In fact, three of the machines had been entered for the 1909 Tourist Trophy event with only one, ridden by Eric Myers, actually starting the race. I mention it because at that time

13

the A-CC considered that two-strokes had an unfair advantage over four-strokes, with their firing or power stroke every revolution of the crankshaft, compared with one firing stroke every two revolutions on the four-stroke motor. Consequently, the regulations stipulated that their capacity should be multiplied by 1.25 in the case of air-cooled machines and 1.32 in the case of water-cooled twins – an item worthy of note when one considers present-day racing machines!

By 1910, entries for the TT had risen to an incredible 80 machines and riders. The motorcycle industry had really switched on to the advantages to be gained from testing, racing and publicising their products in the toughest of all racing events for road machines, the Tourist Trophy. After each and every race, the engineers literally dissected their machines searching for the causes of failures in electrics, frames, motors, etc, hoping to improve on designs for the following year. Fierce competition brought many improvements and it was the customers who bought these machines who harvested the rewards of race development.

As speeds increased, so the need for more effective braking and roadholding became obvious. In four years, the time taken to complete the 158-mile race plummeted from 4 hours, 21 minutes and 53 seconds to 3 hours, 7 minutes and 24 seconds.

The cry went up: the machines are becoming too fast! Already in 1909 Harry Collier had lapped the St John's Circuit at over 52 mph. Therefore, in 1910, the capacity of the twins was restricted to 670 cc. But not even this could deter the flying Collier brothers and, with Charlie in first place and Harry in second, they romped home ahead of the field with W. Creyton, on his Triumph, third.

This race was won at an average of over 50 mph, with an incredible lap of 53.15 mph from Harry Bowen on his BAT twin-cylinder machine. It spelt doom for the St John's Circuit.

If the development of touring machines was to continue along the right lines, it was going to be necessary to put them to a much tougher test – the ultimate, the most difficult and arduous course of all, the Isle of Man Mountain Circuit!

This meant a completely new set of problems for the engineers and manufacturers. It was difficult enough trying to cope with the climb up from Ballacraine to Kirkmichael without pedal assistance and with belt drive; how on earth were they going to overcome the problems of climbing 1,400 feet up the Snaefell mountain from Ramsey to The Bungalow, which was seven miles of sheer torture for engines and transmissions?

For most, it was 'back to the drawing board'. Single speeds were definitely out on this circuit, because the only way to use the restricted power of the fragile motors and complete the climb up Snaefell was with multi-gears.

By 1911, in time for the Mountain course TT, all manner of designs had been completed, some still using the belt drive to the rear wheel hub, which incorporated a three-speed gear somewhat similar to that still used on present-day pedal cycles. Others like Royal Enfield used two-speed all-chain drive, while Douglas appeared using two-speed countershafts on the primary drive.

Needless to say, the manufacturers and riders were undaunted at the prospect of tackling the Mountain Circuit in spite of its very rugged nature. There was, once again, a record entry for the race of 98 machines and riders.

The regulations regarding machinery had been modified providing two classes for the race, 'Senior' and 'Junior'. The Senior section was for single-cylinder bikes up to 500 cc and twins of up to 585 cc, while the Junior catered for singles up to 300 cc and twins up to 340 cc. All told, there were 17 twins out of the entry of 34 for the Junior class, and 24 in the 64 entries for the Senior category. It was a truly magnificent display of support for the 'new look' Tourist Trophy race over the Mountain!

The official pits had been organised in Ramsey and Douglas with the start at the Quarter Bridge Road, Douglas, near Selbourne Drive. The date of the event had been put back to the end of June, and the Senior and Junior races were held separately, the Junior machines to complete four laps of the circuit and the Seniors five. For the first time, except in practice, it wasn't necessary to silence the motors and, for obvious safety reasons, it was now forbidden to push any machine which had broken down against the direction of the course.

Thus, the very well-attended 1911 Tourist Trophy races got under way. The weather was bright and sunny, but I wonder if many riders would have been so optimistic had they known the rigours facing them on the Mountain Circuit.

Basically, the original Mountain course followed the same route as today except that, instead of turning left at Cronk-ny-Mona towards Signpost Corner, the riders turned right along to Willaston and down Ballanard Road to Parkfield Corner, where they turned right again to go down Bray Hill. This made the distance covered slightly shorter than in present-day races, but the 37½ miles which riders had to complete each lap were considerably more arduous.

There were still very few metalled roads on the Island and the Mountain climb and descent, which are very steep, comprised nothing more than loose-surfaced, rutted tracks; dusty when dry and very muddy and slippery when wet. Sheep and cattle wandered across the unfenced tracks and every so often riders would encounter gates on the mountain road which had been left closed! Even Bray Hill, now lined with smart little bungalows, was nothing more than a dusty, muddy country lane on the outskirts of Douglas!

Yet, in spite of all the hazards of the 'new' course, the manufacturers and their heroic riders could not be deterred. The Junior race was held first and it was P. J. Evans on his Humber 340 twin who set the pace with a cracking, race-winning average of 41.45 mph. He also set the fastest lap at 42 mph. The Collier brothers had reverted to a single-cylinder machine for the Junior, but the 300 cc motorcycle just didn't have the steam to catch the flying Humber. Harry Collier finished some nine minutes behind Evans to average just over 40 mph and was followed home over nine minutes later by H. J. Cox on his Forward V-twin.

From the very outset, the Tourist Trophy races could be classified as international events. Although the majority of competitors were British, the machines they rode incorporated a variety of different engines from the Continent. Development of the motorcycle was taking place not only in Britain, France, Germany and Austria, but also in the United States.

The big V-twins of Harley-Davidson and the Indian Motorcycle Company were keeping pace with anything we were producing on this side of the water. Technically, in some ways, they were superior, particularly when it came to the transmission of power from the motor to the back wheel. Belt drive was adequate provided the weather remained fine and the leather or canvas retained its tension. But put a little lubricant on the belt in the form of rain, or oil from the engine, and you have plenty of power but no go!

The most positive drive to the rear wheel is by chain or shaft, and in 1911 the Indian Motor Company proved the point in no mean fashion. The big, flexible V-twins, using two-speed gears with chain drive to the rear wheels, steamed home in first, second and third places in the Senior.

Oliver Godfrey, who, as a pilot in the RFC, was killed in the First World War, led C. B. Franklin and A. Moorhouse in a fantastic Indian clean sweep in the Senior TT. On his Indian, Godfrey averaged 47.63 mph over the 187½ miles of the Mountain Circuit, but a sign of things to come was indicated by the fact that F. Phillip had put up fastest lap on his two-speed water-cooled Scott with a terrific 50.11 mph record.

However, although it appears in the record book that the Indian factory took all the glory, the Matchless twin of Charlie Collier actually finished second. He was unfortunately later disqualified for taking on 'unofficial' fuel. In other words, he did not stop at either of the official pits in Ramsey or Douglas. Rules are rules and Charlie became the first rider in the history of the TT to be excluded for breaking one of them!

There was also to be another tragic first in the TT of 1911, that being the fatal accident involving Victor Surridge. During practice on his Rudge, he crashed on the Glen Helen section. The tragedy brought home to riders and officials precisely how vulnerable the competitors were on their speeding machines, and murmurings were already being heard about safety and proper protective clothing. However, the 'new' Mountain Circuit could not be blamed for this first fatality, because it had happened on a section which had been part of the old St John's course.

After the Tourist Trophy races of 1911, it was blatantly obvious to everyone that the twin-cylinder machines could no longer be considered inferior to the singles on the score of reliability. Twins had proved victorious in both Senior and Junior races and, after the public prize-giving by the Governor in the Palace Ballroom, which started another tradition, thoughts turned to further amendments to the regulations for the following year's races. To simplify matters, it was decided that, for 1912, the capacity classes would be restricted to 500 and 350 cc for the respective Senior and Junior events.

Whether it was because of this change in regulations or because some of the manufacturers found the Mountain course too exacting for their machines, a number of firms decided not to participate in the TT and the entries declined slightly.

Luckily for Alfred Scott, the penalty of capacity multiplication for two-stroke twins had also been dropped during the formulation of the regulations for the 1911 races. Therefore, with Frank Phillip having shown the potential of the Scott twins the previous year, it was no surprise to see F. A. Applebee (Scott) romp home as winner of the Senior ahead of J. Haswell on his Triumph and, yet again, Harry Collier on the Matchless twin.

The Scott two-stroke had a unique, chain-driven disc-valve induction system, a two-speed gearbox and all-chain drive to the rear wheel. It was also the first two-stroke ever to win the Isle of Man Tourist Trophy. Such is progress that we now have water-cooled, disc-valve two-strokes that are chain-driven, and still winning on the Isle of Man!

In the 1912 Junior, a new marque was to show its superiority – the Douglas 350 twin. Yet again chain-driven motorcycles proved that this had to be the transmission of the future, and that belt drive was out. The two-speed countershaft, chain-driven Douglases of W. H. Bashall and E. Kickham finished first and second, with H. J. Cox coming third once more on his Forward.

One of the most incredible aspects of this era of TT history is the remarkable amount of change which took place each year, not only in the regulations for the event, but also in motorcycle design. It was probably one of the most fertile periods in the evolution of the motorcycle. Within a decade, motorcycles had developed from being simply power-assisted, ungainly pedal cycles to reasonably complex, if somewhat unreliable pieces of machinery, capable of attaining speeds never before believed possible. Gearboxes, chain drive, mechanically operated valves, spring suspension, magneto ignition, positive lubrication and many other new principles were tried and proved in the search for reliability and speed.

Every obstacle placed in the path of the manufacturers by the ever-demanding A-CC, which had since become the Auto-Cycle Union, was overcome by the skill of the engineers of those days. As the A-CU made the TT tougher, so the manufacturers made it look easier by not only increasing lap and race records but also building bikes to stay the course. It was like a mechanical game of chess; the A-CU set the problems and the manufacturers and riders overcame them with ingenuity and daring.

However, in 1913 a new A-CU Secretary arrived on the scene, Major Tommy Loughborough. With the improvement in lap speeds in both Junior and Senior TT races, it was obvious to his way of thinking that things were being made a little too easy for the riders and manufacturers. His solution to all these riders finishing the course at such ridiculously high speeds was almost a penal sentence. The Major retained the two classes, Senior and Junior, but decided to give the Mountain Circuit two days in which to break either the men or the machines. The Juniors, wearing blue waistcoats, would now do six laps of the circuit of which two would be run on the morning of the first day (Wednesday). The Seniors, wearing red waistcoats, would do seven laps of the course, the first three being run

on the same Wednesday afternoon. The survivors or three-quarters of the starters, whichever was the smaller, would all be sent off together for their remaining four laps on Friday.

Whether the riders of that time were masochists or lunatics is hard to judge because, in spite of these very tough regulations for the 1913 event, the entries literally doubled! Over 140 competitors had decided to take the punishment meted out to them by the A-CU and a few more manufacturers, including Rudge, were prepared to provide machinery for the battle which was to ensue. Oddly enough, despite the fantastic odds against completing six and seven laps of the very tough Mountain course, this first two-day TT event was to provide the closest finish between rival makes since the series of races began.

It was 'Tim' Wood on his water-cooled Scott twin who just managed to scrape home five seconds ahead of A. R. Abbott on his Rudge Multi, after Abbott had overshot Parkfield Corner on the last lap in his enthusiasm to beat the Scott rider. The third man home was A. H. Alexander on one of those V-twin Indians.

In the Junior it was the NUT twin of H. Mason that managed to beat the 'Duggie' twin of W. F. Newsome across the line by just under a minute with H. C. Newman third on his Ivy Green.

Just to prove that the A-CU couldn't get the better of the riders or manufacturers, both Junior and Senior winners bettered the lap records for the Mountain course.

Unfortunately, a second fatal accident, this time at Keppel Gate and involving Rudge rider T. Bateman, made it quite clear that the threatened compulsory wearing of safety helmets was indeed necessary. There had been other incidents involving head injuries to riders who had taken spills from their racing machines, not only on the Island but also at Brooklands. Therefore, the A-CU had no alternative but to make compulsory the wearing of protective clothing by riders competing in speed events.

With the rumblings of war being heard from across the Channel, the 1914 TT looked all set for disaster, but nothing could have been further from the truth. Some 35 different manufacturers sent teams to the Island for the races and, with the A-CU relenting a little on race distance (it was reduced to four laps for the Juniors on the Wednesday and five laps for the Seniors on Friday), all was set fair for an interesting meeting.

The start line had been moved up to the top of Bray Hill on the schoolhouse corner, where the one and only official refuelling point was set up, the one at Ramsey being abolished.

Whether the manufacturers of the twin-cylinder machines had become complacent due to their run of success in previous TTs is hard to say, but it was apparent from the outset that considerable development had been taking place in the workshops of A. J. Stevens and the Rudge organisation.

Rudge had improved the multi-ratio transmission to a high degree of efficiency providing the rider, Cyril Pullin, with a gear ratio to suit every occasion, whether it was struggling for power on the short, sharp climb from Ramsey to the Gooseneck, or searching for speed on the drop from Kate's Cottage down to Hillberry.

A. J. Stevens had also worked wonders with the transmission on his AJS 350 machines because, with twin primary chains and a two-speed countershaft, he was able to give an effective four-speed gear train to his two riders, E. and C. Williams.

The outcome of this exciting development work was that the big singles came thumping back into the limelight. Cyril Pullin steamed home on his Rudge Multi at an average speed of 49.49 mph, ahead of Howard R. Davies on a side-valve Sunbeam and O. C. Godfrey on an Indian twin, both of whom finished second in a dead heat. However, it was 'Tim' Wood and his Scott who once again broke the lap record with a speed of 53.50 mph.

Tragedy struck yet again in the Junior race, when F. J. Walker was killed riding his Royal Enfield. He had been leading the Junior TT until lap three when his machine had a puncture. After mending it, he hurtled off in hot pursuit of E. and C. Williams riding the AJS machines. Witnesses said that he fell off at least twice during the chase but remounted and rode with such fury that he did in fact finish third behind the two Williamses. Dramatically, he charged head down over the finishing line not knowing that the race had ended. He had either lost count of the number of laps or was completely physically exhausted. Unfortunately, he did not see the barriers which had been placed across the circuit denoting the stopping point and crashed headlong into them. It was a sad end to the 1914 Isle of Man TT, but there was to be even greater sorrow in the world as the Kaiser's army went on the rampage in Europe and Great Britain became embroiled in four years of the bloodiest fighting the world has known.

## The Roaring 'Twenties

Necessity is the mother of invention, so they say, and never have truer words been spoken. Between the years 1914 and 1918, the world witnessed fantastic industrial and mechanical progress. The first tanks crawled across the muddy, battle-torn fields of France; fighting aircraft took to the skies, while submarines prowled the depths of the oceans sinking and destroying. The motorcycle, too, played its part in this terrifying display of inhuman carnage. As a replacement for the outmoded horse, the motorcycle carried the despatch riders, conveyed soldiers into war and generally became accepted as the all-purpose, go-anywhere vehicle, able to work and carry where no four-wheeler could cope.

No longer bothered with the prestige of winning the TT or any other racing award, the motorcycle industry in Britain and Europe spent all its time developing and improving the existing machines and turning them over to mass production to help the war effort.

When sanity finally returned to the world, the motorcycle industry discovered that a considerable amount had been learned about the internal combustion engine by the aeronautical industry. Lighter alloys, stronger steels, improved electrics, better fuel and oils; all had proved necessary in the search for power to become the victor and not the vanquished.

The British motorcycle industry was able to make use of many of the lessons learned in war and, when the Tourist Trophy races were resumed in 1920, it was with a new breed of tourist machines incorporating a number of technical innovations learned during the 'closed season'!

The A-CU took the planning of the post-war TT very seriously and established, for the first time, the pits and grandstand on the Glencrutchery Road alongside Nobles Park. On the opposite side of the road was built the now world-famous scoreboard serviced by the local Boy Scout troops, who received instructions by telephone from marshals' posts around the Mountain Circuit.

With the movement of the pits on to the Glencrutchery Road, alterations had to be made to the course and, instead of competitors turning right at Cronk-ny-Mona, they forked left up to Signpost Corner, where they turned right towards Bedstead Corner, through the Nook and around the tricky Governor's Bridge hairpin and out on to the Glencrutchery Road. It added a further quarter-mile to the course, but established the Isle of Man Mountain Circuit as we know it today.

The length of the Senior and Junior races remained as in pre-war years, 6 laps and 5 laps respectively. But, with the development of lightweight motorcycles, particularly two-strokes, a lightweight 250 cc class was added to the programme.

Neither the Junior nor the Lightweight races could be awarded the splendid silver Marquis de Mouzilly St Mars Tourist Trophy, but it was decided to award the winners of these classes replicas of this magnificent figure of Mercury.

At first, the 250 cc race was to be known as the Junior 250 TT, but its title was changed to the Lightweight 250 in 1922. This was because until 1922 the Junior 250 race was run in conjunction with the 350 event, with riders competing for a separate award, *The Motor Cycle* Cup. In 1922, it became a separate race in its own right.

And so the mechanical lessons learned on the battle fronts were put to the test in the struggles on the Isle of Man racing circuit. The only challenger to British supremacy was from America, where in the Harley-Davidson and Indian factories they too had been learning a great deal about motorcycle engineering.

In the 1920 Senior TT, it was a new name, Sunbeam, that set the spectators gossiping. George Dance on this big, 500 side-valve four-stroke broke the lap record to travel the Mountain Circuit in 40 minutes, 35 seconds at a speed of 55.62 mph. But it was his team mate, T. C. de la Hay, who actually won the race, followed home by D. M. Brown on a Norton with another Sunbeam third in the hands of W. R. Brown.

For the Williams lads in the Junior TT it was almost as if the war hadn't interrupted the proceedings. In 1914, it was Eric Williams on his AJS who had won but, although in 1920 he succeeded in putting up a new record lap of 51.36 mph, his machine didn't last the course and C. Williams stepped in to take the chequered flag from J. Watson-Bourne and J. Holroyd, both riding Blackburnes.

The Junior 250 cc TT of 1920, which I have mentioned was run in conjunction with the Junior 350 cc, almost brought about the biggest surprise of all. The class proved a fantastic clean-sweep for the little two-stroke Levis machines ridden by R. O. Clark, Gus Kuhn and F. W. Applebee and, were it not for the fact that Clark crashed just before Keppel Gate, he might well have won the Junior TT as well, because winner Cyril Williams had to push in his new, four-speed AJS 350 from Creg-ny-Baa. But it was not to be and Clark finished fourth overall to win the 'lightweight' Junior class.

The machines of the 1920s, which had undergone fantastic development during the First World War, were no longer the unreliable, ill-equipped motor-

cycles of the preceding decade. Many of the big, single-cylinder machines had overhead-valve motors, four-speed gearboxes, internal expanding drum brakes, girder-fork front suspension, and magneto electrics. In fact, the four-valve cylinder head, which is considered a modern-day refinement on four-stroke motors, was first introduced in the French-built Alcyon of 1912; while in 1920, the ABC 500 cc motorcycle was the first ever to appear with megaphone-ended exhausts. The rotary disc-valve was featured on the 1922 Sun two-stroke, while the 'steering damper', which is so necessary on the Isle of Man circuit, was introduced by trials ace Bert Kershaw on his New Imperial in 1923! Wire beaded tyres on well-based rims were another innovation of the early 'twenties. In fact, this era might be considered the most fruitful in the development of the roadster motorcycles.

Regulations for the TT remained unchanged for the year 1921, with the Junior race catering for both 250 and 350 cc motorcycles. However, it was to be a memorable year as far as A. J. Stevens and his rider, Howard R. Davies, were concerned, because it was to be the first and only year in which a 350 cc machine won the Senior TT. In fact, Howard Davies used the same 350 Ajay for both Junior and Senior races, coming second in the smaller capacity race to E. Williams on another AJS, with T. Sheard finishing third to make it a 1–2–3 for A. J. Stevens. Meanwhile, in the Junior 250 cc race, the New Imperial four-strokes were putting it over the formerly all-conquering two-stroke Levises. Bert Kershaw set the 250 lap record at 46.11 mph, but failed to finish the race, allowing fellow New Imperial rider, D. G. Prentice, to win ahead of G. S. Davison on the Levis and W. G. Harrison on the new two-stroke Velocette.

To win the Senior TT of 1921, Howard Davies increased his average speed of 51.20 mph in the Junior to 54.50 mph to beat the Indian V-twins of Freddie Dixon and Bert le Vack by a clear two minutes, 13 seconds. There was no doubt that the AJS was one of the most advanced single-cylinder motorcycles of its day.

The surprising thing was that nobody protested about Howard Davies winning the Senior TT on his Junior machine, because he openly admitted after the race that the tyre section of his AJS was at odds with the regulations for a machine entered in the Senior race. Maybe it was because of Howard Davies' outstanding performance on a motorcycle giving away such a capacity advantage to the other competitors that nobody considered it sportsman-like to protest and take away such a well-deserved victory. It must be remembered that the racing of cars and motorcycles in those days was still very much a sport for gentlemen, akin to flying and horse racing!

Speed! Speed! Speed! Once again the cry went up that the TT races were becoming too dangerous. Riders were travelling at ridiculous, break-neck speeds that bore no relation to the needs or requirements of the ordinary touring motorcyclist and, after all, the Isle of Man races were purely for touring motorcycles. It was suggested that the capacity limit be reduced to 350 cc for the Senior event, with the Junior becoming a race for 250 cc motorcycles. Fortunately for the future of the Isle of Man TT, good sense prevailed and the capacity classes remained as they were for 1922, with the exception that the 250 cc race became the Lightweight event run independently of the Junior TT.

Progress was to prove too much for certain machines in the 1922 Tourist Trophy races, because it was the last time that a side-valve engined motorcycle, the Sunbeam of Alec Bennett, was to win a TT. It also spelt doom for the two-stroke era, when Geoff Davison on his Levis scored the last victory for a two-stroke in the Lightweight race until DKW returned to win the class in 1938!

Another notable event in 1922 was the first-time appearance of the one and only Stanley Woods, ten times winner and maker of TT history! Other individuals making their debut were Jimmie Simpson and Walter (Wally) Handley, both to become great racing motorcyclists and stars of the TT circuit.

Although Stanley Woods did not appear in the first three places in the Junior TT on his Cotton, he did cause quite a stir in the pits when he managed to set himself on fire while refuelling! Fortunately, with flames extinguished and no harm done, he rode on to finish fifth.

AJS still retained their supremacy in the Junior TT, when local Manx rider Tom Sheard won the race at an average speed of 54.75 mph, with George Grinton on another AJS finishing second. But it was Bert le Vack on his New Imperial 350 who set a new lap record for the class at 56.46 mph, faster than the previous year's Senior TT lap record. Third was J. Thomas on his Sheffield Henderson.

In the Senior TT of 1922, Alec Bennett on the Sunbeam won at an average of 58.31 mph for the six laps of the Mountain Circuit, with a record lap of 59.99 mph – the 60-mph lap record had yet to be broken! Second was W. Brandish on a Triumph and third, H. Langman on the two-stroke Scott.

Another two-stroke, the Levis of Geoff Davison, won the Lightweight race after dicing for the lead

with Walter Handley on his OK. Walter set the lap record at 51 mph, but retired from the race, allowing Davison to win, followed home by D. Young on a Rex-Acme and S. J. Jones on a Velocette.

Versatility is the hallmark of all great motorcyclists and, whereas today the majority of competitive riders specialise in one particular type of motorcycle sport, when in 1923 a sidecar TT was introduced for the first time, many of the solo competitors also entered for the race. Graham Walker and Freddie Dixon, to name but two, were among the competitors for the newly introduced race, and it was 'Flying' Freddie and passenger Walter Derry, with their unusual and unique 'banking' sidecar outfit powered by a Douglas twin, who romped home as winners of the first-ever Sidecar TT. We all think that disc brakes on motorcycles are modern inventions but, believe it or not, the Dixon-Derry outfit was equipped with a disc front brake, and that was in 1923. This proves once again that there is very little that is new in the world of motorcycling.

Graham Walker and passenger Tommy Mahon, with their Norton outfit, finished second in the Sidecar race, with G. H. Tucker on another Norton coming third. The race was only over three laps of the Mountain Circuit, but even so the machines still put up a remarkably good performance, with Freddie Dixon averaging 53.15 mph.

Wet and windy weather greeted the Senior TT of that year and still the 60-mph lap proved impossible with Tommy Sheard transferring from the Junior AJS to the Senior Douglas to notch up his second win in TT history. G. M. Black finished second, with 'Flying' Freddie Dixon, riding an Indian, taking third place.

Whether it was the wet weather of Senior TT race day, or the brilliance of Stanley Woods beginning to show on the TT circuit, is difficult to say, but the 1923 Junior TT race speed proved faster than that of the Senior, when Woods took his Cotton to victory at an average speed of 55.73 mph. But, although Woods won the Junior, it was still the AJS marque that deserved the manufacturers' laurels because Jimmie Simpson, in his second TT, set a new lap record on the 350 Ajay at 59.59 mph, before dropping out of the running. Another AJS ridden by 'Harry' Harris came second in the race, with A. H. Alexander on his Douglas finishing third.

In the Lightweight 250 race, Wally Handley did a 'Jimmie Simpson' and set a cracking pace on his OK Supreme to break the 250 cc lap record yet again but, as in the previous year, his machine couldn't stand the pace and victory went to Jack

Porter on his New Gerrard, with Bert le Vack finishing second on the New Imperial. Third was D. Hall on the Rex-Acme.

Racing results of the 1920s read like a who's who of the British motorcycle industry . . . Douglas, Triumph, Norton, AJS, Cotton, DOT, New Imperial, Scott, New Gerrard and so on. In 1924, all overseas opposition was temporarily eliminated when Indian motorcycles from the USA finally gave best to the British marques and withdrew from racing on the Isle of Man.

British motorcycle manufacturers were supreme and, in spite of the industrial troubles of the mid-1920s, the industry was able to survive and beat the world in the design and performance of its machines.

Ingenuity was the hallmark of British engineers; witness the Diamond 250 machine, a long-forgotten make, which incorporated a JAP, side-valve motor as the power unit. This was fitted with a 'Zephyr' piston which was of bi-metal construction, having an alloy crown to carry the piston rings and a cast-iron skirt in which the gudgeon pin fitted. The crown and skirt were bolted together with the designer's aim of reducing skirt clearances, eliminating piston 'slap' and reducing cylinder wear!

The speed of machines and riders over the Mountain Circuit was still a bone of contention among critics of the TT races, and in 1924 AJS once again proved that they were still ahead of competitors in engine design. They were the first manufacturers to consider fitting a larger inlet than exhaust valve to the cylinder head to improve 'breathing' of the motor. The result? Jimmie Simpson did another 'Jimmie Simpson' by setting a fantastic lap record of 64.54 mph in the 1924 Junior TT, but once again, as in the preceding year, he failed to complete the gruelling six laps of the Mountain Circuit. In setting the record, Simpson also bettered 'Flying' Freddie Dixon's lap record for the Senior TT of that year. Neither of the two 'aces' won their races, and it was left to Alec Bennett, now riding for 'Pa' Norton, to win the Senior, followed home by Scott fanatic Harry Langman and the unfortunate Freddie Dixon on his in-line, horizontally opposed Douglas twin.

In spite of their obvious superiority in development and performance, the best AJS could achieve in the Junior TT of 1924 was a third place by H. R. Scott. He was beaten to the line by the New Imperial of K. Twemlow and the DOT of S. Ollerhead.

In an effort to pacify the critics of the TT, who believed that the speeds these 'touring' motorcycles were achieving were not only highly dangerous but also unnecessary, the A-CU decided to introduce another capacity class into the 1924 programme of races on the Isle of Man. This was the Ultra-lightweight race for machines up to 175 cc, giving the economy-minded manufacturers of smaller motorcycles the opportunity to test and prove their products. This meant an even more hectic time for manufacturers, with a very full race week encompassing five TT events.

However, 1924 established racing on the Isle of Man for all categories of motorcycles, and the enthusiasts on the mainland flocked to the Island to see this wonderful spectacle, thereby confirming the faith and foresight which Lord Raglan had shown some 17 years earlier.

Meanwhile, on the mainland, mumblings and rumblings about the success of the TT on the Island made people think again about transferring the racing to a road course in Britain. It even went so far as to the mapping out of a 20-mile course in Yorkshire and the presentation of a Bill to Parliament. However, as before, the Government would not consider the closing of public roads for the benefit of a lunatic fringe of hair-brained motorcyclists and, fortunately for the Isle of Man TT races, the Bill was thrown out.

The A-CU themselves had been feeling the post-war financial pinch and, with the cost of running the T T races on the Isle of Man, had even considered taking the British TT races to Belgium! But, luckily, that idea was soon quashed and the 1924 Tourist Trophy races proceeded as before on the now-improving roads of the Island.

In the Lightweight 250 race of that year, Eddie Twemlow on the New Imperial swept all before him to win by over 12 minutes from H. F. Brockbank on a Cotton and J. Cooke on a DOT. Twemlow's lap record of 58.28 mph, on a 'tourist' 250 cc machine, indicates the development which had taken place in the lightweight machines of that era because, to achieve such an average, he must have touched speeds in the region of 80 mph over the $37\frac{3}{4}$-mile circuit. When compared with the performance of present-day touring 250s, it makes one wonder just how much progress there has been in almost 50 years!

Admittedly, we now have improved suspension, better brakes, electric starters and flashing indicators, but how much better is the performance of the 'modern' engine with regard to fuel consumption and top speed? Also, when one considers the road surfaces of the TT circuit in 1924 compared with today, just how much faster would Eddie Twemlow have lapped on the same machine over the present-day TT circuit? Obviously, we will never find out.

The two remaining events during the 1924 series were the new Ultra-lightweight race and the Sidecar TT. Once again, the amazing performance of the 175 cc New Gerrard of J. A. Porter, who averaged 51.20 mph over three laps of the Mountain Circuit to win the event, demonstrates the rapid technical development of Britain's lightweight motorcycles.

Cotton were at this time beginning to make themselves felt in the competition world and, apart from the second place in the Lightweight event of that year, they also took second and third spots in the Ultra-lightweight race, with F. G. Morgan and C. Stead riding.

In the Sidecar TT, Norton were successful with G. H. Tucker winning the race; H. Reed came second on his DOT outfit and A. Tinkler on a Matador was third. Freddie Dixon set the pace with his Douglas, with a lap speed of 53.23 mph, but the twin was not to last the three-lap race distance.

The year 1925 will be remembered in TT history for a number of reasons, all of them milestones in their own right. For example, Howard R. Davies, Sunbeam and AJS works' rider, who had already made his mark on the TT scene, decided to 'go it alone' with his own, now famous, HRD motorcycle.

Howard Davies had learned a tremendous amount as a rider and development engineer with his previous employers and, in spite of its obvious superiority over any other country in the development and production of motorcycles, the British motorcycle business was still very much a 'cottage' industry; literally dozens of small manufacturers making a limited number of basically sound machines.

Howard Davies decided that with his knowledge of motorcycle engineering he could easily build a world-beating motorcycle and in 1925 he proved the point. He took on the might of the then highly successful AJS team and beat them at their own game. He won his second Senior TT riding his own HRD machine.

Although Jimmie Simpson on the AJS once again broke the lap record with an unbelievable speed of 68.97 mph, AJS had to be content with a second place from F. A. Longman as Simpson's machine yet again couldn't stand the pace. Alec Bennett on a Norton was third.

The next milestone in TT history was the outstanding performance of Walter Handley on the Rex-Acme machines. They had been entered in the Junior, Lightweight and Ultra-lightweight races with Wally as their number-one rider.

The statistics show that in 1925 Walter L. Handley not only won the Junior and Ultra-lightweight TTs, but also set up new lap records in all three classes: 65.89 mph for the Junior, 60.22 for the Lightweight and 54.12 mph for the Ultra-lightweight.

Howard Davies, again on his own HRD, finished second in the Junior with Jimmie Simpson finishing third on the AJS.

In the Lightweight TT, Eddie Twemlow repeated his success of the preceding year by winning the race, with C. W. Johnston on his Cotton splitting the New Imperials of Eddie and K. Twemlow who finished third.

C. W. Johnston on the Cotton also finished second in the Ultra-lightweight race, this time to Wally Handley, with J. A. Porter, the previous year's winner, finishing third on his New Gerrard.

In the Sidecar TT, Freddie Dixon set the pace with a lap record of 57.18 mph on his Douglas, but the ill-fated Flying Freddie once again failed to take the chequered flag at the end of a sidecar race. L. Parker on another Douglas won after Freddie had broken down and Norton took second and third places with A. E. Taylor and G. Grinton.

The third milestone, and one which was to change dramatically the appearance of the TT races, was the decision after the 1925 event to cancel both the Sidecar and Ultra-lightweight races. Apparently, the A-CU, manufacturers and certain other individuals were becoming worried about the image that the sidecar race was creating in the eyes of the general public. Sidecar outfits were considered to be sedate, two- or three-seaters for transporting family groups in safety; not hair-raising racing machines that hurtled around corners, sidecar wheels in the air and passengers leaning out trying to regain the stability of the machines. So, the sidecar race had to go and it was not to return until 1954.

A diminishing enthusiasm and entry for the Ultra-lightweight race in 1925 also spelled the end of this event and so, with the A-CU looking for a solution to the pressures and problems of running a successful TT week during a period of intense industrial unrest and unemployment in Britain, they settled on a formula which was to remain until 1950 – one Senior, one Junior and one Lightweight TT race for 500 cc, 350 cc and 250 cc motorcycles respectively.

To sort out the men from the boys, all the races including the Lightweight TT were extended to seven laps of the Mountain Circuit, taking the race distance to a punishing 264¼ miles.

It is also interesting to note that at this time the Italian motorcycle industry was beginning to grow and certain manufacturers including Guzzi and Garelli were studying with interest the success of the British industry with especial regard to racing on the Isle of Man. In 1926, Guzzi and Garelli threw down the gauntlet and arrived on Mona's Isle with lightweight touring 'racing' machines in the hope of claiming some of the glory which had up to that time been, almost without exception, the sole privilege of the British manufacturers.

The Garelli, ridden by Ermino Visioli, was a two-stroke machine, the like of which had never before been seen. It was a twin-piston single-cylinder motorcycle having the incredible number of four carburettors fitted to charge its diminutive 250 cc motor. However, it was the Guzzi of Italian Pietro Ghersi that actually stunned the British manufacturers on race day, because it was this machine that stormed away from the powerful Cotton team to win the Lightweight race! Unfortunately for Ghersi (perhaps he didn't speak or understand English very well), his race declaration entry form showed a different make of sparking plug to that which was actually used in the race, and he was disqualified. It seems a pity that such a trivial item as this should have disqualified Guzzi from the race, particularly after both rider and machine had performed so exceedingly well on their first visit to the Island. But regulations are made not to be broken and, although the Italians went away from the Island feeling a little more than upset, it was not to deter them from returning the following year.

As it was, through the misfortune of Ghersi, the all-conquering Cottons took first, second and third places, giving C. W. Johnston his first-ever TT win after finishing second in the Lightweight and Ultra-lightweight events the preceding year. Second was F. G. Morgan and W. Colgan was third.

Every year of TT history appears to be marked by changes in regulations, alterations in specifications and, of course, new developments in the design of competing motorcycles. The year 1926 was no exception because up to that time 'dope' or methanol was allowed as fuel for the racing machines, but from that year on dope was banned and replaced by petrol-benzole until the outbreak of the Second World War. Also on the machine development side came a brand-new design from Velocette. This was the 350 cc overhead-camshaft model to be ridden by that great TT exponent Alec Bennett.

It was a dream of a debut for the Velocette in the Junior TT; it roared away from the 'big port' AJS of Jimmie Simpson to win by 10 minutes, 25 seconds, raising the lap record to 68.75 mph. Walter Handley on his Rex-Acme finished in third place.

There are a number of reasons why the Senior TT of 1926 should be remembered, the first being the breaking of the 70-mph 'barrier' by Jimmie Simpson on the 500 Ajay. But being Jimmie Simpson, he once again failed to finish the race, and it was Stanley Woods on his Norton 500 who was to record the second of an outstanding run of TT successes. Walter Handley on his big Rex-Acme finished second to Woods, with F. A. Longman bringing his AJS home in third spot.

What can be remembered of the year 1927? Well, I suppose it can be said that this was a period when the advantages of the overhead-camshaft engine were discovered. Velocette had proved the point in 1926 with their extremely fast 350 cc machine, and in 1927 Norton laid the foundations for what must be the most successful overhead-camshaft single-cylinder racing motorcycle in history. Stanley Woods and Alec Bennett, who had transferred his allegiance from Velocette, wheeled out the first-ever overhead-camshaft Nortons on to the start line for the Senior TT.

Stanley Woods set the pace to break the lap record at a speed of 70.90 mph, but Woods' un-proved Norton didn't last the course and it was Alec Bennett who won the race on the other works' machine. As a foretaste of the future, a Scot called Jimmy Guthrie on a New Hudson finished second. Destined to be one of the greatest riders of all time, Guthrie had made his TT debut in 1923, but did not compete again on the Island until 1927. T. Simister on a Triumph was third.

Racing on the Island in 1927 was marred by the death of Archie Birkin. He was killed during practice after colliding with a fish lorry because, although the roads were closed for the race proper, it was only a 'gentleman's agreement' that none of the locals drove or rode on the circuit when TT competitors were out practising. The tragic accident brought home to the organisers and the Manx Government the hazards of riding at race speeds when the roads were still open to the public. Consequently, the following year the roads were officially closed for the practice and the race.

In the Junior race of 1927, Velocette were unable to repeat their success of the preceding year in spite of running their rapid, overhead-camshaft machine. Howard Davies had retired from racing but continued to race-develop his own HRD motorcycles with the 'Flying' Freddie Dixon as number-one rider. And, in spite of Walter Handley (Rex-Acme) setting the fastest lap at 69.18 mph, it was Freddie Dixon, ace sidecar exponent, who won the solo Junior TT on the HRD. Velocette managed to gain second place with H. J. Willis and Jimmie Simpson brought the AJS 350 home in third spot.

In the Lightweight race, everybody was waiting to see what the Italian Guzzi factory could achieve after their disallowed victory the previous year. There was no doubt that the Italian manufacturers had learned a great deal about motorcycles, but it was to be almost another decade before they seriously began to challenge the British racing machines on the Isle of Man.

As it was, Walter Handley on the lightweight Rex-Acme took the honours for Britain, with the Guzzi of L. Archangelli following home some 8½ minutes behind. OK Supreme were third with their rider, C. T. Ashby, although Alec Bennett set the lap record on another OK Supreme at 64.45 mph.

Anything you can do, I can do better . . . such was the motto of the hardcore of British motorcycle manufacturers who year after year supported the TT races. When one manufacturer developed and produced a new idea to give an advantage over competitors, so those competitors left the Island intent on going one better for the following year. Velocette had proved the overhead-camshaft motor to be the single-cylinder power unit of future racing machines, and Norton had immediately responded by demonstrating that they, too, could build a race winner along the same lines. But the thing which stunned everyone who attended the 1928 TT races was the latest in 'one-upmanship' developments by Velocette – the Harold Willis-designed, positive-stop foot-change system for the gearbox.

Up to that time, a rider had had to take his right hand off the handlebar and change gear with a lever situated on the fuel tank or down near the gearbox. This meant a considerable loss in time between gearchanges, as well as being a pretty hazardous operation when travelling at anything up to 100 mph on poorly surfaced roads.

The Harold Willis gearchange caused a mild panic in the camps of opposition manufacturers. It was unheard of that a rider didn't have to take his hand off the handlebar to change gear. And, to prove the value of their high-speed gearchanging mechanism, the 350 cammy Velocettes, in the hands of Alec Bennett and H. J. Willis, took first and second places in the Junior TT, with Alec Bennett breaking the lap record at a remarkable 70.28 mph. K. Twemlow on his DOT finished third.

Bennett's race speed in the Junior of that year proved to be almost 6 mph faster than C. J. P. Dodson, whose Sunbeam won the Senior TT ahead of George Rowley on an AJS and T. L. Hatch on a Scott. Even the great Jimmie Simpson was just over 2 mph slower when, once again, he made fastest lap in the Senior but failed to finish on his AJS.

It was obvious to everyone that positive-stop foot-gearchange mechanisms had their definite advantages over the cumbersome handchange, and so manufacturers and engineers left the Island at the end of the 1928 TT races intent on recapturing or equalling the mechanical advantage which Velocette had gained. This was after F. A. Longman on his OK Supreme had won the Lightweight race, with a new name to the TT result book, Royal Enfield, taking second spot ridden by C. D. Barrow. Eddie Twemlow finished in third place on his DOT.

On the threshold of the 'thirties, it looked as though the race-developed overhead-camshaft machines would have things all their own way on the Island, but Velocette and Norton hadn't reckoned with the mechanical ingenuity still to be shown by other established manufacturers, namely Rudge and Sunbeam. The overhead-camshaft design was still in its infancy, whereas the simple, push-rod operated overhead-valve motor was long established.

Power for any reciprocating piston engine is produced in the combustion chamber and the more fuel-air mixture that can be drawn into the cylinder, the greater the efficiency of the engine. AJS had learned this earlier when they had produced the 'big port' machine incorporating an inlet valve larger than the exhaust. Sunbeam were to use that method almost to its extreme with enormous inlet and exhaust valves on their long-stroke 500; while Rudge were to tackle the task of improving induction in a different manner. They produced a unique valve-operating 'rocker' system, which enabled the single-cylinder head to be fitted with four valves, two inlet and two exhaust.

In 1929, the initial promise shown by the ohc Norton still did not come to fruition. The push-rod single-cylinder Sunbeams ridden by C. J. Dodson and Alec Bennett came home first and second in the Senior TT, while H. G. Tyrell-Smith demonstrated the potential of the Rudge by finishing third.

However, there still appeared to be no way of stopping the triumphant parade of Velocettes in the Junior TT. Yet again Velocette broke the lap record with a speed of 70.95 mph by Freddie Hicks who

23

won the race, with Walter Handley finishing second on the AJS and Alec Bennett third on another Velocette.

In the Lightweight TT, the Italian Guzzi factory was still trying to make an impact on the British domination of the races. Pietro Ghersi made fastest lap in the event at 63.12 mph, but it was S. A. Crabtree on his Excelsior who actually won the race, followed home in second and third places by K. Twemlow on the DOT and F. A. Longman on the OK Supreme. Thus came to an end a decade of vastly improved racing and remarkable development among the British motorcycle manufacturers.

And so into the 'thirties . . .

## The Flying 'Thirties

Apart from the brief foray by Indian and Guzzi, the British manufacturers had had things very much their own way on the Isle of Man. As a testing ground the Mountain Circuit was second-to-none and the British took full advantage of the TT races to develop their motorcycles to the highest pitch. In a way it was similar to the accelerated technical development which had taken place during the First World War when, in order to overcome the enemy, you had to use the utmost in ingenuity and engineering skill to improve at a faster rate than your adversary.

The 'enemy' as far as any one British manufacturer was concerned was his competitor and the tremendous rivalry between British firms at that time created an atmosphere in which all had to improve their products each and every year or fail in the fight for survival in a tough, commercial world.

The pace of progress was incredible and almost without exception the lap records established by the 'latest' race machine tumbled each successive year as improved ideas evolved for brakes, tyres, frames, motors and lubrication. Of course, the TT circuit itself improved as did the riding skill of the competitors.

The 'thirties seemed set fair for the British motorcycle industry and, with the knowledge learned from competing on the Isle of Man, there appeared not the slightest chance that any 'foreigner' might intrude on 'our' motorcycle scene to tarnish the glorious record. But it was not to be. Industrial Europe was awakening and, after shaking off the aftermath of the terrible depression of the 'twenties, the Germans, Italians and Swedes wanted to expand their motorcycle industries and the obvious place to prove their worth was in the Isle of Man Tourist Trophy races.

Unknown to Rudge, Norton, or Velocette, during the next decade there was to be an onslaught on their Isle of Man domain the like of which they had never before encountered. Germany with its DKW and BMW machines, Italy with the Guzzi, Benelli and Gilera and even Sweden with the Husqvarna were to challenge the might of the British motorcycle industry on its own testing ground.

The 'thirties began with the new four-valve radial, single-cylinder Rudge machines sweeping all before them. Although they were only push-rod operated singles, the four-valve 'breathing' gave them an edge with which neither the camshaft Nortons nor Velocettes could compete. In the Senior TT of that year, Rudge scored a first and second place with Walter Handley and Graham Walker as riders, while Norton could only manage third spot in spite of the skill of Jimmie Simpson.

The Junior TT told the same story, with Rudge taking all the first three places: H. G. Tyrell-Smith, first; G. E. Nott, second; and Graham Walker, third. Velocette were nowhere in the hunt while Walter Handley (Rudge) raised the Senior TT lap record to a fantastic 76.28 mph.

Jimmy Guthrie managed to win the Lightweight race for AJS, the last win they were to record until 1954! OK Supreme gained second and third places with C. W. Johnston and C. S. Barrow riding. Walter Handley, probably one of the most outstanding riders of the 'twenties, did his usual 'thing' for Rex-Acme by raising the lap record in the Lightweight TT to 66.86 mph, but it was the last time that this renowned marque was to feature significantly in the TT races.

In an effort to stem the Rudge tide against them, Norton did what all good tacticians do in battle. They surveyed the TT scene and then chose the best 'soldiers' at their disposal: Jimmie Simpson, Stanley Woods, Jimmy Guthrie and ex-Manx GP winner, Tim Hunt. These were four of the best and most promising riders, capable of conquering the most difficult road-racing circuit in the world.

No longer were the manufacturers thinking about touring motorcycles for the average member of the public to ride; they were concerned with racing success on works' racing motorcycles. The gloves were off and now it was definitely a case of succeed or fail, not only on the race tracks, but also with the machines you were selling to the general public.

Norton proved their point in 1931 by completely reversing the Rudge success of the previous year. In the Senior TT they swept to a 1–2–3 victory, with Tim Hunt leading Jimmy Guthrie and Stanley Woods over the line. Jimmie Simpson, as ever, did

*The start of something big! Trials for the Gordon Bennett Cup car race were first held on the Isle of Man, later followed by the Tourist Trophy races for cars. This photograph taken in 1906 shows the extremely rough surface at Ramsey Hairpin. Motorcycles competed in the first TT over the 'short course' the following year, but it wasn't until 1911 that they took on the Mountain Circuit.*

*Because of the advantages of chain drive over belt drive, the Indian V-twins were unbeatable in 1911 in the first Senior TT to be run over the Mountain Circuit. O. C. Godfrey won this race and gained second place in the Senior three years later, dead-heating with Howard Davies on the side-valve, single-cylinder Sunbeam.*

*T. C. de la Hay won the Senior TT of 1920 to gain Sunbeam their first victory on the Island. Note the lack of front braking on the machine on which he averaged 51.48 mph over six laps of the Mountain course. Perhaps that's why he lapped so fast!*

**Above** *The start of the 1920 Junior TT. Some bikes were belt driven, others by chain and all were registered for use as roadster machines. Notice the number of riders with innertubes or tool-kits strapped around their waists!*

**Left** *In 1920, the Mountain Circuit was still very rough and punctures caused many stoppages. Here J. A. Watson-Bourne, who finished second in the Junior TT of that year, scratches around Creg-ny-Baa on his Blackburne.*

*Rough roads became smoother at Governor's Bridge for R. O. Clark and his 2¼ hp Levis in the 1920 Junior TT. Clark finished fourth overall and first in the 250 cc class to win the Motor Cycle Trophy. The races for 250 cc and 350 cc machines were run consecutively at this time.*

**Above** *The all-time great Howard R. Davies pushes off on his 350 AJS in the Senior TT of 1921. It is the only time a Junior machine has ever won the Senior TT! Davies was also a member of the victorious AJS team which took first, second and third places in the Junior TT of 1921 . . . a truly outstanding year for the AJS factory!*

**Left** *A typical scene in a works' garage on the Island. Here the AJS team machines are being prepared to do battle in the 1924 TT races. Jimmie Simpson set an incredible lap record of 64.54 mph in the Junior race, nearly 5 mph faster than the then existing record and even faster than the record set by Freddie Dixon in the 1924 Senior TT. Unfortunately, Simpson failed to finish.*

**Above** *Sidecar racing came to the Island in 1923 and Freddie Dixon astounded critics by taking his 'banking' outfit to victory at an average speed of 53.15 mph. The sidecar passenger operated a lever which raised or lowered the sidecar wheel, causing the outfit to bank to the right or left, depending on the corner being negotiated.*

**Right** *Versatility was the hallmark of many of the great TT riders! Not only did they take part in hill-climbs, long-distance trials and solo road racing, many also competed in the three-wheeler classes. Here the great Jimmie Simpson tackles Ramsey Hairpin in the 1925 Sidecar TT.*

**Above** *Simpson and AJS in action again, this time at Ballacraine in the 1925 Senior TT where he set the fastest lap of 68.97 mph, more than 5 mph better than Freddie Dixon's lap record of the previous year. Yet again, Jimmie Simpson failed to finish the race!* **Below** *The impeccable style of a superb rider! Jimmie Simpson on his Junior AJS approaching the Bungalow.*

The great Howard R. Davies, who won his first TT for AJS in 1921, left the A.J. Stevens concern to build his own HRD machines, and in 1925 won the Senior TT and finished second in the Junior, riding his own bikes!

A challenge to British manufacturers on the Island came from Italy and the Moto Guzzi factory in the Lightweight TT of 1926. Pietro Ghersi set fastest lap and finished second but was disqualified for failing to declare the correct make of sparking plug used in his machine! Note the low, horizontal single-cylinder motor, a design still used by Moto Guzzi today.

**Above** *Stanley Woods, the victor for Norton in the Senior TT of 1926. He averaged over 67 mph for seven laps of the Mountain Circuit, but it was Jimmie Simpson on his AJS who broke the 70-mph barrier for the first time.* **Below** *HRD win again! This time, the Junior TT of 1927 and the rider is Freddie Dixon. Howard Davies can be seen immediately behind Dixon, wearing a flat cap. Also in the picture is Jimmie Simpson, who finished third.*

a 'Jimmie Simpson', by setting a new record lap of 80.82 mph (the first time the 80-mph barrier had been broken), but once again failing to finish the race!

In the Junior TT of that year it was a similar story; Tim Hunt won on the Norton with Jimmy Guthrie, second. Only Ernie Nott coming third in the race saved face for the Rudge concern. Hunt's wins were the first-ever Junior-Senior 'TT double' to be scored on the Island.

Fortunately for Rudge they had not placed all their eggs in the bigger-capacity-class basket and their Lightweight two-valve machine, under the expert guidance of Graham Walker and H. G. Tyrell-Smith, finished first and second in the 250 event, with E. A. Mellors third on his New Imperial.

So began a remarkable run of success for Norton. Their overhead-camshaft single-cylinder machines proved virtually unbeatable, hammering the push-rod Rudges into the ground. Only in the Lightweight class of the TT were Rudge able to maintain their success, but even there they received quite a fright, when in 1933 Excelsior produced a four-valve machine aptly named the 'mechanical marvel', which broke the Rudge hold on the class.

In 1932 the record book for the Senior TT read: Stanley Woods, Jimmy Guthrie, and Jimmie Simpson, a 1–2–3 for Norton. In the Junior TT, it was Stanley Woods, Norton, with Wally Handley and Tyrell-Smith second and third for Rudge. Wally Handley almost won the Lightweight TT for Rudge after raising the lap record to 74.08 mph, but it was the New Imperial of Leonard Davenport which took the chequered flag ahead of Graham Walker and Handley on the Rudge lightweights.

Without any doubt whatsoever, 1933 was Norton's year. They had the first-ever clean sweep in both Senior and Junior TTs. Stanley Woods, Jimmie Simpson and Tim Hunt were first, second and third in the Senior, with Woods, Hunt and Jimmy Guthrie in the Junior.

The best that Rudge could manage in this fateful year was a third place in the Lightweight TT from C. H. Manders, behind the 'mechanical marvel' Excelsior of Syd Gleave and the New Imperial of Charlie Dodson.

Glowing with success from their 1933 results in the TT and knowing that they had the best team of riders in the world, it was surprising that Norton let the double-TT winner, Stanley Woods, be lured away by the Swedish Husqvarna factory for the coming 1934 race season. But with stalwarts Simpson and Guthrie, it was understandable that

they believed they had nothing to fear from any other manufacturer.

In 1934 Stanley Woods raced Husqvarna's new V-twin in the Continental Grands Prix and, of course, on the Isle of Man. However, as Norton had expected, on the Island they had no cause to worry. The two Jimmies, Guthrie and Simpson, did the double act in both Senior and Junior races, with Guthrie winning both events, followed home by his stablemate, Simpson, in second spot. In the Senior, W. F. Rusk finished third on a Velocette and in the Junior, Ernie Nott was third on a Husqvarna.

So, the Swedish Husqvarna factory had made its mark in TT history, particularly as Stanley Woods had set the fastest lap of 80.49 mph over the Mountain Circuit in the Senior.

For Jimmie Simpson, 1934 was his last season in road racing. After 13 glorious years of campaigning on the Island for AJS, Rudge, and Norton, including being the first rider to break the 60-, 70- and 80-mph lap barriers over the Mountain Circuit, Jimmie was to depart the scene in a blaze of glory, leading the triumphant Rudge team with a 1–2–3 in the Lightweight TT. Perhaps the most incredible thing was that Jimmie Simpson only ever won that one TT race in spite of breaking numerous lap records during his racing career on the Island. It was obviously a case of always a bridesmaid and never a bride!

The second and third places in the Lightweight TT of that year went to Ernie Nott and Graham Walker, the other works' riders for Rudge. Graham, of course, was later to become even more famous as a BBC motorcycle commentator and editor of the weekly magazine *Motor Cycling*. In fact, it was in 1934 that Graham first took to the microphone for the BBC who had begun their TT broadcasts as early as 1927.

## Challenge from the Continent

In a way, 1935 was to prove the turning point for the British motorcycle industry on the Isle of Man. Up to that time, apart from the victorious Indian challenge in 1911, the British manufacturers had had things very much their own way. The occasional foray by Guzzi in the late 'twenties showed that things were stirring amongst the manufacturers on the Continent, but nobody could blame Norton, Velocette or Rudge for becoming a little complacent with their exceptional racing record.

Husqvarna had proved in 1934 that 'those Continentals' needed to be watched and, when road-racing ace Stanley Woods signed for Guzzi the following year, motorcycle enthusiasts everywhere waited to see the outcome. And then it happened, Guzzi burst on to the TT scene with machines which could be considered years ahead of their time. Admittedly, the Senior or 500 cc machines were V-twins, but they were overhead-camshaft motors with an outside flywheel on the crankshaft. With the forward cylinder lying horizontal, the centre of gravity for the machine was extremely low, giving exceptional handling characteristics and, to top it all, the new Guzzis had swinging arm rear suspension!

Until that time, virtually every motorcycle made had a 'solid' rear end with the rear wheel being mounted in a triangular section of the frame. This meant the only shock absorption between the rider and the road had been the tyre and the springs under his saddle. Consequently, the rear end of the machine would bounce and leap about every time it hit a bump in the road which was not very conducive to good roadholding characteristics.

The outcome was that Stanley Woods scored the first-ever Senior TT victory for a Continental manufacturer, although it was by a mere four seconds from the Norton of Jimmy Guthrie. Just to show how hot the pace of the race was, Stanley Woods raised the lap record to a remarkable 86.53 mph. W. F. Rusk finished in third place on his 500 Norton.

With no opposition from Guzzi in the Junior TT, Norton made the now quite normal clean sweep of 1–2–3 with riders Guthrie, Rusk and J. H. White. Rusk also set the fastest lap at 79.97 mph.

As with Norton in the Senior TT, Rudge in the Lightweight race received a nasty shock from the Italian Guzzi concern. Without the brilliant riding skill of Jimmie Simpson, the Rudge team found that they were completely outpaced by the flying Guzzi in the hands of Stanley Woods. The horizontal single-cylinder Guzzi 250, with its overhead-camshaft and outside flywheel, was too much for the four-valve, push-rod Rudges, and so Woods led Tyrell-Smith and Ernie Nott over the finishing line on the Glencrutchery Road at an average speed of 71.56 mph and a new lap record of 74.19 mph. The Continental challenge had now arrived!

However, Guzzi lost their number-one rider to the British Velocette factory the following year. That meant that Guzzi no longer had the services of an experienced Isle of Man TT campaigner and, as every racing enthusiast knows, the Mountain Circuit places a very high emphasis on rider ability.

Consequently, the British manufacturers gained a brief respite from the Continental attack on their supremacy on the Island. I say brief because, for the first time, a new sound was heard around the 37¾-mile circuit – the high-pitched wail of the German DKW two-stroke in the Lightweight race.

With the retirement of Jimmie Simpson a new and exciting rider had joined the Norton works' team. His name was Freddie Frith. Norton still had the stalwart Jimmy Guthrie as their number one and it was he who repeated his previous year's winning ride by finishing first in the Senior TT of 1936, followed home by Stanley Woods on the Velocette, with Frith in third place. Stanley Woods broke his own Guzzi lap record on his return to Velocette with a speed of 86.98 mph.

In the Junior TT, Freddie Frith proved his worth to the Norton team by taking the laurels from his team mate, J. H. White, with E. A. Mellors finishing third on his Velocette.

In the Lightweight TT, it was to be the last time that a British machine was to win the class! It was also to be the end of the line as far as push-rod-operated four-strokes were concerned! Not until the 1962 Sidecar TT, when Chris Vincent on his BSA twin won, was a push-rod-engined motorcycle again to see victory on the Island.

A. R. 'Bob' Foster on the New Imperial 250 was the victor, but it was the 'ace' Stanley Woods who set the fastest lap on the howling DKW two-stroke at a speed of 76.20 mph. Meanwhile, Tyrell-Smith had dropped his allegiance to the ailing Rudge concern and rode the sprightly Excelsior into second spot, with the DKW of A. Geiss coming third.

While our aeronautical industry fought battles for the Schneider Trophy with the Supermarine S1 and S2 against the Italians and their Aermacchi monoplanes, the British motorcycle industry fought for supremacy on the world's road-racing circuits. Three of the world's greatest industrial powers, Great Britain, Germany and Italy, attempted to dominate the world of motorised sport. Touring machines . . . to hell with them! Winning meant national prestige and national pride came above all else!

The German BMW factory entered the fray in 1937 along with the flying DKW two-strokes. Guzzi, and soon Gilera and Benelli, were to take up the challenge for the Italian motorcycle industry.

Fortunately, it was still the British riders who held the whip hand with their experience over the Mountain Circuit, but this didn't stop the fiery Italian, Omobono Tenni on his 250 Guzzi becoming the first-ever foreigner to win a TT race, the Lightweight. An Excelsior 250, ridden by S. Wood, split the challenge from the Continent, with E. R. Thomas finishing third for DKW.

The late 'thirties was the era of supercharging. There was nothing in the regulations stipulating that superchargers could or could not be used. In fact, as early as 1931, a supercharged Ariel 500 had actually competed in the Tourist Trophy races. But, because of their mechanical unreliability, machines so-equipped were never considered a serious threat to the standard racing motorcycles of the time. So nothing was done to bar mechanical 'force feeding' on entries in the TT races.

The BMW entry in the 1937 Senior TT proved the point, with none of them managing to halt the Norton run of success. Freddie Frith scored his second TT victory, chased hard home in second spot some 15 seconds later by Stanley Woods on his Velocette. J. H. White finished third on another Norton. Also, the 90-mph barrier was broken by Freddie Frith with a time of 25 minutes, 5 seconds, a lap speed of 90.27 mph.

In the Junior TT, it was Guthrie, Frith and White for a Norton 1–2–3 yet again. But 1937 was to be a sad year. Six weeks after Jimmy Guthrie scored his sixth TT victory, he was tragically killed while racing in the German Grand Prix. It was a terrible loss to the world of motorcycle racing. Jimmy Guthrie's memorial is now a well-known spot on the climb from the Gooseneck up to the Mountain Mile, a tribute to one of the all-time greats on the Isle of Man. Another memorial to him was erected on the Sachsenring Circuit, now in East Germany, where he met his death. It is a shrine to all motorcyclists who have given their lives in pursuit of their sport and a remembrance ceremony is held there every year!

In 1938, supercharging was definitely the name of the game! The Gilera four-cylinder Grand Prix machine was on the drawing board with each of its 125 cc cylinders being blower fed. The BMW twins with their overhead-camshaft engines were also supercharged, while the screaming DKW two-stroke twins boasted a third extra cylinder which was used to pump mixture into the combustion chambers under pressure. Only the British manufacturers adhered to the idea that their thumping single-cylinder, four-strokes should in some way resemble the more sophisticated roadsters of the day.

Instead of aiming for the ultimate in power, the British designers learned their lessons from Guzzi and the Italian manufacturer's ideas for increasing performance through light weight and improvements in suspension and handling.

Plunger rear suspension and then the full swinging arm suspension were developed, along with the first of the telescopic front forks by Norton and Velocette, and for 1938 the gamble paid off. The supercharged machinery from the Continent, with the exception of DKW in the Lightweight race, proved unreliable and both Norton and Velocette managed to stave off the Continental challenge.

Velocette had obviously at last caught up with Norton in the technical development of both their Senior and Junior TT machines. With the riding skill of 'the maestro' Stanley Woods, they proved the point by finishing second to Harold Daniell, Norton, in the Senior, but broke the Bracebridge Street factory's hold on the Junior TT by finishing first and second, with Norton third.

The results of the 1938 Senior and Junior TTs read: Senior – first, Harold Daniell (Norton); second, Stanley Woods (Velocette); and third, Freddie Frith (Norton); Junior – first, Stanley Woods (Velocette); second, Ted Mellors (Velocette); and third, Freddie Frith (Norton). This was a resounding victory for the British single-cylinder 'thumpers'!

Harold Daniell, the 'new' boy in the works' Norton team, also upped the Senior TT lap record to a fantastic 91 mph, a record which was to stand until the great Geoff Duke took over as the Norton 'number one' in 1950.

In the Lightweight TT of 1938, the supercharged DKW two-strokes, with their ear-splitting exhaust note, shattered all British hopes of ever again dominating this class of racing. The speedy German machines were as fast, if not faster, than many of the 350s, and had a shattering fuel consumption of 15 miles-per-gallon. The German, E. Kluge, romped home some 12 minutes ahead of second-placeman, S. Wood (Excelsior), with Tyrell-Smith, on another Excelsior, third.

With the threat of another war looming over the horizon, Norton pulled out of motorcycle racing in 1939 to concentrate on the production of roadsters for the armed services. However, they unofficially supported Freddie Frith on his 1938 ex-works' machine in the hope of keeping the Union Jack flying on the Isle of Man against the German 'invasion' of BMW and DKW machines.

But it was to no avail, because Georg Meier took his supercharged BMW to victory in the Senior TT, followed home in second place by Jock West on another of the horizontally opposed Bavarian twins. Freddie Frith could only manage to bring the Norton home third.

In the Junior TT, Stanley Woods continued his

winning streak for Velocette, beating the Norton of Harold Daniell by a mere eight seconds. Third place went to the DKW two-stroke of H. Fleischmann. And to round off what was a most depressing TT week for British manufacturers, Benelli scored their first-ever TT victory in the Lightweight race with British rider Ted Mellors at the controls; second was E. Kluge on the DKW and third, the redoubtable Excelsior of Tyrell-Smith.

It was blatantly obvious that the tide was turning against the single-cylinder machines. However, the British industry was beginning to experiment with multis. AJS had a supercharged V-4 and Velocette were developing a 'blown' twin. Had it not been for the war, the 'forties could have proved very interesting indeed in the world of Grand Prix motorcycle racing.

The Isle of Man races had developed into an International Grand Prix for highly specialised racing motorcycles which, because the regulations allowed, bore very little resemblance to the motorcycles built by the manufacturers for the average road-going enthusiast. It was true that almost all of the technical advances incorporated in the roadsters during the first 30 years of motorcycle development stemmed from the race tracks, but motorcycle racing had branched out and away from the roadster scene to the extent that it was no longer possible to expect a 'super roadster' to win a Grand Prix.

# CHAPTER THREE

# Courses for horses!

SPEAK OF the Tourist Trophy races and motorcycle enthusiasts the world over automatically think of the Isle of Man Mountain Circuit, the course which for over 50 years has been the ultimate test of man and motorcycle in Grand Prix racing.

The mountain is Snaefell. At 2,034 feet it is the highest peak on the Isle of Man and, although miniature when compared with its counterparts on the mainland and in Europe, it has virtually dominated the development of the world's motorcycle industry. With its lofty peak often shrouded in clouds which sullenly roll in off the Irish Sea, Snaefell is the task master of all competitors who ride in the Tourist Trophy races.

The hairpin bend at Ramsey and the tight uphill bends at Waterworks and the Gooseneck indicate to riders that they are in the foothills leading from the warm June sunshine of sea-level Ramsey to the cooler, damp and often misty mountain air of Snaefell. In a matter of six miles, the temperature can drop anything up to 15 degrees; such is the nature of the $37\frac{3}{4}$-mile Isle of Man Mountain Circuit. On one side of the course competitors may be riding on dry roads in brilliant sunshine, while on the other parts of the circuit they can be crouching behind fairings seeking protection from stinging, torrential rain which smashes into their faces like bullets.

Unless you have ridden as a competitor in either the Manx Grand Prix or the TT races, it is difficult to understand the challenge of the Mountain Circuit. For each lap of the race there are something like 200 bends and corners to negotiate, anything up to 2,000 gearchanges, speed variations from 10 to 150 mph, plus brick walls, kerbstones, trees, telegraph poles and wire fences which wait to trap the careless or reckless rider.

As a road-racing circuit, 'road' being the operative word, the Isle of Man course is one of the very few remaining places where the true or 'thinking' road-race competitor is in his element. Nothing can be left to chance; each and every bend has to be negotiated on a precise line at an exact speed in the right gear to obtain optimum performance. Yet even

all-time great TT competitors such as Stanley Woods, Geoff Duke, Mike Hailwood and Peter Williams admit that they never stopped learning the intricacies of the Mountain Circuit.

Riders either love or hate the TT circuit. There is no in between. Courage is the hallmark of the Isle of Man race competitor and the award, a TT replica, is the badge of that courage. The vast majority of competitors ride a TT race because to them it's there. Like climbing the north face of the Eiger or parachute jumping, it's the personal challenge; man against himself, overcoming fear with courage and determination by fighting his machine over the Mountain. Only more recently, because of the ever-increasing spiral of rising costs in racing, have the financial interest and problems arisen. Professionalism, which has added so much to the sport of motorcycle racing, has in a sad way detracted from the prestige and glamour of the Isle of Man TT races.

It is an accepted fact that it takes a minimum of two or three years' racing to have even an understanding of the TT circuit and, in the past, it was normal for riders to serve an 'apprenticeship' for the TT by riding for at least two years in the Manx Grand Prix, an amateur race run by the Manx Motor Cycle Club in September over the Mountain Circuit.

The 'professionals', riders who earn a fairly lucrative living entertaining the enthusiasts who visit the dozen or so less-demanding courses, see little need or reason for spending a fortnight on the Isle of Man to compete in the TT races. Apart from the fact that they stand very little chance of success on their first racing visit, they believe the financial reward is insufficient to justify them competing in the TT. Cries of 'it's too dangerous!' and 'the start and prize money isn't enough!' have brought pressure to bear on the Auto-Cycle Union and placed a question-mark against the status of the TT as a World Championship event.

Yet, in spite of this, each and every year the number of riders wanting to compete in the Tourist Trophy races continues to grow, and only a select

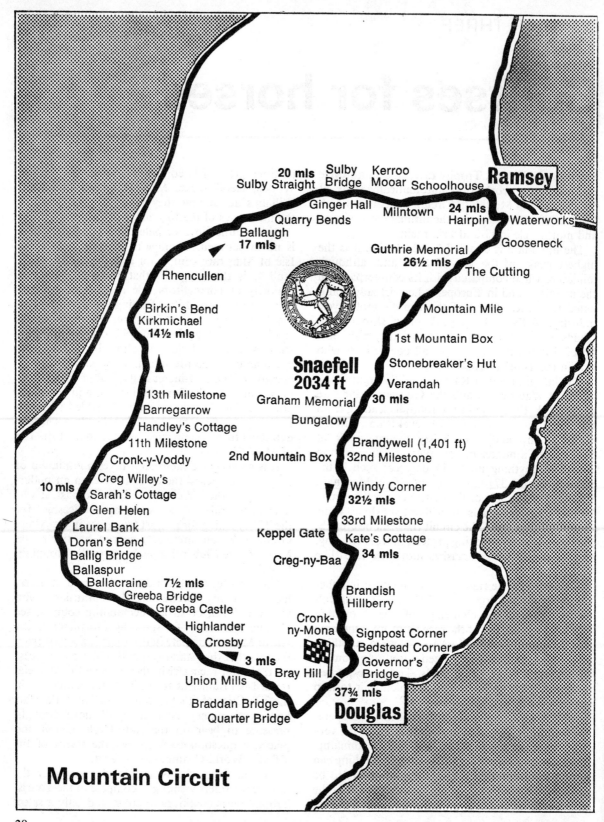

20 mls
Sulby Straight · Sulby Bridge · Kerroo Mooar · Schoolhouse · **Ramsey**

Ginger Hall · Milntown · 24 mls Hairpin · Waterworks

Quarry Bends

Ballaugh 17 mls · Gooseneck

Guthrie Memorial 26½ mls · The Cutting

Rhencullen

Mountain Mile

Birkin's Bend
Kirkmichael
14½ mls · 1st Mountain Box

Stonebreaker's Hut

**Snaefell 2034 ft** · Verandah 30 mls

13th Milestone
Barregarrow · Graham Memorial
Handley's Cottage · Bungalow
11th Milestone · Brandywell (1,401 ft)
Cronk-y-Voddy · 2nd Mountain Box · 32nd Milestone
Creg Willey's · Windy Corner 32½ mls
10 mls Sarah's Cottage
Glen Helen · 33rd Milestone
Laurel Bank · Keppel Gate · Kate's Cottage
Doran's Bend · 34 mls
Ballig Bridge · Creg-ny-Baa
Ballaspur
Ballacraine 7½ mls · Brandish
Greeba Bridge · Hillberry
Greeba Castle
Highlander · Cronk-ny-Mona · Signpost Corner
Crosby · Bedstead Corner
3 mls · Governor's Bridge
Union Mills · Bray Hill
37¾ mls
Braddan Bridge · **Douglas**
Quarter Bridge

**Mountain Circuit**

38

number of the professionals refuse to accept the challenge of the Mountain.

Fortunately, there are riders of the calibre of Peter Williams, Jack Findlay, Mick Grant, Klaus Enders, Paul Smart, Stanley Woods (no relative of the great pre-war rider) and many more, who still consider the TT the greatest road races of all, and each June the 'magic' Isle lures them back to the start line on Glencrutchery Road.

But what does the rider face once the starter has dropped his flag? What does he think about as his machine plummets at over 130 mph down Bray Hill, a few hundred yards after the start? Is it the tricky adverse camber while braking downhill for Quarter Bridge just over a mile away, or the slippery climb out of Glen Helen past Sarah's Cottage, where Mike Hailwood and Agostini both took a tumble a few years back? Let's take a tour of the 37¾-mile course to try and understand what makes the TT Mountain Circuit the greatest *road*-racing course in the world!

Imagine you have just leapt into the saddle of a racing motorcycle, the engine is firing cleanly and you're winding the twistgrip throttle wide open as you change up through the gears and hurtle away from the start line. The short, slightly downhill starting straight is covered in a matter of seconds as you snick the bike into top gear and the road ahead veers slightly to the left and suddenly disappears in the steep drop down Bray Hill. At 110 to 120 mph, the road appears extremely narrow and, at the bottom of the hill, it bears right and rises sharply from a dip at the Bray Hill crossroads.

Crossing from the left side of the road down the hill, you have to clip within a foot of the kerbstone on the right at the bottom of the hill. As you hit the dip, slightly cranked over to get through the right-hand sweep at around 120 mph, the machine's suspension is fully compressed and you slam on to the fuel tank as the G forces pile on to your back as you come out of the dip.

Throttle still wide open you drift over to the left of the road, skimming past privet hedges at 100 mph-plus. On the left as you hurtle up a slight incline is a road junction where photographers and spectators gather to watch the spectacular leaps of faster riders who take off on the hump where the two roads meet.

You have only just really begun to collect your thoughts about the start and how the bike's behaving as the road ahead seems to narrow, disappear to the left and head downhill towards Quarter Bridge. Bad camber here; keep over to the left while braking very hard and changing down gears to take the

tricky, adverse camber, right-hand corner. Can't afford to take it too fast because of the brick wall over on the left as you exit for the straight towards Braddan Bridge.

Ah, smooth road at last; straight as a die and the first real chance to get tucked in behind the fairing.

With the motor just beginning to get wound up in top gear and speeds on the bigger machines topping the ton (100 mph), the warm summer sun disappears behind the giant elm trees which line the right-hand side of the road approaching Braddan Bridge. Must change down a couple of gears here to take the very awkward left bend, followed by an immediate right over the bridge. You'd hardly have time to notice that the public grandstands in the church yard are crammed with spectators eagerly craning their necks to see you tuck down behind your fairing again as you wring the throttle open searching for more speed.

The needle of the rev counter soars up to the 'blood line' as the motor spins towards exploding point in each gear. A full-bore left-hander coming up and after that, Union Mills! Fast right-hander approach, left-hander into the village, then right-hand bend tightening up, flicking over to the left to cross the bridge and then right-hander on to the rise climbing out of the village. Take it easy clipping the corners all the way through using all of the road and you should be all right. Must remember the old rule . . . fast in and you may not come out, slowly in and you can come out fast!

There's only one more village, Crosby, and you're out into the country! A short, sharp, full-power climb away from Union Mills and then you can really get a move on, just 4½ miles from the start. Rolling off the power a fraction to take the fast right-hander leading into Crosby, it's full throttle through the village with roads appearing to become narrower as speeds top the 130 to 140 mph mark. Windows shake to the echo of open exhausts and spectators strain against the course ropes to catch a glimpse of the first of the speeding machines.

Like a grey, granite ribbon, the road undulates towards the Highlander. If a two-stroke's going to seize, then every experienced rider will tell you that it's just after Crosby, with almost two miles of full-bore motoring, that it happens. If it doesn't, then all is well and it's head down below the screen for the 'flying run' through the speed trap set up outside the Highlander pub. Anything up to 150 mph will be achieved by the big bikes on this extremely fast downhill stretch. Spectators at the pub down their pints and almost twist their heads from their necks as they try to spot the race numbers on the flying machines. Some have the good fortune of buying a pint or two for luckless riders who coast silently into the forecourt on their dead machines.

But for those still racing on past the Highlander, the tricky left- and right-hand bends at Greeba Castle are the next challenge. Once again, using all of the road and clipping the kerbs on both sides, Greeba Castle is one of the deceptively fast series of bends in which the true TT 'aces' make up time. Take a car through keeping to the left of the road and 50 mph seems fast, but the real aces are travelling at twice this speed on two-wheelers!

Bridges, bridges and more bridges! There's Quarter Bridge, Braddan Bridge, a bridge at Union Mills, and the next on the circuit is Greeba Bridge. This is another very fast left-hand bend and nothing much can be said about it except that, unless you take the fast line through Greeba Castle and set yourself up properly for the bridge, you'll lose precious seconds in accelerating to maximum speed on the very fast, mile-long run to the sharp right-hand corner at Ballacraine.

Judging the braking distance and changing down gear for the 90-degree corner at Ballacraine are probably the most difficult points about this relatively slow part of the circuit. Wisely, there is a slip road along which riders may detour if they run out of brakes or shut off too late and are going too fast to take the corner.

Ballacraine is also the first of the circuit commentary locations and there, armed with stopwatches and with an unofficial time-keeper, the commentator is able to give the crowds around the circuit a good idea of how individual competitors are progressing after 7½ miles of racing.

Accelerating hard away from Ballacraine, you wring the throttle against the stop on the short, sharp climb which leads to Ballaspur, where the brow of the hill is on a left-hand bend. As the course drops away down to Ballig Bridge, you leave the ground at 80 mph-plus while cranked over for the corner and, drifting sideways with tyres fighting for grip, you hurtle down-hill towards the bridge, where before it was levelled you would have taken off once again!

Over the bridge and it's into a 'blind' left-hander on to a short straight, and here you have to be really skilled to negotiate Doran's Bend, named after the famous TT rider who came to grief here in the mid-'fifties. Leave braking or changing gear too late and precious seconds are lost as you enter Laurel Bank, a deceptive right-hand corner followed by a short straight, and then left and right over another bridge into Glen Helen. The road has been

carved out of solid rock and you can't afford to take chances as you play tunes on the gearbox to keep the racing motor in the power band.

Spectators at Glen Helen Hotel have the advantage of being able to hear the riders on the approach to the tricky left-hand bend leading up to the right-hander at Sarah's Cottage. It was here, on the adverse camber and smooth, slippery surface, that both Agostini and Hailwood came to grief in the 1965 Senior TT.

Even on bright, sunlit, summer days, the Glen Helen section with its sloping banks and trees is sheltered from the sun and, if there has been rain around the course, this is one section where riders have to take extra care because the roads take longer to dry.

But, once past Sarah's Cottage and on up Creg Willey's Hill, you can see bright daylight shining through the trees. A tight right-hand corner, followed by a left and then a right takes you on to the famous Cronk-y-Voddy straight. On a map it appears a fairly straight line, but in fact it is a series of bumps or undulations in the TT circuit, where at 120 mph you spend almost half your time in the air!

Not until you pass the crossroads towards the end of the straight does the pounding cease and, with your brains still rattling in your skull, you aim your racing machine for the double right-hand corner which drops down to the left-hand bend at the 11th Milestone.

Riders of the calibre of Hailwood, Agostini, Read and Williams would reach this point in something like six minutes from the start of the race; in a car on open roads you would be fortunate to see the straight leading to Handley's Cottage in 20 minutes!

Handley's Cottage is a corner where buildings on either side of the road create a chicane three-quarters of the way along a very fast straight. If your line is right for the corner, you can fly through at any speed between 80 and 90 mph. But if it's wrong, then, like the famous Walter Handley, you might well take a spill at this spot. Thus the name, Handley's Cottage!

After Handley's Cottage comes Barregarrow, one of the fastest sections of the circuit. At this point, you approach the top right-hand bend leading down to the tight left-hand corner at the 13th Milestone at around 120 mph-plus. This sort of speed here means foot, footrest and fairing scraping the ground, with the grass-covered wall and hedge getting nearer and nearer as your bike drifts out of the corner on to the straight leading towards the next village on the course – Kirkmichael.

Passing the 14th Milestone on the right-hand corner into the village, the Mountain Circuit leaves the original St John's course, which turns left and heads back towards Peel. The road through Kirkmichael village appears extremely narrow, and white-washed walls close in on you as you clip the kerbstones on both sides of the road trying to 'straighten' the winding strip of tarmac and to urge ever-increasing speed from your machine.

About a mile from Kirkmichael comes the next hazard on the course, Birkin's Bend. It is a very fast right-hander, followed by an equally quick left-hand sweep, which sadly earned its title from Archie Birkin, who in 1927, during practice for the TT races, received fatal injuries after crashing into a lorry which was travelling in the opposite direction to the course. Following this tragic accident, it was decided that, as from 1928, roads would also be 'closed' for practice.

Vantage points for spectators are very limited on this high-speed section and very few bother to witness the skill of the riders here, with the attraction of Ballaugh Bridge just a short distance away. There, in the village, is one of the most spectacular places to watch the racing.

A fast straight, leading down to the hump-back bridge, tests your ability to the full. At any speed over 30 mph, machines leap into the air as they cross the bridge; a delight for photographers and spectators alike. But on landing, you have to negotiate an awkward right- and left-hand corner out of the village and only the foolhardy or very brave play act to the enthusiastic audience.

Only 17 miles have been covered and you are still not half-way around the Mountain Circuit. At Ballaugh there is the second commentary point, which keeps nervous pit attendants on the Glencrutchery Road informed as to how their riders are progressing. But for you it is a race against time. Speed is all important and, with the dreaded leap at Ballaugh past, it is full bore towards Quarry Bends.

Top gear all the way; the road snakes ahead and, with a cottage on the left flashing past, you rapidly approach the road junction by the zoo. Quarry Bends are immediately ahead and this means a right, left, right and left again on to the Sulby Straight. Once more it is mind over throttle – too fast and the line through the bends is completely spoiled for the fast exit on to the straight; too slow and precious seconds are wasted in reaching maximum speed along one of the fastest parts of the course.

To be on the race leader board, you must come out of the left-hand bend on to the Sulby Straight at around 100 mph. Within 200 yards you should have snicked the machine into top gear and, with the throttle wound against the stop, you have a mile-long straight the like of which you have never before experienced. A speed boat ride in a rough sea could be used as a comparison but, with your head down behind the screen on your fairing and the road disappearing towards the horizon in a thin pencil line, you hope and pray that your motor won't explode beneath you as you hold the throttle wide open. 110, 120, 130, 140 mph . . . the speed builds up as Sulby village flashes past and 30-mph restriction signs seem ridiculous as you leap from bump to bump on the roller coaster ride to Sulby Bridge.

The 800-yard marker board is extremely important as it indicates to you that there is a tight, 45-mph right-hand corner ahead and, with anything up to 110 mph to lose, the warning board is very necessary for the safety of the competitors.

Spectators stand behind the brick walls lining the bridge to watch you boot-scraping your way around the corner and accelerating hard towards the Ginger Hall Hotel. Here, others are busy quenching their thirst and gazing in admiration as you crank your racing machine on the left-hander which leads over the hill and down to the tricky left- and right-hand bends of Kerroo Mooar.

Miss a gear or leave braking too late at this point and you are in trouble. The road appears to go straight on but this is simply a slip road or entrance to a farmhouse; the TT circuit goes left and heads towards Glentramman.

On the right can be seen the rolling foothills leading to the Mountain, but you are too busy picking out your personal course markers which indicate a change of gear or direction as you speed towards Ramsey and the next radio commentary point.

Aim to the right of the tree on the straight approaching Milntown Cottage, because here you will find the kerb juts out into the road above the rise! Left-hander clipping the corner on the approach to the cottage, very bumpy if taken too wide. Then heel over for the right-hander past Milntown Cottage and on to the short straight over the bridge towards Schoolhouse Corner.

A fast left-hand bend past the school and it's taken only 15 minutes to cover the 24 miles from the start to Ramsey. The short straight from the school flashes past, and ignoring the 'stop' sign, you heel the bike over to the right to rush into Parliament Square. The crowds wave as you gingerly crank the bike over on a surface which is often slippery due to molten tar. Immediately you take the left-hander out of the square and head up past the bus garage for the right-hand corner at May Hill.

Now comes the make-or-break part of the TT circuit – the Mountain climb! The change in temperature and thinning atmosphere can play havoc with carburation, especially on the high-revving two-stroke machines which make up the bulk of present-day entries in the races. The 1,400-foot climb from sea level begins at May Hill and, as you pitch your bike around the right-hand bend leading out of Ramsey, attempting to avoid the bump in the road by a manhole cover, you hope that the last-minute carburation adjustments you made in the warming up area before the race were correct.

Striving to keep the racing motor 'on song' in its narrow power band, you clip the kerb on the left-hand corner past May Hill and then it's a short, slightly uphill straight climbing to the full-bore, right-hand bend which leads to the notorious Ramsey Hairpin.

Normally, due to the very nature of its design, there is very little engine-braking effect when the throttle is closed on a two-stroke motor, but such is the steepness of the climb to the Hairpin that many riders are surprised at their rate of deceleration as they change down gears to negotiate the tricky 10-mph hairpin corner. Go into the hairpin wide and come out on a tight line, or into the corner tight and exit wide: the lines around Ramsey Hairpin are varied, but every one means taking the corner in first gear and slipping the clutch furiously to keep the racing motors from dying on the ever-steepening road.

The stench of scorching clutch plates pervades the air as you urge your machine away from the Hairpin and uphill towards the bend at Waterworks. The smouldering transmission and motor are just beginning to get into their stride again when the throttle is closed and the struggle to regain power is repeated after taking the double right-hand Waterworks Corner in one, clean swoop. You must forget about the apex you see on the first corner; take it wide and then come in across the road to clip the apex on the second bend.

The scarred brick wall indicates the number of car drivers and other over-enthusiastic riders who have failed to realise just how sharply the bend tightens. With a sheer drop of 100 feet or more down the hillside overlooking Ramsey, it's not exactly the healthiest place to leave the TT circuit.

After Waterworks, the climb eases slightly and the first patches of prickly mountain gorse appear

in the thinning hedgerows. But there is no respite for your hard-working racing motor as you pass the 25-mile marker board. The climb is far from over.

Two sweeping left-hand bends followed by a short straight take you to the Gooseneck, very aptly named and a sharp, right-hand uphill corner, with a badly cambered surface, which climbs steeply, placing ever-increasing stress on the over-worked transmission as you slip the clutch yet again to keep the motor from faltering.

At long last the road ahead is clear. After losing what seems like minutes on the slow, difficult corners from Ramsey, you have to tuck in behind the fairing and wring the throttle wide open as you accelerate up the Mountain. Must make up some time on this fast stretch to Guthrie's Memorial and The Cutting!

In spite of the steep climb, your speed rises as you crouch behind your wind-cheating fairing to take the two, long sweeping left-hand bends after the Gooseneck as one – 80, 90, 100, 110 mph! The sheep grazing gently on the mountain slopes scuttle away when the first of the competitors hurtles by, open exhaust renting the air, shattering the calm and echoing back and forth across the foothills leading up to Snaefell. In two miles, you have climbed almost a 1,000 feet into the cooler mountain air.

If there is any chance of mist, the first microdots of water begin to appear on the fairing screen and on your helmet visor. If the weather is really bad, then it is sometimes possible to run into the clouds down at the Gooseneck, but with a week's practice behind you and, more often than not, two or three year's experience of racing on the Island, you have to ease off only slightly when visibility closes in; most riders know the Mountain like the back of their hands!

As you round the second of the left-hand bends on the high-speed climb from the Gooseneck, you can see The Cutting ahead where Guthrie's Memorial is set on the right-hand side of the road. But, on the tricky left and right 'twitch' through The Cutting taken at around 80 to 90 mph, you have no time to stop and read the plaque which sadly tells of Jimmy Guthrie's untimely death at the German Grand Prix in 1937. All you can think of is taking the bends as fast as humanly possible to maintain speed for the Mountain Mile, which lies just around the deceptive, left-hand bend after Guthrie's Memorial.

Stone walls and hedges have now given way to wire fencing, where little tufts of wool indicate that sheep are the main inhabitants of the area; only in

June and September with the annual pilgrimage of those fanatical, high-speed human beings on two-wheels is their lazy, peaceful existence disturbed.

But this is no time for nature study and, with speeds still rising from 80 to 120 or even 130 mph on the Mountain Mile, the summit of Snaefell can be seen ahead with its radio mast towering into the clear summer sky. A slight right-hand kink in the road takes you over one of the many mountain bridges and leads you on to the short straight heading for the first Mountain Box. Here the road sweeps sharply to the left and, with 28½ miles covered, the climb up the Mountain continues.

Ahead the road bears right over another bridge and beyond can be seen the Stonebreaker's Hut nestling against the mountainside and indicating the point where you sweep left at almost 90 mph on to the Verandah. Here the road has been completely resurfaced and, compared with the approach over the rough, badly cambered mountain road, is billiard-table smooth. The Verandah runs around the side of Snaefell and is a series of four right-hand bends which are taken as one at over 100 mph by the faster competitors.

Roadholding and riding ability are tested to the limit as you accelerate around the Verandah aiming wide on the first corner, taking the second about three-quarters out in the road, the third just over the white line marking the centre of the bend, and finally accelerating hard at the apex of the fourth corner which exits on to the narrow straight towards Stone Bridge. This has recently been resurfaced and is below the Graham Memorial.

The mountain refuge hut, which has been built above Stone Bridge, was set there in memory of that great post-war TT rider Les Graham, who was tragically killed when he lost control of his MV Agusta at the bottom of Bray Hill. The corner over the bridge is deceptively fast and leads on to another short straight which bears right on a 'mini Verandah' towards the Bungalow.

A favourite spot for spectators up on the mountain, the Bungalow can only be reached from inside the circuit when the roads are closed or by electric railway from Douglas and Laxey when the roads are open. The railway continues to the summit of Snaefell, where there is a restaurant and a fantastic view of the Isle of Man. The railway lines actually cross the TT course and you bounce over the tracks on the medium-to-fast left and right sweeping bends at the Bungalow.

As a point of interest for visitors to the Island, there is an exceptionally good motorcycle museum situated at the Bungalow where some of the earlier machines which have competed in the TT may be seen. Also, the Bungalow is the last of the radio commentary points around the circuit and one of the most popular signalling locations to let competitors know their positions in the race. With only just over six miles to go to the finish, a last-ditch effort from a rider can often pick up those vital few seconds which will carry him on to the leader board and possibly a winning place.

Being almost the highest point on the course, the Bungalow is also in the perfect situation to inform the start line officials about the weather conditions on the Mountain. Heavy mist or cloud at the Bungalow has often meant the postponement of the races for an hour or more. But, if mist shrouds the Mountain during the course of the race, competitors are heard before being seen as they sweep across the railway tracks and disappear towards the fast left-hand sweep at Brandywell, the highest point on the circuit.

On a clear day, you can make the most of the downhill stretch from Brandywell to the start and finish line. Only the rise in the road at Hillberry and out of Governor's Bridge stop you coasting all the way home. Riding ability and speed are all that matter to pick up those vital seconds lost on the climb up the Mountain. After the 32nd Milestone, a short straight leads to a triple corner which is taken at around 90 mph by the faster riders in one sweeping bend; then it's downhill all the way to the medium-fast, right-hander at Windy Corner. It's an unusual name for a bend, but understandable as prevailing winds from the sea whistle between the peaks of the two hills off to the left, where the valley drops down to the coast and Laxey, site of the famous 'big wheel'.

If there is another rider just ahead on the road, you will see him on the half-mile straight which leads from Windy Corner to the high-speed, left-hand bend at the 33rd Milestone. The surface is extremely bumpy on the narrow line into the corner which widens considerably before the right-hand bend leading to Keppel Gate.

Over this section of the Mountain, the bike tends to run away from you and it takes extra concentration to bring the bouncing, bucking machine under control as you brake hard for the right and then tight left-hand corner at Keppel Gate. Here the road really begins to plummet down the Mountain and a few hundred yards ahead you see the white-washed walls of Kate's Cottage.

Trying to keep to the right-hand side of the road on the bumpy surface, you aim at the apex and clip the corner of the left-hand bend at Kate's Cottage.

You drift across the road with the grass-covered flint wall rushing closer and closer to your right boot. Impending disaster over, you look ahead and see the sky and in the distance the sea. The road itself disappears downwards below your front wheel and suddenly you realise what it must be like to ski on an Olympic slalom course!

A half-mile straight which drops 300 feet pushes the rev counter needle into the red in top gear! 140 to 150 mph, leaping from bump to bump, and in a few brief seconds the hotel at Creg-ny-Baa looms large through the screen on your fairing. Try and keep the bike over on the left side of the road, brake hard and change down gears to take the corner at about 45 mph. Clip the corner and drift wide on the exit past the sandbag-lined hotel with grass and hedge brushing past a few feet away from the fairing on your bike! You're almost home and if the worst comes to the worst, you could almost coast to the pits from here!

The road is smooth, straight, downhill and extremely rapid. The spectators in the grandstand at Creg-ny-Baa gaze in awe as you drop quickly on to your fuel tank, tuck your head once again behind the protective screen and accelerate away at an incredible pace towards Brandish Corner. The exhaust note rises to a crescendo in each gear and, to the spectators, only the pronounced movement of your right arm at each gearchange indicates that you are wringing as much full throttle power as possible from your speeding machine.

Speeds rise from 45 to 145 mph and, using all of the road, the faster riders are able to roll off the power, change down one gear, then immediately turn on full power again to hurtle through Brandish at around 110 mph. This left-hander leads on to another absolutely smooth downhill straight, and within seconds your machine is in top gear and, once again, reaching towards the 140-mph mark, before slowing slightly to peel off on the rapid Hillberry section, a sweeping right-hand uphill bend which almost immediately swings left and tightens up on the rise at Cronk-ny-Mona.

A short distance along the road and over the rise is Signpost Corner, an acute 90-degree right-hand bend, where course marshals impatiently wait to catch a glimpse of the approaching machines which can be heard but not seen. It is from Signpost that the lights which appear over each and every individual rider's scoreboard at the grandstand are switched on to indicate to the pit staff and officials that a particular rider has rounded the corner and within a minute or so may possibly be pulling into his pit to refuel.

But, although the start and finish line is only a mile away, races have been won and lost over this short distance, because the last part of the circuit is as tricky as the rest. The downhill drop from Signpost to the medium-fast left-hand Bedstead Corner is bumpy and deceptive, while braking hard for the full right bend at the Nook, and immediately swinging left on the steep and slippery approach to Governor's Bridge, is equally difficult.

Nobody in their right mind tries to rush Governor's Bridge, a tight right-hand, downhill hairpin bend followed by a very badly cambered left-hand corner, around which you have to slip the clutch and keep the motor revving to accelerate out slightly uphill on to the home straight along Glencrutchery Road. In trying to save half a second at Governor's Bridge even the most brilliant of riders could lose the race!

As any rider knows, the race isn't over until you've passed the chequered flag and it all happens on Glencrutchery Road in front of the grandstand, where the crowds rise to their feet to acclaim the winner! After completing just one lap of this difficult and demanding circuit, it seems incredible that men and machines can withstand the punishment handed out to them over three or more laps of the course, depending on the race in which they are competing. In the good old, bad old days, from 1926 up to 1959, riders in the Senior and Junior TTs had to complete seven laps of the Mountain Circuit with roads in a far worse state of repair than at present. In fact, in 1957, they had to complete eight laps in the Senior TT and this Bob McIntyre did at an average speed of 98.99 mph and took 3 hours, 2 minutes and 57 seconds to do it. It makes present-day two-hours-and-a-bit races seem like short circuit events!

## The Clypse Circuit

The 'other' course used by TT competitors and still remembered by some, because it was last used in only 1959, is the Clypse Circuit. Originally introduced in 1954 to save the declining Lightweight 125 TT and to reintroduce the Sidecar event to the Island, the Clypse course brought a touch of mainland short circuit racing to the TTs with its massed starts for the 125 machines, and with a clutch start being used in 1956 for the Sidecar race. In 1955, the 250 Lightweight race was also transferred to the Clypse Circuit.

The interesting point about all of the courses which have been used over the years for the TT races is that each and every one of them has incorporated parts of previous circuits. For example,

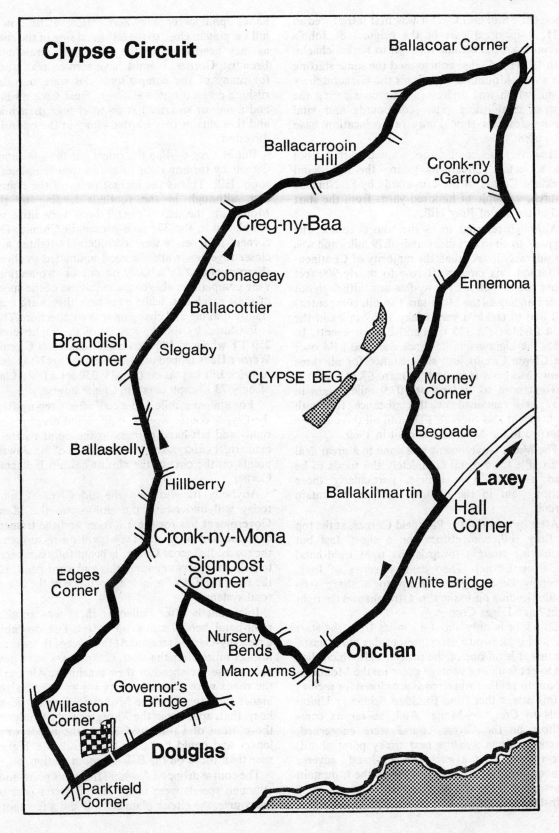

# Clypse Circuit

Ballacoar Corner

Ballacarrooin Hill

Cronk-ny-Garroo

Creg-ny-Baa

Cobnageay

Ballacottier

Ennemona

Brandish Corner

Slegaby

CLYPSE BEG

Morney Corner

Begoade

Ballaskelly

Hillberry

Ballakilmartin

Laxey

Hall Corner

Cronk-ny-Mona

Signpost Corner

Edges Corner

White Bridge

Nursery Bends

Manx Arms

Onchan

Governor's Bridge

Willaston Corner

Douglas

Parkfield Corner

when the Mountain Circuit was first introduced in 1911, it included part of the original St John's Circuit from Ballacraine through to Kirkmichael.

In 1954 the Clypse course used the same starting line as the Mountain Circuit on the Glencrutchery Road, which was understandable considering the cost of establishing pits, scoreboards and vital communications should any other location have been used.

However, the competitors soon departed from the Mountain Circuit by taking the right-hand Parkfield Corner at the crossroads by St Ninian's Church, a couple of hundred yards from the start and at the top of Bray Hill.

Although referred to as the 'short' course, the Clypse Circuit in fact measured 10.79 miles and was considerably longer than the majority of Continental Grand Prix circuits. It rose to nearly 900 feet above sea level after Creg-ny-Baa and, although not as demanding as the Mountain Circuit, competitors still had to tackle a very tricky 107.9 miles in the 1954 Lightweight 125 race and Sidecar events. In 1955, the Lightweight 250 race was also held over the Clypse Circuit, but the distance for all three events had been reduced to a mere 97.14 miles! It was extended to 10 laps or 107.9 miles again in 1957 and remained at this distance for both Lightweight and Sidecar TTs until all three classes returned to the Mountain Circuit in 1960.

The Manx Government had gone to a great deal of trouble to re-metal completely the roads to be used as the Clypse course, particularly those sections 'out in the country' off the Mountain Circuit.

After turning right at Parkfield Corner, at the top of Bray Hill, competitors had a short, fast but undulating straight towards the tight right-hand Willaston Corner. Then came a series of long, sweeping bends tightening up to a sharp left-hander leading on to the short straight and the tight right-hand Edges Corner.

This spot is only about 1½ miles from the start line and is known to many present-day enthusiasts, because it is on one of the many roads which they use to get from one vantage point on the Mountain Circuit to another while roads are closed for racing; in this case, either from Braddan Bridge or Union Mills to Cronk-ny-Mona. And, as far as competitors on the Clypse course were concerned, Cronk-ny-Mona was the next tricky point ahead. For them it was a sweeping left-hand, adverse camber bend which took them on to the Mountain course, but in the reverse direction!

Instead of taking Hillberry in a high-speed, right-hand, uphill sweep, they accelerated swiftly downhill keeping in close to the left-hand side of the road as they headed on to the fast, rising straight to Brandish Corner. It must have seemed really odd for many of the competitors who were one day rushing down towards Hillberry from Creg-ny-Baa and a day or so later having to change their lines and thoughts as they hurtled along in the opposite direction.

But at Creg-ny-Baa the riders left the Mountain Circuit by turning right to head towards Ballacarrooin Hill. This is the highest point of the course and, although in the foothills leading to the Mountain, the actual circuit bore very little resemblance to the 37¾-mile Mountain Circuit. The corners and bends were considerably tighter and closer together, while the road undulated in short, sharp rises and falls. Only on one or two sections were competitors able to make full use of the speed of their machines, while elsewhere they were constantly braking and changing gear or direction. This is indicated by the lap speeds of the Lightweight 250 TT where in 1954, over the Mountain Circuit, Werner Haas lapped at 91.22 mph on his NSU, but in 1955, Bill Lomas on the MV 250 set a fastest lap of only 73.13 mph over the Clypse course.

For almost a mile and a half after Creg-ny-Baa, the Clypse course wound, dipped and dived round right- and left-hand corners to the point where it made riders dizzy. And then came one of the slowest points on the circuit, the almost hairpin Ballacoar Corner.

Anybody travelling on the old Clypse Circuit today will understand the enthusiasm the Manx Government has for the TT races and the tremendous amount of money they spent on re-surfacing the roads. Ballacoar Corner is beautifully cambered to help the riders negotiate this awkward bend, yet the road itself is of minor importance in the Manx road system.

Immediately after Ballacoar there was another right-hand bend leading on to the fast downhill Cronk-ny-Garroo section. At this part of the course, just six miles after the start, competitors were now able to use the speed of their machines. Although the roads were generally narrower and the hedges higher than those on the Mountain Circuit, riders knew that, apart from the 90-degree right-hander at the bottom of Cronk-ny-Garroo, the bends were longer and could be taken faster and in a higher gear than those on the Ballacarrooin section.

The course dropped downhill from this point and, although speeds were rising on this faster part of the course, the circuit planners still had a few more tricky obstacles to test the skill of competitors. The next, after the sweeping left-hander at Ennemona and the 7th Milestone, was the long, long left-hand Morney Corner, which was almost immediately followed by a right-hander on to a short straight leading to another tight left-hand bend at Begoade.

If a rider reached this point in six minutes from the start, he was doing extremely well and also, by this time, the course would have sorted the men out from the boys! In other words, if a competitor could really ride a motorcycle and not rely on out-and-out power and speed, he should have been among the leaders of the massed start race. But the next section was where you lost all the advantage to the high-speed 'works' machinery, because after Begoade came the swerving right and left up to the T-junction at Hall Corner. Here the circuit joined the wide and very fast main road from Onchan to Laxey and, with over a mile of full-bore, top gear racing from Hall Corner to the Manx Arms in Onchan, speeds into the dip at White Bridge approached the 130 to 140 mph mark on the faster machines.

However, as the riders plunged downhill towards White Bridge and took the sweeping right-hand uphill bend into Onchan, the roads narrowed very quickly as the shops and houses closed in on the circuit. Also, the braking point had to be judged perfectly to negotiate the tight, right-hand corner leading sharply uphill at the Manx Arms pub and many a rider found himself having to take to the slip road leading towards Governor's Bridge!

Nine miles covered and a short sharp series of corners – left, right, right and left again through Nursery Bends – chopped the speed once more and then for a short distance it was out into the country on a fast 600-yard straight towards Signpost Corner, where the Mountain Circuit was rejoined, but this time in the right direction. The riders turned left at Signpost, dropped down to Bedstead Corner, through the Nook and on to Governor's Bridge, but for competitors in the Clypse Circuit races, there was no tricky adverse camber hairpin to face! They rode straight out on to the Glencrutchery Road to turn right and head for the finish line.

In a way, it's a pity that the Clypse Circuit was dropped in favour of the Mountain course for the Lightweight and Sidecar TTs, particularly the 125 race which, apart from the years when the Japanese manufacturers sent large teams to the Island, has never been very well supported and has meant quite long boring gaps between competitors for spectators around the Mountain Circuit.

Also, the massed starts for the smaller capacity classes gave the TTs something of the atmosphere

of the short circuit racing found on the mainland. However, with sidecar entrants in both 750 and 500 class now topping 80 machines, it would be hard to imagine the result of a massed clutch start on the Glencrutchery Road with dozens of sidecars attempting to enter Parkfield Corner all at the same time. Maybe only with the 125 TT, where in 1973 there were just 41 starters, could we see a massed start and a truly exciting race once more over the old Clypse Circuit!

## The St John's Circuit

Just imagine stopping to change an exhaust valve on your motorcycle during the course of a race, re-mounting and riding to win by two minutes, 17 seconds! It sounds ridiculous and seems impossible, but that is precisely what Jack Marshall, riding a single-cylinder Triumph, did to win the 1908 Tourist Trophy over the St John's Circuit.

Simplicity in the design of the motorcycles of that era made valve-swopping easier than mending a puncture. Single speeds, belt drives, and total-loss hand-pump lubrication to the side-valve motors were also the reasons why competitors had to use the St John's Circuit for motorcycle racing on the Isle of Man, instead of tackling the Mountain course.

As explained earlier, in 1904 Lord Raglan, the Governor of the Isle of Man, invited the RAC to stage trials for the Gordon Bennett Cup car races on the Island using a 52-mile 'closed-road' circuit that embraced most of the usable roads or tracks between Douglas, Port Erin, Peel, Jurby, St Judes, Ramsey and over the Mountain to Hillberry.

Naturally, the Auto-Cycle Club saw the opportunity of taking motorcycle racing to the Island and immediately requested permission from the Manx Government to establish a 'closed-roads' circuit to run trials to select a team of motorcyclists for the International Cup races, which were at that time being held in Europe. It was obvious to all that the motorcycles could never follow the tough Mountain Circuit laid out by the Royal Automobile Club, but in the west of the Island, where the mountains rolled gently down to the sea, there proved to be an ideal course for the rather fragile two-wheelers.

The course had to be sufficiently demanding to test the skill of the riders and the stamina of their machines, but there was little point in establishing a trial in which none of the contestants would finish. So, after surveying the Island's highways, the A-CC mapped out the 15.8-mile long St John's Circuit.

It earned its name from the location of the start

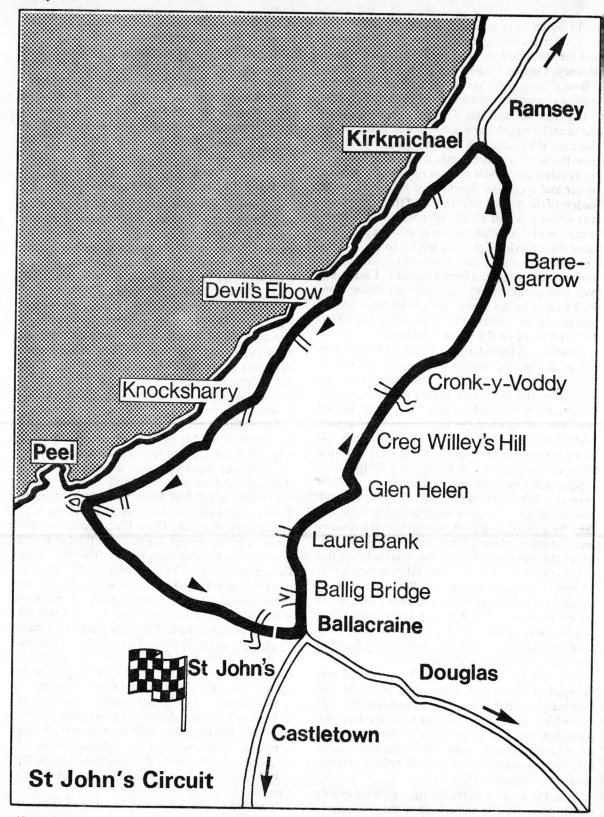

Ramsey

Kirkmichael

Barre-
garrow

Devil's Elbow

Cronk-y-Voddy

Knocksharry

Creg Willey's Hill

Peel

Glen Helen

Laurel Bank

Ballig Bridge

Ballacraine

St John's

Douglas

Castletown

**St John's Circuit**

and finish line at the village of St John's, which had a useful amount of open land alongside the course on which to park machinery and set up the organisers' tents.

The course was plotted from Tynwald Green at St John's, along the then dusty and rutted track to Ballacraine, where competitors turned left to begin the climb towards Kirkmichael. As any TT enthusiast should know, the following 6½ miles of the early St John's Circuit are still part of the present-day Mountain course, although there is little resemblance between the present-day roads and those of over 60 years ago.

On turning left at Ballacraine, competitors in the first-ever TT, held in 1907, had to pedal furiously on the short, sharp climb up Ballaspur and, once over the top, they could take it easy and rely on the engine to get them through to Glen Helen. Actually, it wasn't easy at all because, on the drop down from Ballaspur to Ballig Bridge, the single-gear bikes picked up a fair speed and the bridge was in those days very 'hump backed' with the result that many of them literally took off. Next came the tight left-hand corner, now known as Doran's Bend.

The roads were little more than hard-packed mud, strewn with flint and rocks. They were also badly rutted and very bumpy, even making handling in a straight line difficult for competitors. Many riders took the corners speedway-style with a foot trailing the ground to steady the sliding machine.

From Doran's Bend, through Laurel Bank and over the bridge into Glen Helen meant a hair-raising ride for the dare-devil competitors, who had little braking on their machines. Solid rock and brick-built bridge walls flashed past as they tried to build up sufficient speed to round the left-hander at Glen Helen and climb past Sarah's Cottage and up Creg Willey's Hill without pedalling too strenuously. But normally it was to no avail and long before they had reached the Cronk-y-Voddy straight, they were puffing and panting in their efforts to assist the tiring motors. So slowly did they travel at this point that friends or mechanics would often trot alongside the struggling riders encouraging them to greater effort, and shouting instructions or competitors' positions.

Once over Creg Willey's Hill and on to the Cronk-y-Voddy straight, it was downhill all the way to Kirkmichael. On the drop from the cross-roads on Cronk-y-Voddy to the left-hander at the present-day 11th Milestone, Rem Fowler's 1907 Norton must have been touching almost 60 mph for him to achieve his lap speed of 42.91 mph. And, when one considers that this was over a dusty,

muddy lane on a bike with barely any suspension and very poor brakes, it makes one realise just how tough and enthusiastic those riders had to be to complete 10 laps of the circuit. Apart from being good riders and mechanics, I should imagine that they also had to be extremely athletic and fit!

Continuing on from the 11th Milestone, the first sign of habitation seen by the contestants in the 1907 TT, after the farmhouses up on Cronk-y-Voddy, were the cottages at either side of the road at Handley's Cottage. Of course, it wasn't known by that name at the time, because it wasn't to earn its title until some years later when the great TT rider, Walter Handley, pitched his machine down the road at this tricky chicane.

And so, the riders continued on to the fast Barregarrow section with the steep drop from the crossroads down to the difficult double left-hander at the present Mountain Circuit 13th Milestone, once again another high-speed but dangerous spot for those early TT competitors. With poor brakes, the steep descent from Barregarrow took a great deal of courage and skill to negotiate and they were no doubt pleased to arrive on the fairly level stretch leading through long sweeping bends to Kirkmichael.

For the present-day TT competitor, the entry to Kirkmichael is a fairly fast right-hand bend sweeping past the straw-bale lined walls of fairly modern cottages. For the 1907 TT rider, it meant a very slow approach to the right-hander, where he negotiated an awkward left-hand corner taking him away from civilisation yet again as he headed out along the coast road towards Peel. If you look at an Ordnance Survey map of the Island, you will see this marked as the present-day A3 main road leading from Ramsey to Peel.

Without a doubt this is one of the prettier coast roads around the Island with a fabulous view out over the sea. Today the road is well-surfaced and both car and bike drivers have time to snatch a glimpse of the scenery as they enjoy the undulating, smooth road to Peel. But, apart from the same glorious view of the sea, the early TT riders were far more occupied with trying to negotiate the treacherous Devil's Elbow, give assistance to flagging motors on the short, sharp hills and negotiate the right-hander at Knocksharry, which aims them to Peel and away from the finishing point at St John's.

At Peel, the competitors entered the outskirts of the tiny fishing village to turn left immediately and head towards Douglas and the home straight to St John's.

The fastest lap recorded in the first-ever TT over

the St John's Circuit in 1907 was 42.91 mph and took 22 minutes, 6 seconds. It was made by the winner, Rem Fowler, on his Norton and even with present-day smooth roads, it is not an easy performance to match on a modern machine. Just imagine what it must have been like having poor brakes, only a single gear machine with pedals and roads more fit for a horse and cart than a motorcycle. Yet the incredible thing is that, in the four years that the St John's Circuit was in use, the lap record was raised by over 11 mph to an incredible 53.15 mph by H. H. Bowen on his BAT twin-cylinder machine. Is it any wonder that there were complaints that the machines were getting too fast and that in 1911 the A-CC decided to put the riders and motorcycles to the ultimate test – the Isle of Man Mountain Circuit?

Fortunately, for those like me who have a hankering after the past, particularly when it comes to motorcycles and their history, the Veteran and Vintage MCC stage a rally every year around the original St John's Circuit. Normally, it's held on the Thursday of TT week, so any visitor to the TT races can see some of those truly magnificent machines out and about on the circuit where British motorcycling virtually was born!

# CHAPTER FOUR

# 1947 to 1954 . . . End of an era

IMMEDIATELY AFTER the Second World War began a period of austerity, 'pool' petrol, and rationing of food and clothing, with very little indeed to brighten the lives of the British after six dreadful years of war! Yet, two years after peace had returned, the Isle of Man TT races bounced back in 1947 as though nothing had really happened!

The same riders were there – Frith, West, Daniell, Cann, Anderson, Barrington and many more besides. They had a few more grey hairs and were a little portlier, but still the same band of enthusiasts riding the same kind of machines that they had left at the finishing enclosure in 1939! The big-finned Velocettes were there, together with the 'garden gate' Manx Nortons, and the spritely, outside flywheel Guzzis.

As far as the A-CU was concerned, 1947 was going to be a great year for motorcycling on the Isle of Man. In spite of the fact that FIM regulations now banned the use of superchargers and competitors could only run their bikes on low-octane 'pool' petrol, the organisers wanted to make it a TT to celebrate the return of motorcycling to the Island. Therefore, they decided to introduce duplicate 'Clubman's' races of the actual Senior, Junior and Lightweight TTs.

Clubman's machines had to be based on proper roadster motorcycles, with kickstarters which had to be used at the beginning of the race and to start the engine after a compulsory second lap refuelling stop. The Senior Clubman's race had a capacity limit of a 1,000 cc, but only one machine, a 600 cc Scott twin, actually exceeded the normal 500 cc Senior restriction. The Junior and Lightweight entries had the usual 350 and 250 cc limits.

Megaphone exhausts were banned and lighting sets had to be fitted to the Clubman's machines, making many a TT enthusiast wonder what was happening to his favourite race. Meanwhile, others questioned the wisdom of allowing inexperienced riders to 'race' around the Mountain Circuit during TT week, particularly as the Manx Grand Prix was to return later that year.

Luckily, the A-CU had the wisdom to run the practice periods for the TT proper and Clubman's races at separate times, with the result that riders did not seriously hinder each other and the whole idea progressed quite smoothly, much to the dismay of the critics.

The other difference between the Clubman's race and main TT was that the roadster classes were run together, with the Senior and Junior riders covering four laps and the Lightweights completing three. The incredible thing was that the Lightweights started first, in pairs, at 15-second intervals, followed by the Junior and then Senior entries. This, of course, meant that the faster Juniors had to pass the Lightweight machines and the leading Senior riders would have to overtake virtually the entire field!

The object of the exercise was to have all three winners arriving at the finish line at approximately the same time, but one can imagine the hair-raising experiences of the slower Lightweight rider who had high-speed machines hurtling past him on all sides during the course of his first ride in a Clubman's TT race!

The other interesting point about the Clubman's TT was that in no way could it be considered an amateur race like the Manx Grand Prix. Prizes for first, second, third and fourth places were £50, £40, £30 and £20 respectively and, in addition, all riders who finished within six-fifths of the winner's time received a free entry in the 1947 Manx Grand Prix.

Surprisingly, in spite of riding what were virtually standard roadsters, the clubmen lapped the TT Mountain Circuit at speeds which compared favourably with those of the TT race experts. In the Lightweight class, W. McVeigh (Triumph) won at 65.30 mph; B. E. Keys (AJS) was second at 64.27

mph and Les Archer (Velocette) finished third at 63.73 mph.

In the Clubman's Junior TT, Denis Parkinson (Norton) was first at 70.74 mph; R. Pratt (Norton) was runner-up at 68.87 mph and W. Sleightholme (AJS) was third at 68.28 mph. While in the Clubman's Senior TT, E. E. Briggs (Norton) won at 78.67 mph, with A. Jefferies (Triumph) second at 75.23 mph and G. F. Parsons (Ariel) third at 71.26 mph.

But the real interest in the Island races centred around the established TT where the pre-war battle between the factory Velocette, Norton and AJS teams continued to dominate the scene in both Junior and Senior events.

Norton's long run of success in the Junior TT, when they won seven events in a row, had been brought to an end in 1938 by Velocette who, with Stanley Woods and Ted Mellors, had taken first and second places ahead of Freddie Frith on his Norton. In an attempt to overcome the opposition from Velocette, in 1938 Norton had shortened the stroke and increased the bore of their machines to improve power output. Although they continued with the same idea in 1947, it could not stop the obviously superior Velocette team making a clean sweep with a 1–2–3 in the first post-war Junior TT race. Bob Foster led the Velocette team to victory at an average speed of 80.31 mph over the seven laps of the Mountain Circuit, although it was runner-up M. D. Whitworth (Velocette) who set the fastest lap of 81.61 mph, with J. A. Weddell (Velocette) finishing third with an average of 76.15 mph.

Fortunately for Norton, in the Senior TT it was a different story, with their pre-war campaigner and lap-record holder, Harold Daniell, setting the pace to win at an average speed of 82.81 mph. He was followed home by Artie Bell on another Norton some 22 seconds behind at an average of 82.66 mph. Third was P. J. Goodman (Velocette) at 82.46 mph.

Perhaps one of the most ironic stories to be heard after the TT was that Harold Daniell had been turned down as a despatch rider when he went to sign on for military service in 1939!

As you will see in the results' section at the end of the book, the fastest lap speed in the Senior TT of 1947 was a mere 84.07 mph, set jointly by Artie Bell and P. J. Goodman. When compared with the 91 mph set by Harold Daniell in 1938 this seems incredibly slow; but one has to remember that, because of the extremely low-octane rating of the 'pool' petrol used in 1947, compression ratios had to be lowered considerably. Consequently the power output of the machines was way below pre-war figures.

It was a pity that in the 1947 races the AJS marque didn't have a better showing with their new 'Porcupine' double-overhead-camshaft twin 500. Originally designed to incorporate supercharging before the war, it could only manage a ninth place in its first post-war TT, but for AJS better things were to come. As far as Velocette were concerned, the 500 contra-rotating, supercharged 500 twin-cylinder machine, aptly named 'the roarer', had been completely scrapped.

In the Lightweight TT of 1947, run on the Friday of race week because the Clubman's events had taken over on the Wednesday, Moto Guzzi proved that the low centre of gravity, flexibility and road-holding of their machines, so well-developed in pre-war years, still held good. In spite of a little furor over timekeeping, which credited M. Cann with the fastest lap of 74.78 mph, it was M. Barrington (Guzzi) who won the race at an average of 73.22 mph. Cann was second on his Guzzi at 72.97 mph, while B. Drinkwater on an ageing Excelsior finished third at 70.14 mph.

The late 1940s were definitely times of change for the TT races. The Clubman's events had added another complication to what had until 1939 been a stable pattern in the running of TT week. Nothing could have been simpler than a Senior, Junior and Lightweight series of TT events. But for 'clubmen', the 1947 experiment was repeated the following year, with a change in regulations in 1949 giving a new 500 class separate from the 1,000 cc machines, making four classes in all. In 1951, because of the lack of entries, the 250 cc class was dropped, along with the 1,000 cc class in 1954. In 1955, the 350 and 500 were run on the Clypse course. However, after a 'last fling' over the Mountain Circuit in 1956, the Clubman's events were relegated the following year to short circuits on the mainland.

In some ways, of course, it was a pity because, similar to the present-day Production Machine TT, which is the very essence of the Tourist Trophy races, the Clubman's TT developed roadster machines which were to have considerable success in sales to the general public. The BSA Gold Star and the Triumph Tiger 100 were two such machines.

However, nothing could stand in the path of the TT as an event for true, thoroughbred Grand Prix racing motorcycles. With a world championship for racing motorcycles only a year away as British and Continental manufacturers lined up for battle on the Glencrutchery Road in 1948, the challenge to British supremacy was about to begin.

Because of the lack of entries in the 1948 Lightweight TT, the race was a massed-start affair, but it did not stop Maurice Cann proving that his fastest lap of the previous year was no fluke, because he won the race at an average speed of 75.18 mph. The ancient four-valve Rudge of Roland Pike finished second, almost ten minutes behind, at an average of 71.86 mph, while D. St John Beasley (Excelsior) was third.

However, for spectators, entrants, manufacturers, sponsors, the 'trade', in fact the world, the true interest at the Tourist Trophy races lay in the outcome of the Senior and Junior events. Norton were intent on re-establishing their pre-war superiority, while AJS, with their rapidly developing 'Porcupine', were aiming to gain some of the glory. Meanwhile, Velocette, having signed up Freddie Frith, wanted to maintain their supremacy in the Junior TT. One of the dark horses at the time was Moto Guzzi who, having conquered the Lightweight class, were still aiming for higher honours in the Senior race.

Perhaps the Senior TT of that year gave a good indication of the future. Guzzi rider Omobono Tenni set the fastest lap at 88.06 mph, which was considerably quicker than the winning speed of Artie Bell (Norton), who won at an average of 84.97 mph from his team mate, Bill Doran, 80.34 mph, and J. A. Weddell (Norton), 79.56 mph. Fortunately for Norton, their long-lived, single-cylinder design was maintaining its reputation for reliability, and the high-flying Italians were still some way from challenging the supremacy of the British machines in the bigger capacity classes. The incredible fact about Artie Bell's victory was that his 10 minute 45 second win over Bill Doran was the largest margin ever recorded since the Senior's introduction in 1911.

In the Junior TT of 1948, Velocette continued their domination of the class. Flying Freddie Frith not only set the fastest lap at 82.45 mph, but he also led team-mate Bob Foster over the line with Artie Bell on the Norton finishing third. Frith's time for the seven-lap race was 3 hours, 14 minutes and 33.6 seconds, giving an average speed of 81.45 mph. This was still considerably slower than the time he had set in 1937 when he produced a fastest lap of 85.18 mph on a Norton!

The year of 1949 brought the World Motorcycle Road Racing Championship and, with Les Graham signing for AJS in 1947, it was fitting that this great TT exponent should become the first 500 cc World Champion. Yet surprisingly, in spite of Graham's victories on the Continent on the extremely fast 500 twin, AJS had very little success on the Isle of Man.

Bob Foster, having signed for Moto Guzzi, proved yet again that the Italian machines were very quick, by raising the Senior lap speed to 89.75 mph. However, it was Harold Daniell (Norton) who once again brought victory to the British factory with an average speed of 86.93 mph. Johnny Lockett finished second at 86.19 mph with Ernie Lyons (Velocette) third at 85.50 mph.

Freddie Frith, who retired in the Senior race, was to have his last winning ride in the Junior TT of 1949, when he rounded off his Isle of Man career magnificently with a superb victory for Velocette at an average speed of 83.15 mph, setting fastest lap at 84.23 mph. Freddie led team-mate Ernie Lyons over the line by 32 seconds, followed by Artie Bell some 41 seconds later.

In the Lightweight race, Moto Guzzi continued their domination of the class, when M. Barrington and T. L. Wood scored a 1-2 victory. This was Guzzi's third win in succession.

Meanwhile, in the Manx Grand Prix later that year, a young rider by the name of Geoff Duke was attracting considerable interest from the factory 'scouts'. (He had been leading the 350 Manx of 1948, but retired with a split oil tank, and in 1949 had actually won the Clubman's TT, which set him on the path of success.) His stylish and very neat riding impressed many of the people who could spot a star in the making. In spite of not appearing on the practice leader board, he was runner-up in his second Manx Grand Prix and won his third, the Senior GP of 1949, and in 1950 he was snapped up by the works' Norton team!

Unfortunately, 1949 was a sad year for Velocette, because at the end of the season their number-one rider and World Champion Freddie Frith announced his retirement from road racing.

As a fitting climax to his motorcycling career (which included being among the select band of riders who have won a TT at their first attempt, and recording the first-ever 90-mph lap around the Mountain Circuit), after winning the 1949 350 World Championship, he was awarded the OBE (Order of the British Empire) for his services to the sport, the first rider to receive the award.

However, 1950 was a memorable year for Joe Craig and his works' Norton team! With the departure of Freddie Frith from road racing, Norton had everything their own way on the Island. Their new signing, Geoff Duke, made his TT debut and confirmed all that had been forecast about his road-racing ability.

'Pool' petrol was out and record speeds were in; for the first time in 12 years, lap records tumbled in all three classes of the TT races. It was Geoff Duke who set the pace in the Senior, which was still being run over seven laps of the Mountain Circuit, to win at a superb average speed of 92.27 mph, faster than the standing lap record of 91 mph set by his team-mate Harold Daniell in 1938. Duke also raised the lap record to 93.33 mph.

Artie Bell finished second on another works' Norton with an average of 90.86 mph and Johnny Lockett (Norton) was third. Once again, the pre-war-designed AJS 'Porcupine' twin, in spite of its comparatively advanced specification, could not match the pace of the works' Nortons, and Les Graham finished fourth behind the all-conquering Bracebridge Street gang.

Norton repeated the story in the Junior TT. But this time it was Artie Bell who climbed on to the winner's rostrum, with Geoff Duke (second) and Harold Daniell (third) alongside him. Similar to Duke's Senior victory, Artie Bell's average speed of 86.33 mph for the seven-lap Junior was faster than the previous lap record of 85.30 mph set in 1938 by Stanley Woods (Velocette). Artie also set the new lap record at 86.49 mph. Meanwhile, although Velocette were unplaced on the Island, their team of Bill Lomas, Cecil Sandford and Bob Foster continued to achieve success on the Continent. Bob Foster, in fact, won the 350 World Championship in 1950.

Harold Daniell, who had begun his TT career way back in 1934, was at this time the 'old man' of the Norton team, but with his fifth place in the Senior and third in the Junior, he had demonstrated that experience was still all-important for racing on the Island. But at the end of TT week in 1950, Harold decided to call it a day. Speeds were rapidly increasing and, although still a rider of great ability, he wisely decided that it was time to hand over to the younger generation of up-and-coming road racers.

Artie Bell, who had a terrible crash at the Belgian GP, also made his last appearance for Norton in 1950, which meant that, for the following year, Norton had the job of selecting a new team of riders for the Island.

Leader of that 1951 team was, of course, that superb stylist Geoff Duke. Jack Brett, Bill 'Cromie' McCandless and Johnny Lockett were the back-up riders.

However, some interesting developments had been taking place in the Lightweight 250 cc TT race. There the Italian factories were making a deter-

mined effort to maintain the superiority they had earned just prior to the outbreak of the Second World War.

Moto Guzzi relied on light weight, roadholding and the reliability of their well-proven horizontal layout, single-cylinder machine; while Benelli, who had developed a fantastic, four-cylinder super-charged 250 just prior to the war, dropped this in favour of a single-cylinder, double-overhead cam-shaft design. The four-cylinder design was to return much later to win the World Championship in the hands of Kel Carruthers.

On the Island in 1950, an Italian rider, D. Ambrosini, scored the second of Benelli's TT victories, at an average speed of 78.08 mph and also set a new lap record for the Lightweight class of 80.91 mph. Maurice Cann, who had won the 1948 Lightweight race for Guzzi, had to be content with second spot, but it was one of the closest fought races in the history of the TT.

It seemed impossible that, after $264\frac{1}{4}$ miles' racing, the time difference between Ambrosini and Cann should only be two-tenths of a second! Ambrosini's race time was 3 hours, 22 minutes and 58 seconds, while Cann on his Moto Guzzi took 3 hours, 22 minutes and 58.2 seconds. For Cann it was a disappointment, but for Ambrosini, on his second visit to the Island, it was a superb victory. Third was R. A. Mead on a Velocette.

However, as usual in road racing, times were changing and, apart from the new Norton team for 1951, AJS were having a re-think about the design of the 'Porcupine'. During the winter, drastic modifications were made to the motor. It changed from being a horizontal twin to one of 45 degrees, along with alterations to the frame, which included shortening the wheelbase.

Unfortunately, their number-one rider, Les Graham, was tempted away by a newcomer to the world of road racing – MV Agusta! The machine that Graham was to ride in the Senior TT was a four-cylinder 500 designed by Rondine, the engineer responsible for the development of the pre-war Gilera 500-four.

Les Graham, in fact, was the 'test pilot' for MV Agusta who, although able to develop a complex and powerful motor, knew very little about the handling and roadholding for high-speed racing motorcycles. But as results have since proven, they learned exceedingly fast and well under the guidance of a number of British riders.

Meanwhile, in the AJS camp, Bill Doran took over the responsibility of developing and riding the works' twin-cylinder 500 and single-cylinder 7R 350 racing machines. And Velocette produced a new double-overhead camshaft 250 for Sandford, Lomas and Foster to race.

In a way, I suppose 1951 could be described as the turning point for road racing after the war. The motorcycle industries of Europe were getting back on their feet; the age of austerity was gradually coming to an end and racing on the Isle of Man became even more International with the influx of riders from the 'colonies'.

Ray Amm from Southern Rhodesia, Rod Coleman from New Zealand, Ken Kavanagh from Australia, to be followed by all-time greats like Tom Phillis, Jim Redman, Hughie Anderson and many more, were all road racers of great skill and determination who were to ride the world's fastest racing motorcycles as works' team men on the Island.

Also in 1951, the Auto-Cycle Union added another race to the TT calendar, the Ultra-Lightweight 125 cc event. It was to be a two-lap race over the Mountain Circuit and from its introduction was obviously to be a benefit race for the Italian manufacturers who, at that time, dominated the lightweight classes.

The A-CU had also made alterations to the Clubman's events by scrapping the 1,000 cc and 250 cc races, leaving simply a Junior and Senior Clubman's TT which were to be dominated by BSA with their 'Gold Star' machines . . . but that's another story.

In the TT proper, it was 'the Duke' who set the circuit alight. He became the first rider to lap the Mountain Circuit at more than 90 mph in the Junior TT, and apart from doing the double – winning both Senior and Junior TTs – he also broke lap and race records for both classes.

In the Senior, Duke led Bill Doran on the revamped 'Porcupine' over the line by over four minutes, in a time of 2 hours, 48 minutes and 56.8 seconds for the seven laps. Cromie McCandless was third on his Norton. At last AJS had made a dent in the Norton supremacy by splitting the works' team.

But there was still no stopping Norton in the Junior event. Works' riders Duke, Lockett and Jack Brett were first, second and third respectively, with Duke upping the lap record by almost 5 mph to a remarkable 91.38 mph. For Johnny Lockett, who had begun racing Nortons on the Island in 1939, his second place behind Duke and his unsuccessful ride in the Senior, four days later, marked his retirement from racing.

If you study photographs of racing motorcycles of this era, you will find that the machines are unadorned by fairings or screens. The handlebars were mounted on top of the front forks, as on roadsters, and the speeding riders simply crouched as low as possible on the fuel tanks, hoping to get a little protection from flying stones and insects behind a wire mesh screen mounted above the front racing number plate. But things were soon to change because, in the Lightweight events in 1951, the Italian manufacturers, who had been experimenting with streamlining for their machines, appeared with half-fairings.

Admittedly, in no way did they resemble the full streamlining that we see on racing bikes today. However, it was the beginning of a period of rivalry between machines of brute power and speed, and those which were less powerful, but superbly streamlined, light in weight and very manageable.

Moto Guzzi were among the first to introduce partial streamlining, and in 1951 it was Fergus Anderson, who had ridden for DKW in 1939, who set the fastest lap at 83.70 mph. But he wasn't destined to win the race, and it was team mate, Tommy Wood, who took the chequered flag to win from Dario Ambrosini on the Benelli. It was almost a repeat of the previous year's event, because there was a gap of only 8.4 seconds between the leading two riders. Another Moto Guzzi, ridden by Enrico Lorenzetti, finished third. As a matter of interest, in 1951 the race length had been reduced from seven laps to four, mainly due to the declining number of entries for the Lightweight class.

The Ultra-Lightweight TT over two laps of the Mountain Circuit proved a clean sweep for the Italian Mondial team. Cromie McCandless rode the dimunitive single-cylinder, four-stroke to win from Carlo Ubbiali and G. Leoni at an average speed of 74.85 mph. McCandless also set a fastest lap of 75.34 mph which, when one considers the road performance of the average 125 in those days (50 to 55 mph was good), was an outstanding debut for the new Ultra-Lightweight TT.

With the retirement of Johnny Lockett from the Norton team, a new and fast-improving rider, Reg Armstrong, was signed up for the 1952 season. He had first raced on the Island in the 1949 TT and, like many Irishmen before him, found the Manx circuit very much to his liking. Also, Jack Brett had left Norton to join AJS, who had temporarily lost their number-one rider, Bill Doran, through injury. With the development of AJS machines, including the new treble-knocker 350, which was a single-cylinder motor having two inlet and one exhaust valve, each operated by its own camshaft, the scene was set for some really hectic and close racing in the larger capacity events.

The 1952 TT week opened with Geoff Duke maintaining his winning streak in the Junior. He finished over a minute ahead of his new team mate, Reg Armstrong, with AJS works' rider Rod Coleman from New Zealand finishing third. As he wasn't pushed, no lap records were broken by Duke, but he did set a new race record of 90.29 mph.

In the Senior TT, Geoff retired on the fourth lap with clutch trouble after setting a fastest lap of 94.88 mph. Team mate Armstrong won the race 27 seconds ahead of Les Graham on the MV 500-four, which was at last beginning to show its true potential under the development and guidance of the skilful Graham. Third to finish in the Senior was Ray Amm, the Rhodesian, on another Norton.

The Lightweight 250 race, with Benelli no longer competing, proved a clean sweep for Moto Guzzi, with Fergus Anderson winning at an average speed of 83.82 mph from Enrico Lorenzetti and Syd Lawton. But it was Bruno Ruffo who, on his first visit to the Island, raised the lap record to 84.82 mph and after striking trouble finished sixth.

At that time, there was not a single machine that could live with the amazing, single-cylinder Moto Guzzi, the design of which had been developed in the late 1920s. However, the German motorcycle industry was re-awakening after a massive post-war rebuilding programme, and the following year the Italian domination of the Lightweight classes on the Island was to encounter severe competition from both DKW and NSU.

Meanwhile, in the Ultra-Lightweight TT, Mondial had suddenly found a new challenger for their neat little 125 cc four-stroke. The Mondial team were far from complacent about the preceding year's 1–2–3 victory and, with Carlo Ubbiali, a fiery Italian and master of lightweight motorcycle road racing, as their number-one rider, it looked as though Mondial would have no problem in winning yet again. But MV had different ideas; they were making their mark in the Senior against the world's best riders and machines and, with Cecil Sandford at the controls, they took the Lightweight title away from Mondial.

Sandford won the two-lap race at an average speed of 75.54 mph to beat Carlo Ubbiali and A. L. Parry, both Mondial-mounted. Sandford also set a new lap record of 76.07 mph.

Velocette, even with the great Les Graham riding for them in the 250 and 350 classes, could make no impression on either Norton or Guzzi domination of the TT. And the motorcycle world were ab-

solutely stunned, when Velocette announced their withdrawal from road racing at the end of the 1952 season.

The name Gilera appeared on the Isle of Man for the first time in 1951, without success. The machine, a single-cylinder, overhead-camshaft model named the Saturno and ridden by a private entrant from Australia, W. A. McAlpine, had retired. However, although the factory had won the 1950 500 cc World Championship, it wasn't until 1953 that they arrived on the Island with their four-cylinder 500 cc bikes, having enticed both Geoff Duke and Reg Armstrong from Norton to become their 'success' team for the TT.

MV had Les Graham; Ray Amm and Jack Brett were with Norton; while AJS still had Rod Coleman and Bill Doran. They were all superb riders, and all capable of winning on the Island. It really was destined to be a battle of light weight and handling versus the brute power of the four-cylinder 'fire engines'.

Other riders in the Gilera camp were Dickie Dale and Alfredo Milani, while Les Graham was backed up by Italian Carlo Bandirola.

In an attempt to combat the sheer speed of the Italian four-cylinder machines, Norton had developed a 'kneeler' which was a fully streamlined machine. In fact, ridden by Ray Amm, it appeared in race practice with a 350 cc motor, but it wasn't actually used in any of the races.

Fortunately for Norton, their far superior handling was still just about a match for the straight-line speed of the four-cylinder Italian machines. However, on the opening lap of the Senior TT, Geoff Duke proved that speed was still important by shooting into the lead and breaking the existing lap record from a standing start! Duke completed the lap in 23 minutes, 30 seconds at a speed of 96.38 mph, but on the fourth lap he took a tumble at Quarter Bridge, allowing Norton rider Ray Amm to win, followed home by Jack Brett (Norton) and Reg Armstong (Gilera). Ray Amm also set a new record lap of 97.41 mph.

The tragedy of the 1953 race was, of course, that one of Britain's most outstanding riders, Les Graham, was killed on the second lap. He was lying second to Geoff Duke at the time and, after plunging into the dip at the bottom of Bray Hill, he lost control of his machine and crashed a few seconds later. He was killed instantly, a very sad end to an outstanding week's racing.

In the Junior, the Nortons of Ray Amm and Ken Kavanagh proved superior to anything that AJS had yet to offer, and it was only the Moto Guzzi of Fergus Anderson taking third place that stopped the now-established 1–2–3 for Norton, because Jack Brett on the other works' Norton finished fourth. Ray Amm also set a new lap record for the race with a speed of 91.82 mph. As it was, the best AJS could manage was a fifth place by Bill Doran, with Rod Coleman retiring from the race.

Perhaps one of the most outstanding rides in the 1953 TT series was that of Werner Haas on the very quick, brand-new twin-cylinder 250 cc NSU in the Lightweight race. As in the previous year, Fergus Anderson rode the Moto Guzzi to victory, at an average speed of 84.73 mph, and set the new lap record at 85.52 mph. But it was Haas, on his first visit to the Island on the NSU, who set the tongues wagging. He finished second just 17 seconds behind the very experienced TT exponent, Anderson. The DKW of S. Wunsche finished third over four minutes later.

The German challenge to the Italian lightweight machines had arrived and, although it was only to be a brief encounter, a matter of three years, the Germans simply set out to prove their point: beat the best in the world and retire to reap the commercial benefits. Witness the similar efforts by Mercedes in the car world at approximately the same time.

NSU were also entered in the Ultra-Lightweight race, which had been extended to three laps. Once again, Werner Haas proved to the Italians that any machine they could build, NSU could do the same if not better.

Admittedly, Haas finished second yet again, but he split the MVs of Les Graham and Cecil Sandford which, considering the riding skill of these two masters of the TT circuit, proved that Haas was not only an outstanding rider, but that the NSU was a superbly engineered racing motorcycle.

The Ultra-Lightweight TT of 1953 was Les Graham's first and only victory on the Island and yet, among the riders of his day, he stood head and shoulders above most of them with his honest and sportsmanlike approach to motorcycle racing. Consequently, it is no wonder that the Les Graham Memorial Hut was established on the TT Mountain Circuit, just before the Bungalow. It is a tribute to a sportsman who gave everything to the 'game' he loved most.

With Geoff Duke (Gilera) and Les Graham (MV) leading the Senior TT of 1953 until their unfortunate crashes and Ray Amm winning due to the misfortunes of his adversaries, it was obvious that the writing was on the wall for the good old, thumping British single-cylinder machines. After years of development on frames, brakes, etc, to improve roadholding, it was evident that too little attention had been paid to development of the motors.

Modifications, such as shortening strokes, increasing bore and valve sizes, using stronger steels on con-rods, etc, to withstand higher revs, were just not good enough to compete with the brand-new, imaginative ideas coming from the Italian manufacturers. As far as the Italian and Germans were concerned, winning was all that mattered no matter what the cost. The fact that the racing machines in no way resembled their roadster models was of little consequence. The money spent on developing and producing highly specialised, hand-built racing machines in superbly equipped competitions' workshops was necessary to establish a brand image of which every road-going owner could be proud. Therefore, the tremendous expenditure was justified by the world-wide publicity gained by winning races.

The fact that Britain was at that time producing what were probably the finest roadster motorcycles in the world, because of the lessons learned on the race tracks, this to all intents and purposes held back the development of our racing machines. British motorcycle management could not, or did not want to understand that it was necessary to spend money to build highly specialised race-winning machines.

Thus we come to 1954. It was the last year in which we were to see a British machine win the Senior and Junior TTs until 1961 when, due to the mechanical failure of the lone works' MV Agusta, Norton won virtually by default.

The Sidecar TT also returned to the Island in 1954 and, along with the Ultra-Lightweight 125 race, was run over the newly established Clypse Circuit. These massed-start races brought a touch of mainland short circuit racing to the Island and it was possibly this which saved the 125 race from being dropped completely from the TT programme.

It is interesting to note that the unpredictable weather on the Isle of Man was partly responsible for Ray Amm and Norton gaining another Senior TT win that year. But it came about after a controversial order from the race stewards for the Senior to be stopped at the end of the fourth lap and the leader at that time to be declared the winner.

Out in front at the end of the third lap was none other than Gilera's Isle of Man expert, Geoff Duke, but he stopped to refuel and lost precious time as Ray Amm went storming past the pits without halting for petrol. The result was that, at the end of the fourth lap when the race finished, Ray Amm was declared the winner by 1 minute, 5.8 seconds. At that time, there were still three laps of the race to complete and it is anybody's guess who would actually have won if the race had been run over the full distance.

Admittedly the weather had been getting progressively worse during the first three laps but, when the race was stopped, the cloud was clearing and on the finishing line the sun was actually beginning to shine! But to Ray Amm's credit it must be recorded that he had gained 12 seconds on Duke on the second lap and was only two seconds behind at the start of the third lap. At the end of that lap, Amm had picked up another 30 seconds on Duke and it is still in doubt whether the Gilera rider could have made up the deficit after taking on more fuel.

Anyway, the records show that Norton was first, Gilera second and Norton (Jack Brett) third. Ray Amm set the fastest lap with a speed of 89.82 mph, giving some idea of the very bad weather conditions encountered around the circuit.

Very few but the diehard TT enthusiasts remember the name of Ray Amm, the Southern Rhodesian who first came to the Isle of Man in 1951 and literally took the place by storm. There are no memorials or sections of the TT circuit named after him but, out of eight races on the Island, he won three, set three outstanding lap records, retired in two races and earned replicas in all the others. Had he not been tragically killed while racing the following year in the Italian Grand Prix, it was clear to everyone that he was among the top six riders in the world and could certainly have become a legendary figure to match the Guthries, Simpsons, Woods and other great racing exponents on the Isle of Man.

In the Junior of 1954, Ray Amm set an outstanding lap record of 94.61 mph, but he was to retire with mechanical trouble before the end of the race which, due to bad weather, had been shortened to five laps.

For the first time in 24 years, AJS won the Junior TT, with Rod Coleman proving that at long last the Plumstead factory's faith in the 'treble-knocker' was well-founded. Another AJS was ridden into second spot by Derek Farrant, with Bob Keeler (Norton) finishing third. AJS had at last succeeded in beating their Isle of Man jinx and their win was no hollow victory, because Rod Coleman had averaged 91.51 mph, almost as fast as the previous year's lap record set by Ray Amm.

But if the British manufacturers thought they were doing well, it was the Germans in the Light-

weight 250 race who really stole the show, with their beak-nosed 'dolphin' fairing NSU 250 machines. Not satisfied with their previous year's results, the race development engineers had built a completely brand-new motor for the 1954 season. It was still a twin-cylinder, four-stroke with a double-overhead camshaft, but the gear drive to the camshafts was different and the new motor developed 33 bhp – only a fraction below that produced by the British 350 racing machines! In fact, had the German rider, Werner Haas, been competing in the Junior TT on his lightweight machine, he would have finished in second place behind the AJS of Rod Coleman.

As it was, the powerful NSU team swept aside all opposition from Italy and, out of the first six places in the three lap-race, they claimed five – first, second, third, fourth and sixth. Werner Haas also set a remarkable lap record of 91.22 mph, which was to stand until 1960 when the Lightweight 250 race returned to the Mountain Circuit. (In 1955, it was relegated to the Clypse course to join the Ultra-Lightweight and Sidecar TTs.) In second and third places behind Haas came fellow countryman R. Hollaus and Reg Armstrong from Ireland.

Over the Clypse course, the German manufacturers didn't get things exactly their own way because, in the Ultra-Lightweight race of 1954, the fiery little Italian, Carlo Ubbiali on his MV, chased and harried R. Hollaus all the way during the ten-lap race. But the German managed to win by a mere four seconds from the Italian, with Cecil Sandford (MV) coming third.

Racing on the Clypse course proved popular with the crowds and the re-introduction of the Sidecar TT added a new dimension to spectating on the Island. Not since 1925 had motorcycle enthusiasts seen the three-wheelers dicing through the narrow Manx village streets with passengers hanging precariously out of their 'chairs', elbows and shoulders almost scraping the road, as they fought to maintain the stability of the unwieldy sidecar outfits.

Sidecar racing machines of this era were little more than ordinary solo racers with a sidecar attached, unlike present-day three-wheelers which are very specialised, low profile, purpose-built outfits incorporating many of the design features of racing cars. Even the riding positions were totally different, with the riders of 1955 sitting on their machines as a solo rider, whereas today the competitor kneels 'in' his machine.

Perhaps the only thing in sidecar racing that hasn't changed is the continued success of the German BMW marque. This outstanding horizontally opposed, overhead-camshaft twin, which was introduced in supercharged form in the late 1930s, has proved the ideal power unit for three-wheeler racing. Apart from Eric Oliver's 1954 win for Norton and Chris Vincent's BSA win in 1962, BMW powered outfits have won every single Side-car TT since its re-introduction on the Clypse course.

In fact, had it not been for the outstanding riding skill of four-times World Sidecar Racing Champion Eric Oliver, it is very doubtful whether a British machine would have won the 1954 sidecar race. As it was, Eric raced a Norton/Watsonian outfit with considerably advanced streamlining for the period, and led the ten-lap event from start to finish. He also set the fastest lap at 70.85 mph but, with the BMWs of F. Hillebrand and W. Noll finishing second and third respectively, it was obvious to everyone that, as in the solo racing classes, the British manufacturers, with their antiquated designs, were soon to lose out completely to the rapidly improving Continental challengers. Eric Oliver, who paid so much attention to machine design, could be considered the instigator of the 'kneeler' outfit, where the rider actually kneels on his bike instead of sitting on it.

It was a very sad, sad era for the British racing teams. Because of lack of development to their racing motorcycles, they were losing their top riders to the Continental teams, which in turn meant that the British manufacturers began to lose more and more races. It was a vicious circle and, while managements were unprepared to take up the challenge on behalf of the British industry, it meant that, from the mid-1950s, enthusiasts saw a rapid decline in the superiority of British raceware not only on the Island but throughout the Grand Prix circuits of Europe. The old, single-cylinder Norton and AJS racing machines were to remain the backbone of road racing until the mid-1960s, with famous tuners such as Joe Potts, Francis Beart,

Steve Lancefield, Tom Arter and more besides urging a little extra power from the design, long after the factories and designers who had built the original bikes had given up.

But even as early as 1952, the writing was on the wall for Britain's motorcycle manufacturers who were competing in road racing. They failed to heed the warning and failed to keep abreast of Grand Prix racing machine development. Consequently, in 1956, in spite of rumours that in the Norton race development shop at Bracebridge Street, Birmingham, there was a brand-new racing four-cylinder design on the stocks, the Norton, AJS and Matchless factories stunned the motorcycle world by pulling out of racing!

After almost 50 years of total domination of the Senior and Junior TT races, the British manufacturers finally capitulated to Italian and German engineering skill and determination; it was the end of an era and, on reflection, could be seen to be the beginning of the end of almost the entire British motorcycle industry.

Fortunately, in spite of the demise of the British works' teams, the TT races continued in all their glory. The Continental manufacturers remained to battle for the prestige of winning a Tourist Trophy race, still considered to be the ultimate test of man and machine, as well as being the most prestigious event in the World Championship series.

However, the Continental manufacturers were also beginning to feel the financial pinch after running exotic Grand Prix racing machines. Their glory was to be short-lived, as the Island was to echo to new motorcycle sounds which had been created thousands of miles away . . . sounds from Japan and a vital, young industry which was going to breathe new life into the dwindling world motorcycle markets and bring new and exciting glamour to motorcycle sport.

# CHAPTER FIVE

# 1955 to 1960...Italy all the way!

WITH THE NORTON and AJS/Matchless works' teams mounted on what were virtually standard production racers for the 1955 Senior and Junior TTs and the cream of British riders 'going Continental' in order to have the fastest and most modern raceware on Europe's racing circuits, it came as no great shock to the spectators on the Island that year to see the Italian factories sweep all before them and prove victorious in the four solo races.

The day of reckoning had arrived with a vengeance and, although the racing itself was as exciting and stimulating as before, there were long faces in the British pits along the Glencrutchery Road. There was no way in which the long-established Manx Nortons and 7R Ajays could compete with the high-flying, high-revving multis from Italy. The only solace that could be found in the results of that TT week was the gallant performance of that great TT exponent, Bob McIntyre, who rode his heart out in the Junior on Joe Potts' privately entered Manx Norton, to split the Guzzis of winner, Bill Lomas and third placeman, Cecil Sandford.

It had been left to the privateers and entrants to experiment with fairings, cowlings and supplementary fuel tanks on over-the-counter raceware from Norton and AJS. The canny Scot, Joe Potts had prepared and streamlined a Norton which almost proved a match for the fully faired, low, light and fast Moto Guzzis. The Guzzis were, at that time, also single-cylinder machines, still built along pre-war lines, with the overhead camshaft motor lying horizontally in the frame. But their low centre of gravity and light weight gave them superb handling qualities and the small frontal area, which was fully faired and streamlined, gave good air penetration and, consequently, a very high top speed considering the power output from the motor.

Bill Lomas set a new race record of 92.33 mph for the seven-lap Junior, but failed to beat Ray Amm's Norton lap record set the previous year.

Moto Guzzi were at that time one of the first manufacturers to make use of a wind tunnel in the efforts to improve streamlining and it paid off, because in 1955 Bill Lomas not only won the Junior TT but also the 350 World Championship.

In the Senior, Geoff Duke gave Gilera their first-ever TT victory, at an average speed of 97.93 mph and, had he been hard pressed to take the win, he would in all probability have been the first rider ever to have clocked the magic 100-mph lap of the Mountain course. At the time, almost everybody in the pits on the Glencrutchery Road thought he had done so but, when the timekeepers eventually worked out his speed, the TT maestro had missed the 'ton' lap by one second, to record a speed of 99.97 mph!

Following the German challenge for honours in the Lightweight TT classes, MV had temporarily withdrawn from the Senior to concentrate their efforts on winning back their supremacy from the NSU camp. The Lightweight 250 race had been transferred from the Mountain to the Clypse course and, over nine laps of the circuit, MV completely dominated the events.

In the Lightweight 125 event they took first, second, fourth, fifth and sixth places, with Carlo Ubbiali, the winner, setting a new lap record at 71.65 mph. Luigi Taveri, in the first of his many Isle of Man rides, finished second, followed home by G. Lattanzi riding a lone Mondial.

MV completed the Lightweight double that year, when Bill Lomas took the vertical-engined MV 250 to victory over the horizontal single Guzzi of Cecil Sandford, at an average speed of 71.37 mph. NSU, who had withdrawn from the 125 class, finished third, with rider H. Muller completing the course more than four minutes behind the flying Lomas.

Meanwhile, in the Sidecar TT, BMW gained the first of a long line of victories. Two out of their three works' entries retired, but their lone finisher,

60

Walter Schneider, went on to win at an average speed of 70.01 mph, while Wilhelm Noll (BMW) set a new record lap of 71.93 mph. Bill Boddice (Norton) finished second and 'Pip' Harris (Matchless) was third.

In the 'closed season' before the 1956 World Championship series began, considerable developments had been taking place in the Continental manufacturers' racing workshops. MV Agusta had completely revamped the four-cylinder 500, and their new, number-one runner was a youngster by the name of John Surtees. The main modifications to the bike were to the frame and the replacement of Earles-type forks with telescopic units.

Moto Guzzi, too, were developing what can only be considered a masterpiece in motorcycle engineering, a 500 cc V-8 water-cooled, four-overhead camshaft motor, reputed to produce over 90 bhp. A top speed of over 160 mph made it a fearsome contender in the 500 World Championship but, unfortunately, although its straight-line potential was beyond the wildest dreams of any rider seeking absolute performance, its roadholding and braking were no match for the lighter four-cylinder MV and Gilera machines. Unfortunately, the eight-cylinder machine was not ready for the 1956 TT and Bill Lomas, Dickie Dale and Ken Kavanagh only had the 500 single-cylinder bike, while MV chose John Surtees as their lone rider for their 500-four in the Senior TT of that year.

Unfortunately, Gilera were not entered for the Senior and the expected clash between the four-cylinder 'fire engines' and the eight-cylinder Guzzis never materialised.

In a way, this gave a little consolation to the works' Norton team of Jack Brett, John Hartle and Alan Trow who were riding the ever-faithful single-cylinder 500s which, although considerably down on performance, were still able to out-corner and out-brake the faster and heavier raceware from Italy.

The result was that John Surtees won his first Senior TT for MV, with John Hartle and Jack Brett finishing second and third for Norton. Alan Trow finished seventh to help Norton win the Manufacturers' Team Prize. Guzzi's luckless effort ended with a fifth place for Bill Lomas, while both Dickie Dale and Ken Kavanagh retired from the race.

Still the 'ton' lap remained to be achieved, because, without the pressure of Duke, Armstrong and Milani on the Gileras (they had been suspended from racing until after the TT by the FIM) the fastest lap recorded by Surtees was 97.79 mph, with a race average of 96.57 mph over the seven laps.

The Junior was another of the TTs to be won by an Italian manufacturer in 1956 and, although MV had produced a 350 version of their all-conquering 500-four, John Surtees was excluded from the race, allowing the super-streamlined Guzzi of Ken Kavanagh to win at an average speed of 89.29 mph. Records show that there was nothing outstanding about the Junior TT of that year, although the consistency of the AJS team brought them the Manufacturers' Team Award.

By 1956, the format for racing on the Island had settled down to an established pattern: seven laps for the Junior and Senior events over the Mountain Circuit and nine laps for both Lightweight and Sidecar races over the Clypse Circuit.

MV had established complete domination of the Lightweight events and Carlo Ubbiali became the first foreigner ever to achieve a TT double by winning both the 125 and 250 races of that year. He was also to finish the season as World Champion in both capacity classes.

However, he was not to have things all his own way in the 250 race, because NSU rider H. Baltisberger established the fastest lap of 69.17 mph. But this did not stop MV claiming first and second places, with Ubbiali and Colombo taking the honours for the Italian factory. Baltisberger eventually finished third.

In the 125 race, MV encountered new opposition, this time from Spain. The Montesa factory had entered a team of single-cylinder two-strokes, but they proved nowhere near a match for Ubbiali and his high-revving Italian four-stroke.

A great deal had yet to be learned about two-stroke technology and, although the Montesas were sufficiently fast and reliable to finish in second and third places in the 125 race, Ubbiali finished almost five minutes ahead of M. Cama (Montesa), who in turn was almost six minutes ahead of team mate, Gonzalez. When one considers that Ubbiali's fastest lap was only 9 minutes, 9.8 seconds, giving a lap speed of 70.65 mph, it is surprising that he finished over half a lap ahead of his rivals. The event had developed into a rather boring procession.

With three factory entries for the Sidecar TT, it was almost a foregone conclusion that BMW would once again take the honours in this event. The enthusiasm of the British privateers just was not sufficient to overcome the sheer speed and performance of the horizontally opposed twins from Munich.

Once again, Willi Noll set the pace with a fastest lap of 71.72 mph, but it was his team mate, ex-Luftwaffe pilot Fritz Hillebrand who gave BMW

61

their second successive Isle of Man Sidecar race victory. He lead the Nortons of 'Pip' Harris and Bill Boddice over the finishing line, taking 1 hour, 23 minutes and 12.2 seconds.

Perhaps the most stunning thing of all about the 1956 race season was that after almost 50 years involvement in the TT races, both Norton and AJS announced their withdrawal from the sport. The successes of Gilera, MV, Moto Guzzi and BMW had sealed the fate of the British works' teams. Admittedly, the British manufacturers were to continue building the established Manx Nortons, Matchless G50s and AJS 7Rs for road-racing enthusiasts but, as far as the British public were concerned, we had given best to the Italians and Germans and were in effect handing over the British motorcycle empire! It was now up to the 'privateers' to take on the high-flying Italians and their super four-cylinder specials.

However, behind the scenes, things were also happening in the Italian camps, where the cost of Grand Prix racing was being questioned by their masters in the boardrooms. Admittedly, they produced and developed even better machinery for 1957 and had the pick of the best riders in the world but, unknown to all but a few, the Italian glory was to fade rapidly.

Meanwhile, on the other side of the world in Japan, a new industry was being born. From power-assisted pedal cycles and copies of European light-weights, Soichira Honda was creating his dream, a range of machines to sell not only in Japan but on the world's motorcycle market.

The little Japanese engineer had paid his first visit to the Isle of Man in 1954 and was amazed at the speeds and complexity of the motorcycles he saw in the races. But he knew that he would have to improve on these if his company was to win world markets. But more of the Honda story later . . .

1957, the Golden Jubilee of the TT, was Gilera's year! Without Geoff Duke, due to injury, or Reg Armstrong who had retired, on Duke's advice they had signed up another great Isle of Man exponent, Bob McIntyre, and to back him up had offered Bob Brown from Australia a chance to ride the flying four-cylinder machines. Unfortunately, with Bill Lomas 'off sick' and unfit to ride the eight-cylinder Guzzi, Dickie Dale took over the entry and Keith Campbell rode the single-cylinder 500 Guzzi.

These Guzzi riders, together with the lone MV Agusta of John Surtees, were to do battle with the Gileras of Bob McIntyre and Bob Brown, and what a battle it proved to be, with the quiet Scotsman making TT history by completing the first over-100 mph lap! The crowds went wild when they heard that Bob Mac had rocketed the Gilera around the course at an incredible 101.12 mph in a time of 22 minutes, 23.2 seconds, to become the first rider to top the 'ton'.

Bob McIntyre went on to win the 1957 Senior at an average speed of 98.99 mph in 3 hours, 2 minutes and 57 seconds over a distance of 302 miles. (In Jubilee Year, the Senior TT had been extended to cover eight laps of the Mountain Circuit; the longest TT race in history.) Following Bob Mac home 2 minutes, 7.2 seconds behind came John Surtees on the MV, and 3 minutes, 57.8 seconds later was Bob Brown on the other Gilera. Dale finished fourth on the V-8 and Campbell fifth on the single-cylinder Guzzi.

The result was a repeat of what had happened earlier in the week in the Junior race, confirming Bob McIntyre's TT double on his debut with the works' Gileras. However, in the Junior, it was Keith Campbell on the Moto Guzzi who split the highly successful Gilera team men, while John Surtees' MV finished fourth.

In his triumphant ride in the Junior, Bob Mac had raised the lap record to a remarkable 97.42 mph and established a new race average of 94.99 mph for the seven-lap event.

Back on the Clypse course, the race length for the Lightweight and Sidecar races had been extended to ten laps and, with most spectators expecting to see Carlo Ubbiali, the World Champion, repeat his previous year's double, they and MV were in for a shock. Mondial, another Italian manufacturer equally deft at producing exciting, high-performance lightweights, had signed-up a slim, but fiery Irish rider by the name of Sammy Miller, now universally recognised as probably the greatest-ever trials rider. His team mates were Tarquino Provini and Cecil Sandford, both experienced lightweight riders of no mean ability.

In the Lightweight 250, it was Provini who established an incredible lap record of 78 mph, but retired with mechanical trouble leaving Sammy Miller to lead Cecil Sandford on the last lap. Unfortunately for Sammy Miller, a spill on the last corner of the circuit, Governor's Bridge, allowed Cecil Sandford to win for Mondial, while Sammy pushed home to finish fifth. The MVs of Luigi Taveri and R. Colombo finished in second and third places.

Provini, a virtual newcomer to the Island, made certain of the 125 TT by setting a scorching pace and notching up another new lap record, this time at 74.44 mph. After ten laps, Tarquino was chased home by World Champion Ubbiali and Luigi Taveri, both on MVs. Miller and Sandford on the other two Mondials finished fourth and fifth.

By now the Sidecar World Championship, which included the TT as one of the qualifying events, had become a BMW benefit. The horizontally opposed, overhead-camshaft twins developed the type of power needed to haul the heavy outfits out of corners and provide maximum acceleration. Unless the German factory team machines struck mechanical trouble, there was not an outfit to touch them on performance.

This proved to be the case in the 1957 Sidecar race with the works' BMWs making a clean sweep, with first place going to the previous year's winner, Fritz Hillebrand; Walter Schneider was second and Florian Camathias came third. Hillebrand established a new lap record of 72.55 mph and won at an average speed of 71.89 mph.

The late 1950s was a critical period for Grand Prix racing in Europe because, like the British manufacturers, the Italians were also finding the cost of developing highly specialised racing machines too expensive in relation to the existing market potential of their roadsters. There was no doubt that, at this particular time, world motorcycle sales were declining and, without commercial success with roadster machines, it was not possible for manufacturers to spend a fortune on racing.

Therefore, at the end of the 1957 season, Gilera, as had Guzzi earlier in the year, withdrew from Grand Prix racing. Only MV Agusta, a factory which had more lucrative and diverse interests in the aircraft industry, continued its support for the World Championship events. Therefore, with Surtees as their number-one rider in the large capacity classes, and World Champion Carlo Ubbiali and Tarquino Provini in the lightweight events, they had everything very much their own way at the start of the 1958 racing season. Mondial, too, had officially withdrawn from racing, but a newcomer, Ducati, had decided to contest the lightweight championship.

Although racing on the Island in 1958 appeared and was, in fact, very much an MV Agusta benefit (they won all four solo classes that year), it was an interesting series of races for a variety of reasons. First, there was the return of Geoff Duke on a BMW in the Senior and on a Reg Dearden Norton in the Junior. Secondly, there was the appearance of a likely lad by the name of Stanley Michael Bailey Hailwood. Then, of course, there was the first-ever showing of the East German MZ light-

weight machines, indicating that things were also happening behind the 'iron curtain'. Finally, 'dustbin' fairings were out and 'dolphin' fairings were in! The machinery and the riders in their skin-tight, one-piece leathers appeared much as we see them today, apart from the brightly coloured leathers and full-face 'space' helmets which the riders wear nowadays. Even the sidecar outfits had become streamlined, integral units with small sidecar wheels and fairings behind which the passenger could lie to improve streamlining and performance.

In 1958, John Hartle had been signed up by MV Agusta as the back-up rider for Surtees and, with only the privateer Nortons against them, it was not surprising that both Johns were at the head of the practice leader board. In the Senior itself, Surtees led from start to finish over the seven laps. He also clocked up his first 100-mph racing lap on the Island.

However, Bob McIntyre on Joe Potts' Norton did not allow MV to have things all their own way, because at the end of the first lap he was only five seconds behind Surtees and leading Hartle by seven, proving that McIntyre's knowledge of the TT course and the superb handling of the Norton were almost a match for the high-speed MVs.

Unfortunately, after the second lap, Bob Mac's Norton cried enough, letting Hartle into second place behind his MV teamster. On this lap, Hartle also lapped at over the 'ton' joining the elite of TT aces. But even Hartle's good fortune was not to last, because, on his fourth lap while pulling out of Governor's Bridge, his machine caught fire and had to be left in the hands of the fire brigade.

This left Surtees to press on, followed by a pack of Nortons all snapping at his heels and hoping that the mighty four-cylinder MV might falter. Alistair King led this chase and would have been runner-up but for a spill at Kirkmichael. This allowed Bob Anderson to pip Bob Brown, both riding Nortons, for second place. In fact, as in so many Senior TTs before, Norton filled the next six places with Dickie Dale bringing home the BMW solo racer in tenth spot. Geoff Duke on the other BMW had retired on his second lap, while the young Mike Hailwood finished 13th to gain a silver replica, making four replicas from four races on his first appearance on the Island.

Progress in the Senior was really a repeat of the Junior race earlier in the week, when Surtees had led from start to finish on the MV Agusta. Hartle had suffered the first of his MV retirements allowing Bob McIntyre to take up the chase after the flying 350-four. However, retirements among the ranks of

Norton owners came thick and fast with the favourites, such as Geoff Duke, Jack Brett, Dickie Dale and then Bob McIntyre, dropping out of the hunt.

The final result was that Dave Chadwick, who had started a lowly tenth on the first lap, had worked his way through the field to finish 4 minutes, 12.2 seconds behind Surtees, leaving Geoff Tanner (Norton) in third position. Another outstanding achievement was that of Norton rider Terry Shepherd, later to have the offer of a works' MV, when he came through from 26th position on the first lap to finish fourth. In this race, Mike Hailwood finished 12th.

In the Lightweight 250 race over the Clypse course, there was little to challenge the MVs of Provini and Ubbiali and the interest lay not so much in any competition against MV, but the obvious battle which took place between the two World Champion riders.

It was a ding-dong struggle right from the start, with Ubbiali leading for the first few laps, but Provini harassed the Champion all the way and, during the course of setting a new lap record of 79.90 mph, passed Ubbiali to win at an average speed of 76.89 mph. A similar battle had taken place for third spot between Mike Hailwood and Bob Brown aboard their production racer NSUs, with the young Hailwood eventually getting the better of Brown.

The Lightweight 125 race was a totally different proposition for the MV pair, Ubbiali and Provini. They had far stronger opposition from the Ducati factory, which had developed a superb lightweight machine with a desmodromic valve motor.

Desmodromic valve operation is when the valves are opened and closed mechanically instead of being opened mechanically and closed by valve springs, as is the normal case on a four-stroke motor. In consequence, engine revolutions are not limited by the speed at which the valves can open and close. Theoretically, a desmodromic valve motor will rev faster without encountering the problem of valve bounce.

Luigi Taveri (Ducati) was the initial challenger to the MV pair and managed to take the lead at the end of the second lap. Leading positions constantly changed around the course, until Provini retired on the third lap and Taveri two laps later. This left Ubbiali substantially in the lead, being chased hard by the remaining Ducati team of Romolo Ferri, Dave Chadwick and Sammy Miller. In fact, they finished in that order.

The rotary-valve MZ two-strokes from East Germany, ridden by Ernst Degner and H. Fugner finished fifth and sixth, while Hailwood gained yet another replica by coming seventh on his Paton. This time Hailwood had to be content with a bronze and not a silver replica to add to his collection.

Highlight of the Sidecar race of this year was the return of one of Britain's greatest sidecar aces, Eric Oliver. He had originated the 'kneeler' outfit a few years earlier and had set the trend for future racing outfit design. But on this occasion, instead of competing seriously against the all-conquering BMW team, Eric chose to race a standard Norton Dominator equipped with an ordinary Watsonian Monaco sports sidecar. His passenger, Mrs Wise, was to remain seated as ballast for the entire ten hectic laps around the Clypse course.

Florian Camathias and Walther Schneider were the BMW riders who set the pace and, in spite of spirited efforts from 'Pip' Harris and Cyril Smith on their Nortons, there was no catching the Munich twins. Schneider romped home the winner 1 minute, 6.2 seconds ahead of Camathias, with Jack Beeton (Norton) finishing third almost six minutes later.

As for Eric Oliver and his brave passenger, Mrs Wise, they finished in a very creditable tenth place on their standard roadster outfit. His speed? Believe it or not, Eric Oliver averaged 59.95 mph, including pit stop, to win a bronze replica.

With Gilera, Moto Guzzi and then MV Agusta completely dominating the Senior and Junior TTs, it was not surprising that the A-CU eventually decided to do something to allow the British manufacturers to gain some of the prestige to be earned from victories on the Isle of Man. And in 1959 it happened, a brand-new formula which would rule out the 'specials' and encourage riders who could only obtain production racing machines. Of course, this meant British production racing machines, because there was no such thing as an over-the-counter MV or Gilera-four. Therefore, as Norton, AJS and Matchless were probably at that time the only companies building racing bikes for sale to the public, the entire entry for the new formula comprised these marques plus a couple of BMWs and a BSA.

The title for the new race was simply Formula 1 (500 and 350) and the races were run on the Saturday before TT race week over three laps of the Mountain Circuit. The event was a grand opening to the 1959 TT week and, with no opposition from the Italian manufacturers due to the 'production-machine' regulation, Formula 1 gave the tuner-sponsors a chance to prove their abilities.

**Above** *Low-level flying in the Senior TT of 1927. Freddie Dixon takes off on the HRD at Ballig Bridge. Although he won the Junior, 'flying' Freddie could only finish sixth in the Senior.*

**Right** *The Norton camp 1929 style! Stanley Woods and Jimmie Simpson study their new overhead camshaft machines, but it was Sunbeam and Rudge who held the whip hand that year in the Senior!*

**Right** *Weighing-in time. A sight that has hardly changed to this day, when bikes are checked by the scrutineers and A-CU officials as they pass into the paddock. This photograph was taken just before the 1930 Junior.*

**Above** *The last AJS victory for 24 years was scored by Jimmy Guthrie in the Lightweight TT of 1930, when he took over four hours to cover seven laps of the Mountain Circuit, at an average speed of 64.71 mph. A great rider on a great machine!*

**Left** *Jimmie Simpson roars through the Cutting (where the Guthrie Memorial now stands) on his way to third place in the 1930 Senior.*

Norton came back with a bang in 1931 when they scored a first and second in the Junior and took the first three places in the Senior. Jimmie Simpson also broke the 80-mph lap barrier. Seen here after the Junior race is the victorious Norton team of Tim Hunt (winner) right, Jimmie Simpson (eighth) centre, and Jimmy Guthrie (second) left.

Riding for the first time in the Junior and Senior TTs of 1936, Freddie Frith scored a fantastic win for Norton in the Junior, setting new race and lap records, and finished third in the Senior. Frith gained his knowledge of the Isle of Man course as a competitor in the Manx Grand Prix, which he won in 1935.

A record lap of 91 mph by Harold Daniell on the works' Norton stood for 12 years until broken by Geoff Duke on another works' Norton in 1950. Not only did Daniell win the 1938 Senior, but he also rode to victory in the Senior TT of 1947, when racing was resumed on the Island following the Second World War.

**Above** *Rider's eye view of Union Mills, one of the many fast and tricky series of bends on the course. Straw-filled sacks give riders a little protection against hazards around the course.*

**Left** *Kirkmichael, where the streets seem to get mighty narrow at speeds of over 110 mph!*

**Right** *The superb stylist Geoffrey Duke, OBE.*

**Below** *Geoff Duke wins his first Junior TT in 1951 at a faster average speed than the previous lap record! He also clocked the first-ever 90 mph-plus lap for a 350, with a record of 91.38 mph.*

**Above** *Geoff Duke left Norton to join the Italian Gilera team and in 1955 gave them their first Senior TT victory. He also came within a fraction of becoming the first man to lap the Mountain Circuit at over 100 mph, with his record lap of 99.97 mph.* **Below** *The challenge to Norton's supremacy in the Senior TT in 1952 came from the Italian MV factory. Here the late, great Les Graham, aboard the powerful four-cylinder 500 MV, leads Reg Armstrong out of Parliament Square, Ramsey. Oil leaks later slowed the Italian bike.*

Scotsman Joe Potts was perhaps the most canny of the backroom boys who wielded the spanners with great effect at that time. His Norton and AJS machines proved as fast as the best of the works' singles and, with Bob McIntyre returning to ride for Joe in 1958, after Gilera had withdrawn from racing, they made a perfect tuner-rider team. This was proved without any doubt in the Formula 1 500 race when Bob McIntyre led from start to finish on Joe Potts' Manx Norton, at an average speed of 97.77 mph.

Bob McIntyre won by over a minute and at no time was he challenged for the lead by second placeman, Bob Brown or by the third runner home, Terry Shepherd. In fact, apart from Dickie Dale on the BMW dropping out of the race on the second lap while holding third spot, the Formula 1 500 class proved quite uneventful. Norton machines took the first six places with the lone Matchless of Derek Powell finishing seventh ahead of another gaggle of Norton runners.

The Formula 1 350 event provided another winner for Joe Potts, this time with Bob McIntyre's close friend and fellow Scot, Alistair King at the controls of Potts' AJS 350 machine. As Bob McIntyre led from start to finish in the 500 class, so did Alistair King in the 350 race. But this time there was only ten seconds between Alistair King and Bob Anderson who took second place. Young Mike Hailwood, showing all of his previous year's promise, finished third.

The incredible thing about the race was that from start to finish there was not a single change on the leader board; in fact, such was the reliability of the British production racers, that all first ten finishers maintained their same positions for all three laps of the race.

The Formula 1 race experiment was not to be repeated on the Island again, but it did provide the riders with additional race practice in 1959, prior to what most considered to be the real TT races.

During practice, John Surtees and John Hartle on the MV Agusta four-cylinder machines had demonstrated that there were few challengers to the high-speed Italian bikes. Only Bob McIntyre and Alistair King on the Potts-tuned motorcycles appeared capable of splitting the two MVs. But there was a new noise on the Island that year, the sound of high-revving lightweights from Japan.

Tanaguchi, S. and G. Suzuki and Tanaka were the Japanese riders with Bill Hunt, the American team manager, making their debut on the Isle of Man for the Honda Motor Company; a name that in a few years was to set the world's racing circuits

alight and rekindle the enthusiasm for road racing which, with the withdrawal of all factory support but that of the MV Agusta team from Italy, was beginning to wane.

Throughout practice week, the Honda 125 twins had aroused the curiosity of everyone on the Island. They had not proved very fast and many a spectator in the pit area had smiled with amusement at the sight of the unwieldy looking lightweights surrounded by a swarm of Oriental mechanics. Soon it would be the turn of the Japanese to smile.

Meanwhile, in the first of the larger capacity races, the Junior TT, John Surtees demonstrated his and the MV's superiority by storming to another TT victory at an average speed of 95.38 mph. He led from start to finish in the seven-lap event, and for four laps Bob McIntyre on Joe Potts' AJS held second place ahead of John Hartle on the other MV-four. However, the strain of winning the Formula 1 350 race for Alistair King and then having to contend with the high-speed MVs proved too much for the 350 AJS and, at the end of lap four, Bob McIntyre pulled into the pits to retire. Vibration on his bike had caused the streamlining mountings to break and he was unable to continue the race.

This allowed John Hartle to finish second, ahead of Alistair King on a 350 Norton, followed home by the great Geoff Duke on another Norton in fourth place. It was to be Duke's last race on the Isle of Man and, at the age of 36, he retired from the road-racing scene to take up residence on the Island. However, to this day he has maintained his interest in motorcycle sport, and in 1965 was Clerk of the Course when the Isle of Man played host to the International Six Days Trial.

The Clypse course was used for the last time in 1959 and in the first of the ten-lap races, the Lightweight 250 event, MV Agusta gained the second of their four solo TT wins of the week. Works' riders Carlo Ubbiali and Tarquino Provini were engaged in a race-long, record-breaking dice with none other than that rising motorcycle ace, Mike Hailwood, on a Mondial. In fact, on lap six, Mike actually took the lead from the World Champions and held them precariously at bay for another two laps. But on lap eight his Mondial gave up the fight and he retired to leave the two Italian champions to fight it out for the last two laps.

First Ubbiali and then Provini led, but on the last lap Provini managed to take the lead and cross the line a mere two-fifths of a second ahead of his team mate. It was a most exciting race and, to complete an MV 1–2–3, Dave Chadwick came home third on his private MV machine. Tommy Robb on the GMS (Geoff Monty Special), which was a sleeved-down Norton in a special lightweight frame, finished fourth ahead of five NSU machines.

MV were also expected to fare extremely well in the 125 race, with Provini and Ubbiali once again favourites to take the honours for the Italian factory. But generally it was accepted that the race would be more open because tiny Luigi Taveri had put in some extremely fast practice laps on the East German MZ. Also, there were the Ducatis of Hailwood and Spaggiari to contend with. Interest, too, lay in the Honda entry, although, judging by practice times and lack of rider experience on the Island, they were never seriously in the hunt for a first-time win.

Taveri and his MZ set the pace and stormed into the lead, breaking the lap record with a speed of 74.99 mph on his third lap. Carlo Ubbiali, who had been chasing him hard on the first two laps, pulled into the pits to make adjustments to his machine, allowing Provini to take up the chase. Hailwood on his Ducati had managed to pass Ernst Degner on the other MZ and, at the end of lap nine, Provini had managed to overtake Taveri, whose two-stroke was rapidly going off-tune.

Provini won the race for MV by seven seconds from Taveri, who finished just ahead of Mike Hailwood and H. Fugner on another MZ two-stroke.

The Hondas finished sixth, seventh, eighth and eleventh in their first Isle of Man TT and were justifiably awarded the Manufacturers' team prize. It was a remarkable demonstration of reliability from the Japanese factory and a marvellous debut which obviously encouraged and inspired them for the future.

Another interesting fact which emerged from the Lightweight 125 race was that a new breed of two-stroke had been designed and was proving extremely competitive against the long-established four-strokes. The MZ single-cylinder two-stroke used a rotary valve induction system, which allowed fuel to enter directly into the crankcase over a much longer induction period than that which was possible with the normal piston-port-controlled two-strokes of the period.

A tuned exhaust system (or expansion chamber) was also used in conjunction with the rotary valve induction to make use of the power pulses to extract the burned gases from the combustion chamber. The result was a tremendous increase in power output over the accepted two-stroke designs and the Japanese in particular were quick to recognise the advantages of the design which had emerged from East Germany.

BMW, BMW, BMW, there was no way of disputing the German factory's supremacy in the sidecar class. Even Pip Harris, who had for so long campaigned on a Norton outfit, decided that if you can't beat them you have to join them, and in 1959 he was mounted on one of the extremely fast horizontally opposed, overhead-camshaft twins. Everyone recognised that Pip was among the top riders in sidecar racing and, now that he had the machinery, there was every chance that he would give Walter Schneider, the reigning champion, a run for his money. Pip did just that.

In the first of the ten laps over the Clypse course, Pip Harris led Walter Schneider around the twisting circuit and, with a two-second lead at the end of lap one, looked all set to gain his first-ever TT victory.

Unfortunately for Harris, in spite of having equal machinery, his outfit struck clutch trouble on the second lap. He continued to race without a clutch and, even after Walter Schneider had passed him, he still chased hard after the champion. But with no clutch, the gearbox took too much punishment and, while lying second on lap seven, Pip had to retire from the race.

This allowed the BMWs of Florian Camathias and Fritz Scheidegger up into second and third places and that is how the race finished; Schneider first, Camathias second and Scheidegger third, a 1–2–3 for BMW. In fact, they took the first five places, with the first British machine, a Triumph ridden by Owen Greenwood, finishing sixth.

The weather on the Isle of Man can and does sometimes seriously affect the racing. Rain invariably means mist on the mountains and, with riders exposed to gale-force winds or torrential rain, is it any wonder that race times are somewhat unpredictable? This proved to be the case for the Senior TT of 1959, when visibility on many parts of the course was practically nil and racing had to be postponed from the Friday to Saturday.

This had happened once before in 1935 when conditions on the Saturday had proved ideal, but the riders were not so fortunate on the second occasion, because, after the first lap of the 1959 Senior, the weather broke making conditions almost impossible for competitors.

However, the race was run in its entirety and, as conditions worsened, so spectators sitting miserably under their umbrellas around the course saw speeds slump. It was one of the slowest Senior TTs for a decade or more.

However, Surtees on the MV set a cracking pace on the first lap and, in fact, beat McIntyre's old

Gilera lap record from a standing start with a speed of 101.18 mph. Hartle on the other MV-four lay second and Bob McIntyre went through in third spot at the end of lap one, but it was obvious that the flying Scotsman was having problems and at the end of the second lap he pulled into his pit and calmly started to dismantle his clutch. Repairs effected, he went on his way well down the field and was not expected to finish on the leader board.

This allowed Bob McIntyre's fellow countryman, Alistair King, up into third place and, when John Hartle crashed the MV on the third lap, Alistair moved up to second behind the slowing Surtees. The weather at this point dramatically worsened, and with speeds slumping into the 80s many wondered why the race was not stopped.

Realising that he had slowed the pace a little too much, Surtees increased speed for the last three laps and romped home the winner over five minutes ahead of King, with Bob Brown on another Norton finishing third. Meanwhile, Bob McIntyre set an astounding pace considering the race conditions and, possibly because of his outstanding knowledge of the TT circuit, worked right through the field to finish in a creditable fifth place. And so ended a TT week which few spectators realised was the start of something big. The little Japanese gentlemen with their cine-cameras, note books and polite smiles knew that they still had a lot of development work ahead of them if they were to beat the superior handling and speed of the Italian racing machines.

In 1960, all of the TT races reverted back to the Mountain course, with both Junior and Senior events being reduced to six laps, the Lightweight 250 covering five laps, while the Lightweight 125 and the Sidecar event were run over three laps. As mentioned previously, the Formula 1 races were disbanded after a one-year experiment. With MV Agusta fielding works' teams in all four solo classes, it looked as though there was nothing to stand in their way, particularly as they had taken Gary Hocking, who had been harassing them in the world's Grands Prix, into the team to ride the lightweight machines in place of Tarquino Provini, who had transferred his allegiance to Morini.

Honda appeared with works' teams for both 250 and 125 races in 1960, but up to that time they had not signed up any European riders for their teams, although they had engaged Australians Bob Brown and Tom Phillis to assist in the development of their Grand Prix racing machines.

Race week began on Monday with the Sidecar and Lightweight 125 races and, for the first time since 1925, racing sidecar outfits were seen speeding over the Mountain course. Surprisingly, the BMWs did not get things all their own way as they had done over the Clypse Circuit. The favourites, Camathias and Scheidegger, both struck trouble during the three laps, but the win still went to BMW, with Helmut Fath scoring his first-ever TT victory to set a new lap record of 85.79 mph.

Pip Harris was still out of luck, but at least on this occasion he finished the race on his BMW, 1 minute, 25 seconds behind Fath. Third place went to Charlie Freeman riding a Norton, but he arrived at the finishing line over seven minutes after the winner.

In the Lightweight 125 race, MV made certain of a victory by ensuring that they had the best riders in the world available to pilot their machines. In the previous year, little Swiss ace Luigi Taveri had given the MV team a hard time riding the East German MZ machine. MVs solution to the problem was to employ him to ride their bikes, and this they did with the result that they scored a 1–2–3 runaway win. World Champion Ubbiali finished first, Gary Hocking second and Luigi Taveri was third. MZ finished fourth and fifth. Fastest lap was set by Ubbiali in a time of 26 minutes, 17.6 seconds at a speed of 86.10 mph, which compares very favourably with a fastest lap in 1974 of 88.78 mph . . . so the question might well be asked – 'What is progress?'.

In the Lightweight 250 race, MV scored their second win of the week, when Gary Hocking confirmed Count Agusta's faith in his riding ability by leading Ubbiali over the line for an MV 1–2. In fact, the Italian factory achieved this remarkable first and second place in all four solo classes in 1960, the first time any manufacturer had done so to date.

However, although Hocking set the new race record at 93.64 mph for the five-lap race, it was Carlo Ubbiali, making his last TT appearance, who set the lap record of 95.47 mph with a time of 32 minutes, 42.8 seconds. Tarquino Provini finished third on the single-cylinder Mondial.

The two Johns, Hartle and Surtees, were on the books as virtual dead certs for the Junior race. They lapped top of the leader board during practice and only Bob McIntyre on his Joe Potts' AJS showed any likelihood of upsetting the form book. As was usual, Surtees stormed into the lead on his four-cylinder MV 350 chased hard by McIntyre and Hartle.

In spite of giving away up to 15 mph on top speed, Bob McIntyre was able to out-corner and out-brake the faster, heavier four-cylinder machines from Italy. Also, with his fantastic riding ability on

75

the Island (even to this day he is considered to be among the top six riders in the history of the TT), he was able to split the two works' machines.

Surtees came close to breaking the 100-mph barrier for the first time on a Junior machine, with a record lap of 22 minutes, 49.4 seconds, a speed of 99.20 mph, as he began to pull away from his pursuers, but then he struck mechanical trouble and lost the lead to his team mate Hartle, who went on to win at an average speed of 96.70 mph. Surtees finished 1 minute, 55.4 seconds later, just 26.2 seconds ahead of Bob McIntyre.

Surtees was without question the number-one rider in the MV team and the maestro proved why with his absolutely faultless ride in the Senior race of that week. He led from start to finish at the fantastic average speed of 102.44 mph which was 1.26 mph faster than the previous lap record.

Weather conditions were perfect and Surtees achieved his personal all-time best lap speed with a new 500 cc record of 104.08 mph. In his wake followed his team mate, John Hartle, who became the second man in the history of the races to average over 100 mph over six laps of the Mountain Course, but even so he still finished 2 minutes, 39 seconds behind Surtees. Mike Hailwood, the youngster who was taking Britain's short circuits by storm and winning virtually every race he entered, finished a gallant third at an average speed of 98.29 mph.

In 1960, the first-ever 100 mph lap by a single-cylinder machine was recorded. Mike 'the bike' Hailwood's father had offered a £100 prize to the first rider to top the 'ton' on a single-cylinder machine over the Mountain course and the ironic thing was that his own son almost claimed the award. As it was, Derek Minter achieved the 100-mph target on the Steve Lancefield-tuned Norton, just one lap before Mike actually recorded his first 'ton' average for his lap. Unfortunately, Minter failed to finish the Senior race, so the Hailwood-Minter dice, which was virtually a continuation of their constant battles on the mainland short circuits, failed to materialise.

Meanwhile, as far as the Japanese Honda factory was concerned, it had astounded everyone with a completely new range of racing lightweights for the 1960 races, the 250 four-cylinder machines and the 125 twin-cylinder models. The specification of double-overhead camshaft, four-valves per cylinder, six-speed gearboxes and engines which peaked at around 14,000 rpm brought an incredible new sound to the Island.

They may not have won the races, but they had impressed everybody with their outstanding reliability. In the Lightweight 250 race, all three entries finished to gain fourth, fifth and sixth positions; while in the Lightweight 125 event, all six entries completed the tough Mountain course with sixth, seventh, eighth, ninth, tenth and 19th positions. All that was required was to combine the outstanding engineering skill of the Honda company and the riding ability of a select few European riders and it was obvious to all that a new challenger had arrived on the Grand Prix scene.

# CHAPTER SIX

# The rising sun shines

WHILE EUROPE'S motorcycle industry suffered the pangs of contraction, which in turn meant the reduction in the efforts to sustain world championship racing teams, on the other side of the world an exciting new industry was struggling to its feet. With a collosal home market for lightweight, economy transport, it was not surprising that the infant motorcycle industry in Japan flourished, but Soichira Honda had dreams beyond the imagination of his European counterparts.

To succeed as a motorcycle manufacturer, it was obvious to Honda that he had to build motorcyles for the entire world and to impress the world he had to achieve one thing . . . beat all opposition on the Isle of Man in the Tourist Trophy races!

Honda's visit to the Island in 1954 had opened his eyes to the fierceness of competition between the European manufacturers, and he returned to Japan aware of the vastness of his undertaking, but undaunted by the challenge. While Norton, Velocette, AJS, Matchless, MV Agusta, Gilera, Moto Guzzi and many others continued their struggle for supremacy on Europe's Grand Prix circuits, Soichira Honda was quietly building up his company and developing the motorcycles which only a decade later were to sweep the world markets.

In 1959, Honda arrived on the Isle of Man. Established manufacturers and trade representatives were very aware of if somewhat amused by the quaint Japanese machines. Their styling and technical specification left a lot to be desired by European standards and, initially, they were not really considered as a threat to any of the existing racing teams or manufacturers.

The riders, except Bill Hunt, who was their American team manager, were all Japanese, with absolutely no experience of the intricacies of riding the 37¾-mile TT circuit. Also, although the machines had proved they were reliable, they had no exceptional performance or handling qualities.

However, in 1960, when five out of six entries in the Lightweight 125 race finished close behind established Grand Prix riders on World Championship-winning machines, a niggling doubt must have crept into the minds of the European manufacturers and racing team managers. Should the challenge from Japan be taken seriously? Did they really have anything to worry about from a country that until that time had been renowned for copying everything from cameras to bicycles?

The answer came in 1961 when, for the first time in the history of the Isle of Man TT races, a Japanese manufacturer achieved a TT double and scored a hat-trick with first, second and third places in both Lightweight classes.

Soichira Honda's dream had come true; he had challenged Europe's established manufacturers of racing motorcycles and won. However, it was achieved very shrewdly by employing the best British and European riders, namely, McIntyre, Hailwood, Phillis, Redman and Taveri, backed up by the Japanese riders, Tanaguchi (125 and 250 classes), Takahashi (250 only) and Shimazaki (125 only). The high-revving, four-cylinder 250s and twin-cylinder 125s were more than a match for anything that MV or MZ had to offer, and all European opposition wilted under the onslaught of Honda's superiority in numbers, performance of machinery and the quality of riders employed in their new works' team.

For the Isle of Man races, it was like a breath of spring air blowing through the pits on Glencrutchery Road. Once again, the atmosphere was alive with that sort of electric that is generated by a sense of urgency, of purpose and the will to win no matter the cost. 1961 was the start of something big which was soon to involve the entire Japanese motorcycle industry and herald the return of fierce rivalry between works' racing teams which had almost died on the Island a few years before. Of all the highly esteemed Italian manufacturers, only MV Agusta were to stand firm against the Japanese opposition.

With Ubbiali and Surtees retiring from motorcycle racing at the end of 1960 and Luigi Taveri signing on for Honda, Count Agusta was left with a problem for the coming season. MV had only one superb, world-class rider, Gary Hocking. This meant MV's virtual withdrawal from the Lightweight TTs and only one entry in the Senior and Junior races.

Now the field was wide open for the Honda team, and in the larger capacity classes the pressure was on Hocking to keep at bay all the established aces on their tried and trusty Manx Nortons and AJS machines.

Another interesting feature about the 1961 Senior is that Norton returned to the Island with a works' machine known as the Domiracer. It was a 500 cc twin-cylinder, push-rod motor based on the roadster machine. Ridden by Tom Phillis, it had given a fair account of itself during practice and, in fact, became the first-ever push-rod engined motorcycle to lap the Isle of Man Mountain Circuit at over 100 mph.

The pattern of racing in 1961 was the same as for the preceding year, with both Senior and Junior events over six laps of the course, the Lightweight 250 over five laps, and both Sidecar and Lightweight 125 races over three laps of the Mountain Circuit.

The racing itself can only be described as classic because in all classes, except the Senior, lap records were shattered and in the Lightweight events shattered beyond all belief. The week was also to prove the most outstanding of all in the career of Stanley Michael Bailey Hailwood who, at 21 years of age, came within an ace of winning all four solo classes of the TT races. As it was, because of a crankpin failure on the last lap in the Junior event, when he virtually had the win in his grasp, Mike had to be content with three out of four wins on the Island.

The first of Hailwood's successes came in the Lightweight 250 race when he rode the Honda-four. After dicing with the wily Scot, Bob McIntyre, for the lead, Bob Mac's Honda failed and Mike went on to win at a fantastic race average of 98.38 mph. This was 2.91 mph faster than the previous lap record set in 1960 by Carlo Ubbiali on the MV 250 machine!

Actually, at the time, everyone agreed that, had Bob McIntyre's Honda not struck mechanical trouble, it was almost certain that he would have won the race, because it was he who almost became the first rider to lap the TT course on a lightweight machine at the magic 'ton'. Bob's lap and record speed was 99.58 mph and this indicates the tremendous pace set by these two fantastic Isle of Man exponents.

Honda, of course, had no need to worry about the outcome of the race, because behind McIntyre,

when he dropped out of the running, was a whole host of their howling four-cylinder machines. Second to Hailwood at the finish was Tom Phillis; then came Jim Redman, followed by Takahashi and Tanaguchi. One, two, three, four, five of the red four-cylinder flying lightweights from Japan, all at speeds almost equal to racing machines double their capacity.

The story was repeated in the Lightweight 125 race with all seven starters finishing the three-lap race, in first, second, third, fourth, fifth, eighth and twenty-second places. Mike Hailwood did the double by claiming his second win of the week, but it was nowhere near as decisive as his victory in the 250 race. He was pushed hard all the way by the dimunitive little Swiss ace, Luigi Taveri, who finished only 7.4 seconds behind the young lad from Oxfordshire.

Mike set a new race record of 88.23 mph, which was once again over 2 mph faster than the existing lap record, but it was Luigi Taveri who set a new record lap of 88.45 mph. Third to finish was Tom Phillis, the first non-Japanese rider to join the Honda team in 1960 and the man greatly responsible for the development of the Honda racing machines. Without Ubbiali or Taveri, MV completely faded from the Lightweight scene and even Hocking was out of luck in the 250 race when he struck the first of the mechanical problems which were to plague him for the entire week on the Island.

It seemed incredible that the positions could be reversed so suddenly from one year to the next. In 1960, everything had gone the way of MV Agusta when they won all four solo classes and yet, just one year later, they were having great difficulty in even being placed on the leader board in the lightweight classes.

Fate almost struck another blow against MV and Hocking in the Junior race. Although Hocking shot off into the lead on the first lap, being chased hard by Hailwood on his AJS, by the end of the third lap it was obvious that something was wrong with the four-cylinder Italian machine. Cheers echoed around the course as Hailwood took the lead because it looked as though there might be the first British Junior victory since 1954. Hailwood continued to open the gap between himself and Hocking on the ailing MV 350, and then Phil Read caught and passed the mighty four-cylinder power bike.

The crowds were on tenterhooks as Mike headed for home and his third successive victory of the week. Then it happened, just 14 miles from the end of the race, the AJS 350 cried enough and Mike was left stranded at the roadside only to watch despondently as first Phil Read and then Gary Hocking flew past on their way to the finishing line.

Hocking had set the fastest lap at 99.80 mph on the MV, but it was Read who took the chequered flag to win at an average speed of 95.10 mph, 1 minute, 17.8 seconds ahead of Hocking. Third was Ralph Rensen on his Norton. Not surprisingly, Phil Read could not believe he had won the race. It was his first appearance in the TT and, although he had won the previous year's Senior Manx Grand Prix, a first-time-out win in the Tourist Trophy races seemed beyond belief for the young rider from Luton.

In the Sidecar TT, it was the established runaway win for the BMW twins from Germany. Both race and lap records fell to the World Champion, Max Deubel, who completed a faultless race at an average speed of 87.65 mph and broke Helmut Fath's lap record with a speed of 87.97 mph. Fritz Scheidegger finished second some 32.8 seconds behind Deubel, and Pip Harris on his BMW came third.

The race of the week, and the one which was to establish the name of Hailwood in the record books as probably one of the greatest riders in TT history, was Friday's Senior TT. For the first time a rider was to win three TTs in a week!

The race began as expected according to the previous week's practice times and speeds. Hocking on the big MV lapped at over 101 mph to lead Mike Hailwood by 15.4 seconds at the end of the first lap. But it was obvious to all that Mike was trying his hardest, for he averaged over 100 mph from a standing start on his Manx Norton. Hocking turned on the pressure, but still he could not shake off the determined young Hailwood and only 29 seconds separated the first two men at the end of the third lap. Mike was trying everything he knew to keep within striking distance of the four-cylinder MV and, in doing so, clocked an incredible lap of 101.31 mph on the single-cylinder Norton. By the end of the fourth lap, Mike had reduced Gary Hocking's lead to 15.2 seconds and the atmosphere around the circuit was incredibly tense as Hocking pulled into the pits at the end of the fourth lap to make frantic adjustments to his machine. The seconds ticked rapidly by for Hocking, but incredibly slowly for the crowds around the course.

When Hocking finally pushed off to start his fifth lap, he had lost the lead to Hailwood and the commentators around the course went wild with excitement. Everyone except the MV pit staff were urging Mike on to win. Spectators, all dedicated to giving the young 21-year-old Hailwood their support, waved with programmes and handkerchiefs. For the second time in the week, it was to be a British machine with a British rider aboard actually winning a TT race, something which had not happened for far too long.

At the end of lap five, the race was clinched for Hailwood. Although Hocking had completed the lap and lay fourth on the leader board, for him the race was over. The throttle had kept sticking wide open, making the machine virtually uncontrollable, so on lap five Gary Hocking pulled into the pits to retire from the race.

This left Mike with a lead of almost two minutes over his Scottish friend and rival, Bob McIntyre, who in turn held only a very slender 3.4 second advantage over Tom Phillis. On the new Domiracer twin Phillis had clocked up the magic 'ton' for the Norton factory on a push-rod twin-cylinder machine.

On the last lap, the result was never really in doubt but, realising the misfortune that had robbed him of a victory in the Junior TT earlier in the week, everybody kept their fingers crossed until Mike and his Norton crossed the finishing line on the Glencrutchery Road. It was a fantastic finish to a marvellous week's motorcycle sport on the Island.

Although MV had virtually pulled out of Grand Prix racing in 1961 and Gary Hocking had to be content with riding the previous year's machinery under the MV 'privat' banner, it was not surprising that Mike Hailwood, having proved to all that he had developed into one of the world's greatest road racers, should be offered MV 350 and 500 cc machines for the 1962 season.

Both Hocking and Hailwood were to race the MVs as 'privat' entries and not works' machines. This meant that Honda temporarily lost one of the best riders in their all-conquering team. In fact, considering that Mike Hailwood won the World Championship 250 class for Honda in 1961, it was surprising that they let him go without too much of a fuss. Probably, they felt that with riders of the calibre of McIntyre, Phillis, Taveri, Redman and their new signing for 1962, Tommy Robb, there was was no need to worry unduly about Mike leaving the camp.

However, although Mike was obviously pleased about the chance to ride the MVs, he was left without a ride in the lightweight events and snapped up the opportunity to race the new Benelli four-cylinder 250, which had been developed by the

Italian concern. As it worked out, the Benelli-four did not materialise for the TT and Mike had to be content with riding one of Fron Purslow's early single-cylinder bikes.

In the 125 race, Mike demonstrated his versatility by riding the EMC two-stroke, which had been developed by Dr Joe Erhlich in conjunction with the de Havilland aircraft company. The bike had a single-cylinder, disc-valve motor and was very similar in design to the East German MZ. Another of these British lightweights was ridden by Rex Avery, the rider responsible for much of the development and test riding programme.

The programme of the races was altered for 1962, with the 250 event being extended to six laps, while a brand-new 'tiddler' race was introduced for 50 cc machines. With Suzuki, Honda and Kreidler taking a remarkable interest in the TT, it was not surprising that the A-CU went along with other Grand Prix organisers and provided a race for the tiddlers. A World Championship had been established for the class and with four works' entries each from Honda and Suzuki, as well as works' interest from Kreidler in Germany, the competition over two laps of the Mountain course was fierce. The 50 cc racing class had become quite popular in Britain, mainly due to the relatively low cost and the easy availability of over-the-counter racers such as the Itom from Italy.

In fact, the entry for the 50 cc TT was comprised mainly of these miniature two-strokes which were completely outpaced by the high-revving Suzukis, Kreidlers and Hondas, all of which had anything up to 12 gears to cope with the ridiculously narrow power band of the motors. With the Kreidlers, changing gear was accomplished by the dual-operation of a twist-grip gearchange and also a foot-operated gear pedal. How any of the riders of these factory specials knew which gear they were in at any given time is still a mystery. It seemed that it was simply a matter of changing up or down gears, while attempting to keep the engine in the power band, until there were literally no more to select or use.

Another little piece of TT history was established this year and that was the entry of a woman into the 50 cc TT. Other women had competed in the TT as passengers in sidecar racing outfits, but Mrs Beryl Swain became the first and only woman to ride in a TT race for solo motorcycles. One year later, the FIM banned women from holding international racing licences for solos and so Beryl Swain, who finished 22nd in her race, made TT history.

The sidecar race opened TT week and, true to form, the BMWs, that had dominated the event since 1955, streaked into the lead with Deubel and Camathias battling for first place. At the end of the first lap, it was Deubel who led Camathias by 16 seconds, while Chris Vincent on his BSA lay third, well over a minute and a half behind the BMW twins.

Unfortunately for Camathias, he crashed on the second lap and retired from the race leaving Vincent in second spot quite a considerable distance behind the record-breaking Max Deubel. His first lap on the BMW was the first-ever 90 mph-plus lap of the Mountain Circuit by a racing outfit, and this was from a standing start. By comparison, Vincent's lap speed was almost 5 mph slower.

But it is not always the hare that wins the race. On his third and last lap, Max Deubel's engine seized solid at Ballig Bridge, leaving Vincent 30 seconds ahead of the BMW of Otto Kolle, who had a precarious lead over Colin Seeley on his Matchless. And that is how the result read at the end of the race, with Vincent winning the first-ever Sidecar TT for BSA, at an average speed of 83.57 mph. He finished 37.4 seconds ahead of Kolle, who in turn beat Seeley by 8 seconds.

The Lightweight 250 race which had been extended to six laps, the same as the Junior and Senior TTs, lacked entries. In fact, the list was down to 37 riders and of these 11 were non-starters! But what it lacked in quantity, the entry definitely made up in quality.

Reg Armstrong had been appointed Honda team manager and, with virtually no opposition in the 250 class, it was obvious that Honda were going to win the race; but who would be the lucky rider? McIntyre, Phillis, Redman and Minter were all on the list of possibles and all had lapped the Island at 'over the ton' and were capable of winning.

McIntyre stormed away from the rest of the runners at the start of the race and by Ramsey had gained over half-a-minute on Derek Minter. Leading on the roads and the race, Bob Mac streaked past the pits at the end of his first lap with a 34.6-second lead over Jim Redman, who in turn was 9.2 seconds ahead of Derek Minter. Phillis and Kitano on another two of the screaming Honda-fours lay fourth and fifth, with Mike Hailwood on the single-cylinder Benelli just making it on to the leader board in sixth spot.

Bob McIntyre's standing-start lap was an incredible 99.06 mph. At the beginning of his second lap it looked as though he had every chance of recording the first 100-mph lap in the Lightweight TT.

But, as in the previous year's race, the Isle of Man jinx struck yet again and Bob McIntyre did not get beyond Kirkmichael before the flying four expired with mechanical trouble. This allowed Jim Redman into the lead, chased very hard by Derek Minter.

Tom Phillis, who was lying third, also encountered mechanical problems with his Honda and had to call into the pits to cure a misfire. Trouble corrected, Phillis returned to the fray after losing several places and Mike Hailwood took over third place behind Minter and Redman on the second lap.

And so the race progressed, with first Redman and then Minter leading, with the single-cylinder Benelli of Hailwood chugging along behind. In the tremendous dice between Redman and Minter, the lead changed five times, but it was Minter who led at the start of the last lap.

Meanwhile, Tom Phillis, who had been making haste on his repaired Honda, had carved his way through the field from eighth position to relegate Mike Hailwood from third to fourth place. But Mike had had problems with the Benelli and at the start of the last lap pulled into the pits to remove the fairing from his bike. Vibration had shattered the mountings and he continued the race without the streamlining, but only for a short distance because the ageing single-cylinder Benelli gave up the ghost at Braddan Bridge, allowing veteran Arthur Wheeler into fourth place on his single-cylinder Moto Guzzi.

The incredible point about the 1962 Lightweight 250 event was that out of 37 entries only seven machines actually completed the race, but Honda were satisfied because their machines finished first, second and third.

Derek Minter won the race at an average speed of 96.68 mph, followed by Jim Redman and then Tom Phillis. At the time, many spectators were under the illusion that Minter was a member of the Honda works' team. In fact, this was not the case for he had been loaned his Honda 250-four by Hondis, the British importer of the Japanese machines. The bike Minter used was the 1961 model and Honda were far from pleased that Minter had beaten their works' riders who were contesting the World Championship. Whether Minter would have won the 1962 250 TT if Jim Redman's petrol filler cap had not kept flying open during the race, which meant an extra stop for fuel, is debatable. But the win is recorded in the books, and for Derek Minter it was his first victory and equally as satisfying as being the first rider to clock the 'ton' lap on a single-cylinder machine.

To some, Honda's win in the 250 race rang a little bit hollow because both Suzuki and Yamaha had dropped out of the class for the simple reason that they did not at the time consider their 250 two-strokes competitive. They had literally 'gone back to the drawing board' to produce brand-new GP machines for the following season.

In the Lightweight 125 race, Hugh Anderson from New Zealand, Frank Perris and Ernst Degner were the team fielded by Suzuki to combat the six works' riders from Honda. Mike Hailwood, Paddy Driver and Rex Avery were competing on the British EMC 125 singles, but nobody really expected any challenge to the obvious supremacy of the Honda team.

However, Mike Hailwood had other ideas and, demonstrating his extraordinary adaptability and riding skill, he set about proving that not even a manufacturer the size of Honda was invincible. Aboard the diminutive, single-cylinder two-stroke EMC, Mike chased hard after little Luigi Taveri on the Honda. In fact, so hard did Mike push the Swiss ace, that Taveri's race average of 89.88 mph broke the previous lap record and his fastest lap of 25 minutes, 7 seconds gained him the first over 90-mph lap by a 125 racing machine on the Island. It seemed incredible that, just 11 years after the great Geoff Duke had cracked the 90-mph barrier on his Junior machine, lightweight 125s were lapping as fast!

Unfortunately, Mike's gallant efforts on the EMC were in vain, because, although he held second place behind Taveri for the first two laps of the race, on the last lap the EMC stopped on the Glen Helen section of the course. This allowed Irishman Tommy Robb into second place on his Honda, followed closely by Tom Phillis. Honda were back in the old routine, taking the first five places in the race, with Rex Avery on the EMC finishing sixth.

The best that Suzuki could manage was an eighth place by Ernst Degner, with both Frank Perris and Hugh Anderson failing to complete the course.

The weather for the 1962 race week was superb and, when the machines came to the grid for the start of the Junior race on Wednesday afternoon, the crowd around the circuit could sense that the record book was about to be re-written. Hocking and Hailwood on the MV-fours were teammates but deadly rivals on the track. Against them and obviously in with a chance of winning were Bob McIntyre and Tom Phillis on over-bored 250 Honda-fours. In practice, the Hondas had proved extremely fast and there could be no let up for the MV pair.

From a standing start, both Hailwood and Hocking lapped at over the 'ton', with Tom Phillis lying third at the end of lap one, closely followed some 7.8 seconds later by Bob Mac. Hocking had caught and passed Hailwood on the roads and led by 11 seconds at the end of lap one; all he had to do was stay with Mike for the rest of the event to win the Junior TT. And that's how it was for virtually the entire race with first Mike and then Gary slip-streaming one another at speeds up to 150 mph with no more than 8 or 10 feet between them.

The Honda team where shattered when Tom Phillis crashed and was fatally injured on the second lap and, although his team mate, Bob McIntyre, took over in third place, he was to retire on the third lap with mechanical trouble at Keppel Gate. Honda were out and, with both Ron Langston and Alan Shepherd also retiring from the race, Franta Stastny on the Czechoslovakian Jawa 350 four-stroke twin moved up into third place, followed by the usual gaggle of British Norton and AJS machines.

Meanwhile, after both Hailwood and Hocking had taken precisely the same length of time over their refuelling stop, their battle for the lead continued. Mike managed to repass Gary on the fifth lap, but all Hocking had to do was keep Hailwood in his sight and he must win. Mike had other ideas and, using every ounce of riding skill he possessed, he set about pulling away from the MV of Hocking which was beginning to feel its age.

Mike's last lap was completed at over 101 mph to give him victory from Hocking by a mere 5.6 seconds, with Stastny gaining a well-earned third place. The previous year's winner, Phil Read, finished seventh on his Norton.

Mike Hailwood's time for the race was 2 hours, 16 minutes and 24.2 seconds at an average speed of 99.59 mph, which was a new race record, and his fastest lap took 22 minutes, 17.2 seconds to set another new lap record of 101.58 mph.

Perhaps the race with the greatest curiosity value during the week was the two-lap, 50 cc 'tiddler' event. Three works' teams were competing, Suzuki and Honda from Japan and Kreidler from Germany. The remainder of the entry comprised rather slow production 'over-the-counter' racers which stood very little chance against the multi-speed works' specials.

Many thought the race would be just a boring procession, but the fierce competition between Suzuki, Honda and Kreidler for the 50 cc World Championship stakes ensured that the race was as hotly contested as any of the bigger capacity events.

Incredibly, Ernst Degner reeled off a standing start lap of over 75 mph on his screaming Suzuki two-stroke single, while Luigi Taveri on the double-overhead camshaft Honda single lapped only 15.2 seconds slower at just under 75 mph. At the end of the first lap, the leader board read Degner (Suzuki), Taveri (Honda), Robb (Honda), Anscheidt (Kreidler), Ichino (Suzuki) and Itoh (Suzuki) and, apart from Ichino and Itoh swopping places on the last lap, that is how the results read at the finish.

Ernst Degner set a fastest lap of 75.52 mph in 29 minutes, 58.6 seconds and, with the Suzuki, Honda and Kreidler machines filling all of the first 12 places, this left the privateers on their Itoms and suchlike to fight it out for a finisher's medal.

The climax to the week's racing was the expected duel in the Senior between Hailwood and Hocking on their 'privat' MV 500-fours. Mike already had the Junior race to his credit that week and his aim was obviously to score a TT double. The battle royal commenced and on the first lap lived up to the expectations of the enthusiastic crowds around the course. At the end of lap one, Hocking was in the lead on the roads and held a precarious 1.6-second advantage over Hailwood, with Alan Shepherd lying third.

But instead of being able to close the gap, Mike Hailwood soon learned from pit signals that Gary was pulling out all the stops, and slowly but surely increasing his lead by averaging over 103 mph. Mike was having clutch trouble with his MV and at the end of lap four he pulled into his pit and lost 12 minutes while the unit was dismantled and re-built. Mike rejoined the event way down the field and Hocking had the race in the bag. Hocking won by a clear 5 minutes, 52.8 seconds from Ellis Boyce (Norton) and Fred Stevens (Norton).

During the course of his struggle for the lead with Hailwood, Gary Hocking had raised the lap record to 105.75 mph and averaged 103.51 mph for the six-lap event.

The feud between Hocking and Hailwood continued on the world's Grand Prix circuits and Gary openly admitted that the pressure was hell. In fact, at the end of the 1962 season, Hocking retired from motorcycle racing to return to Rhodesia, where he was tragically killed while testing a racing car.

Another tragic loss to motorcycle sport in general and the TT in particular was the death of Bob McIntyre at Oulton Park over the August Bank Holiday meeting. In torrential rain, Bob Mac crashed into a tree and sustained severe injuries from which he died a few days later. Bob was a quiet person, a brilliant rider and a clever engineer who could hold his own with any other Isle of Man TT exponent.

During the 'closed season' between 1962 and '63, the Japanese race development engineers worked like demons to produce new and even more shattering machines. Honda, who had so successfully conquered the Grand Prix scene in 1962, suddenly found at the start of the 1963 season that Suzuki and Yamaha had been working wonders in their development workshops.

The rotary disc-valve Suzuki twins in the 125 cc class and the rotary valve, water-cooled 50 cc singles were considerably quicker than the Honda counterparts and, for that year, Honda withdrew their existing 50 cc overhead camshaft single until something better could be produced.

In the larger capacity classes, the 250-fours were still just about holding their own, but were coming under increasing pressure from Yamaha and in 1962 had almost lost the World Championship to Provini on his lone single-cylinder Morini. Another interesting event that happened at the start of the new road-racing season in 1963 was that Geoff Duke managed to talk Gilera into making a comeback into racing, using the old four-cylinder 350 and 500 machines which had been in mothballs since 1957.

Gilera agreed and Geoff Duke, as team manager, picked Derek Minter and John Hartle as team riders. However, due to injury, Derek was replaced by Phil Read. This meant that Hailwood on the MVs not only had Jim Redman and Tommy Robb on Hondas to contend with in the Junior race, he also had the additional challenge from Gilera with Phil Read and Hartle in both 350 and 500 cc events.

In many ways, the 1963 TT week could be considered one of the most widely supported race weeks in TT history. There were works' teams from Italy, Japan and Germany. It was almost like returning to the mid-1950s, when all the European manufacturers were competing for the honour of winning the races.

The formula for the 1963 races was much the same as the previous year except that the 50 cc race had been extended from two to three laps. The Sidecar TT opened the week's events and, although the record books show that the FCS (Florian Camathias Special) won the race at a new record average speed of 88.38 mph, the outfit was based on a BMW power unit with only the chassis design and construction being carried out by the Swiss rider, Florian Camathias.

In fact, as was normal and accepted, the BMW-powered machines scored the usual 1–2–3 with

Camathias winning by 38.2 seconds from Fritz Scheidegger, with the British pair, Alan and Peter Birch, finishing third. Max Deubel, the favourite to win the event, again, as in the previous year's race, struck trouble and limped home to finish eighth.

Interest in the 250 race lay in the challenge to Honda's highly successful team of riders (Taveri, Redman, Robb and Takahashi on their flying fours) from the brand-new, water-cooled 'square four' two-stroke Suzukis of Anderson, Schneider, Degner and Perris. Yamaha had three official works' entries in the race, all ridden by Japanese riders – Fumio Ito, Sunako and Hasegawa. Unfortunately for the spectators that year, the Suzuki-fours' entry was withdrawn and the expected Honda/Suzuki confrontation was postponed for another year. However, Honda did not exactly have an easy time winning the race, because Yamaha with their rotary disc-valve twins were able to match the performance of four-stroke fours. In fact, Fumio Ito, on his second visit to the Isle of Man, harassed Jim Redman for the entire length of the race.

For the first time, the renowned Honda reliability was in doubt, with both Taveri and Takahashi dropping out of the race. This left Redman and Robb to do battle with Ito and Hasegawa, with Bill Smith on his Honda production racer twin supporting the works' machines. The final outcome of the race was that Redman beat Ito by 27.2 seconds, with Bill Smith finishing third over five minutes after the two works' bikes. Hasegawa on the Yamaha took fourth place ahead of Tommy Robb on his Honda-four.

No race or lap records were broken by Jim Redman who set a fastest lap of 97.23 mph and averaged 94.85 mph for the six-lap race.

In the three-lap Lightweight 125 race, which took place on the Wednesday morning, the Honda team were completely out-gunned by the fantastically fast water-cooled Suzuki two-stroke twins. Tohatsu and Yamaha, two other Japanese manufacturers, were also entered for the race, but at the time Yamaha were still developing their raceware. They did not have a competitive machine for the class and so withdrew their entry. Dave Simmonds rode the lone Tohatsu, but it could not rival the works' Suzukis or Hondas.

Surprisingly, even EMC, with riders Peter Inchley and Rex Avery, dropped their entry along with the East German MZ factory. In fact, what had promised to be an interesting race with so many works' teams on the starting line turned into a straight confrontation between Honda and Suzuki, with all the cards stacked on the side of the two-strokes.

From the drop of the flag, New Zealander Hugh Anderson rocketed into the lead. He started ten seconds behind the Honda of Tommy Robb and within half a lap had caught and passed the Belfast-born Honda works' rider. From then on nobody in the race saw the going of the flying Kiwi. Anderson led from start to finish and averaged 89.27 mph to beat team mate Frank Perris over the line by 1 minute, 20 seconds. Ernst Degner finished third to give Suzuki their first 1–2–3 victory on the Island, with Hugh Anderson raising the lap record to 91.23 mph.

Luigi Taveri finished fourth for Honda; Bertie Schneider on the remaining Suzuki came fifth and Honda then filled the remaining places from sixth to twelfth. It was obvious to the Honda racing team that the Suzuki two-strokes were far superior to the twin-cylinder four-strokes and that something would have to be done to win back the advantage from Suzuki.

The first race of the week for Mike Hailwood on his MV 'Privat' 350 was the Junior TT on the Wednesday afternoon. Virtually no development work had been done on the MV and Hailwood was well aware of the challenge from Jim Redman and Tommy Robb on the very rapid Honda 350-fours. And, of course, there was the return of Gilera under the Scuderia Duke banner, with Read and Hartle, both experienced TT campaigners, riding to win.

Redman and Hailwood started with racing numbers one and two, Honda versus MV from the drop of the flag. The crowds in the grandstand rose to their feet as both the fighting fours screamed into life, with the slightly higher-pitched Honda leading the MV on the steep drop down Bray Hill. Thirty seconds later, Tommy Robb and John Hartle were away, followed a further ten seconds behind by Phil Read on the other Gilera 350-four.

With five four-cylinder works' specials, each in with a chance of winning the Junior, there were all the ingredients for a fantastic race. However, as far as Jim Redman was concerned, it was his week and he had the machine to show the ageing MV and Gileras the way home. The roads ahead were clear and, with nobody to baulk him or slow him down, all Redman had to do was use his speed and acceleration advantage to pull away from Hailwood. He did just that.

There was no way Mike could catch the flying Honda and eventually, in his efforts to stay with Redman, Hailwood's MV expired leaving the

Rhodesian to cruise home the winner by a clear 6 minutes, 50 seconds. Both Read and Robb had retired from the race with mechanical trouble, leaving Hartle to bring the Gilera home in second place. Third was Franta Stastny, who repeated his previous year's performance on the Czech Jawa twin.

Redman's fastest lap on the Honda was 22 minutes, 20.8 seconds at a speed of 101.30 mph, just outside Hailwood's lap record. But it was obvious that he had no need to hurry once Mike had dropped out of the running, because the race average of 94.91 mph was only a fraction faster than Redman's speed in the 250 event.

With no Hondas in the 50 cc TT, Friday morning's race was to all intents and purposes a straight duel between the six works' Suzukis and the four Kreidler machines. Tohatsu had two entries with the Simmonds brothers riding and, although Dave Simmonds' machine had an incredible twin-cylinder power unit, neither Tohatsus were considered serious opposition to the Suzuki or Kreidler machines.

The event had been extended to three laps of the Mountain Circuit and, although the speeds of the buzzing 50 cc racers were quite outstanding, the race itself was rather boring for spectators. There were far too few entries and there were long gaps between competitors, which meant that spectators had to wait anything up to 20 minutes to see a racing bike on the roads.

In an attempt to make things more interesting, the A-CU started the event with the opposing Kreidler and Suzuki teams setting off in pairs: Bertie Schneider (Suzuki) with Hans Anscheidt (Kreidler), Alberto Pagani (Kreidler) with Hugh Anderson (Suzuki), Ernst Degner (Suzuki) against Ramon Torras (Kreidler), followed by Itoh, Ichino and Morishita, all on Suzukis.

Ernst Degner set the pace with an absolutely incredible lap of 79.10 mph on his diminutive Suzuki, breaking the lap record by 3.58 mph. But the extra lap proved too much for his machine and the German retired on the last lap with mechanical trouble. This left Itoh and Anderson to fight it out for the lead, with Hans Anscheidt pressing them hard on his Kreidler.

The final outcome of the race was that Itoh became the first-ever Japanese rider to win a TT, at the record speed of 78.81 mph, with Hugh Anderson finishing 26.8 seconds later. Anscheidt, who was 4.6 seconds behind Anderson, gained Kreidler third place.

The Senior TT of 1963 could almost be conidered a repeat of the 1957 event, when Gilera clashed with MV for race honours. Then, Bob McIntyre and Bob Brown had taken on John Surtees with his lone MV 500-four. Surtees had come off second best when Bob Mac on the Gilera had achieved the first 100-mph lap of the Mountain Circuit.

However, the situation was slightly different for the Senior race in 1963, because, whereas MV had continued to race and had the advantage of further development over the period, Gilera's 500s had literally been stripped, cleaned and rebuilt, fitted with new tyres and streamlining, filled with petrol and oil and put back on the track for Hartle and Read to ride.

Practice times showed that the Gilera was still reasonably competitive and, with nothing else to see other than the usual Manx Nortons and Matchless G50s, it was interesting for spectators to witness a possible challenge to MV's virtually unbroken winning streak in the Senior. With the exception of 1961, when a mechanical failure lost them the race, MV had won every Senior TT since John Surtees rode to victory in both Junior and Senior in 1958.

Hailwood started the race ten seconds after Hartle, with Read on the other Gilera setting off a further ten seconds behind Hailwood. Considering that it was Read's first time out on one of the extremely rapid four-cylinder Gileras, he rode extremely well to average just over 100 mph for the six-lap race. However, it was the battle between the ex-MV teamster Hartle on the Scuderia Duke Gilera and Hailwood on the 'Privat' MV 500 that had the crowd on their toes.

With a ten-second lead on the roads, Hartle was at an immediate disadvantage because all that the young Mike Hailwood had to do to win was catch Hartle and stay with him for the rest of the race. But Hailwood did more than that because he caught up and passed Hartle on the first lap and promptly started to open up an unassailable lead. Mike's fastest lap, which established a new record of 106.41 mph, took him well clear of the rest of the field and, although he was able to cruise home the winner some 1 minute, 13.4 seconds ahead of Hartle, Mike also established a brilliant race record average of 104.64 mph.

In a way, it was a pity that Hailwood defeated the Gilera team because, had they succeeded in winning the TT, it may well have inspired them to return to Grand Prix racing in 1964. As it was, they could see that the existing raceware was no match for the Hondas in the 350 class and could not beat

the World Champion MVs and Hailwood in the 500 cc category. Consequently, Gilera decided at the end of the year that, rather than become involved in spending a fortune on developing new race-winning machines, they would gracefully slide back into retirement.

One of the most interesting points about this era of TT history was the development which took place in the lightweight range of racing machines. In the 350 and 500 classes, development had virtually stagnated apart from Honda's 350, and the Senior and Junior races maintained their status more because of tradition than by being exciting and stimulating to watch. In the lightweight races, the advantage swayed to and fro between the four-stroke Hondas and the two-stroke Yamaha and Suzuki machines.

If a manufacturer scored an overwhelming victory with their new racing machine one season, before the year was out the opposition had developed, produced and race-tested something just that little bit better. In the lightweight classes, any racing design more than a year old was obsolete and the European manufacturers could only watch from the sidelines and wonder how the Japanese industry could, at the drop of a hat, produce a brand-new, race-winning motorcycle.

The engine configurations were numerous, from twin-cylinder two- and four-strokes of only 50 cc, to square and V-four two-strokes of 125 cc and 250 cc, five-cylinder 125 cc four-strokes, four- and six-cylinder four-strokes from 250 to 500 cc; all producing unbelievable power outputs with performance to match. The computer-designed Japanese machines attained unbelievable peaks; 14,000 rpm was commonplace with the 250s, and 22,000 rpm from the double-overhead-camshaft, twin-cylinder Honda 50 cc was probably the ultimate.

Works' riders and mechanics practically carried commuter airline tickets in their hip pockets. One week they would be in Japan secretly testing the latest racing machine; the next, returning to Europe to unveil the new brainchild of the racing engineers before a stunned audience of press men, race officials and, of course, the opposing teams.

After Suzuki had stolen the glory from Honda in the Lightweight 125 and 50 cc races of 1963, works' riders Taveri, Redman and newcomer Ralph Bryans spent some considerable time in Japan testing the new raceware that was to show Suzuki that Honda four-strokes were the best. Meanwhile, Frank Perris and Hugh Anderson were busy testing the new square-four 250 cc Suzuki that they hoped was going to beat the Honda 250-four.

Yamaha still retained their rotary-valve 250 twin, but the decision was taken to sign-up Phil Read, Mike Duff and Tommy Robb to campaign the works' machines in Europe.

And so the stage was set for another clash on the Isle of Man between the giants of the Japanese motorcycle industry. Mike Hailwood sat on the sidelines, quietly confident of scoring another fairly easy win in the Senior on the MV 500, knowing that he had problems in winning the Junior against Jim Redman and wishing for all the world that Count Agusta would allow him to ride other marques in the Lightweight races.

Mike must also have been wondering when MV would do something about the Japanese threat to the larger capacity classes and how long it would be before the inevitable happened and Honda built a 500 cc machine capable of easily beating the ageing MV.

The 1964 TT week began with the Sidecar race. This was something of an anticlimax with many of the favourite runners dropping out with mechanical trouble before the end of the three laps. Florian Camathias had managed to get Gilera to lend him one of their 500-four motors to build into his outfit, but to no avail. Although the Italian motor produced considerably more power than the BMW twins, Camathias, who had won the previous year's sidecar race, could manage no better than 15th place.

Scheidegger and Otto Kolle on their BMWs also failed to complete the race distance and it was Max Deubel who won at an average speed of 89.12 mph. Colin Seeley rode Florian Camathias' FCSB into second place, 1 minute, 55.4 seconds behind the winner, and Georg Auerbacher finished third on another BMW over 2 minutes behind Seeley, to make it the accepted 1–2–3 for the German factory.

The race which all the spectators had been waiting for, the Lightweight 250, took place after the sidecar event. With three of the new Suzukis and three works' Yamahas against the Honda team, it should have been one of the most hotly contested events of the week. But great expectations often create great disappointments and, although initially there was a tremendous dice for the lead with Read setting the pace on his Yamaha with a record lap of 99.42 mph, one by one the works' machines failed. All three Suzukis were not able to complete the race; only Tommy Robb finished for Yamaha, in seventh place, and five out of the six Honda team failed before seeing the chequered flag.

Fortunately for Honda, Jim Redman kept going to win at an average of 97.45 mph from Alan Shepherd, who rode an MZ into second place ahead of Pagani on the Paton. In the search for power, it appeared that the manufacturers were pushing their machines to the limit of reliability.

In the 125 race later in the week, Suzuki encountered exactly the same problem, lack of reliability. Whereas the previous year they had scored a superb victory over Honda, in 1964 all three Suzuki entries failed to complete the three-lap race. Without opposition, it was a Honda benefit, with Redman and Taveri setting the circuit alight with a tremendous demonstration of riding skill as they battled for victory.

Redman was very much the quiet man of the Honda team. He was a dedicated professional able to analyse precisely the machines he rode and tell the Japanese exactly what was needed to improve or correct the racing bikes. Probably, for this reason Redman finished races where others failed. But in the Lightweight 125 event, it was the fiery little Swiss ace, Luigi Taveri, who not only pipped Jim Redman at the post by a mere 3 seconds, but also pushed the 125 lap record up to 93.53 mph. Honda's new teamster, Ralph Bryans finished third. Only a lone CZ finishing fourth stopped a Honda clean sweep from first to eighth places!

The question in everybody's mind at the start of the Junior race was, could Mike Hailwood beat Jim Redman? It was a straightforward two-man race, with the rest of the competitors there to fill up the leader board behind the winner. The answer was immediately apparent as Redman and his Honda set the pace and, as had happened the previous year, Hailwood's MV self-destructed in the attempt to stay with the speeding Rhodesian. MV Agusta had to spend time and money on further development if they hoped to beat Honda on the Island.

With Hailwood out of the race, Redman was able to cool the pace and win at leisure. His average speed of 98.50 mph was sufficient to carry him over the finishing line some 7 minutes, 14.2 seconds ahead of Phil Read on his AJS, while Phil's Yamaha team mate, Mike Duff, finished only 11.8 seconds behind him on another of the Plumstead 350 singles.

The one consolation for Suzuki in the entire race week was their domination of the three-lap 50 cc race. Hugh Anderson led from start to finish and won the race at the unbelievable average speed of 80.64 mph, faster than the previous year's lap record. Honda's Ralph Bryans finished second to Anderson after a race-long scrap with Morishita on a Suzuki. In fact, Bryans just managed to pip Morishita at the post by six-tenths of a second.

Surprisingly, Honda's lightweight ace, Luigi Taveri, rode for Kreidler in the 50 cc race and came seventh. Another Kreidler ridden by Hans Anscheidt finished fourth and the overall conclusion at the end of the event, which was a three-cornered fight between Suzuki, Honda and Kreidler, was that Suzuki still had the edge over the other two manufacturers.

The Senior TT did nothing more than confirm that Mike Hailwood and his MV had absolutely no opposition in the 500 cc class. He gave his accepted faultless display of high-speed riding skill to the spectators around the 37¾-mile course, and literally toured to victory. There was little point in pushing the MV to its limit and, with a race average speed of 100.95 mph, Mike Hailwood finished 2 minutes, 22.8 seconds ahead of his short-circuit rival, Derek Minter. In turn, Minter won a comfortable second place by 2 minutes, 58 seconds from Fred Stephens on a G50 Matchless.

With the failure of the Suzukis to make any impression on the Honda domination of the Lightweight TTs in 1964, it was back to Japan for a hectic winter of research and development. Yamaha, too, were determined to break the Honda domination of the Grand Prix road-racing scene and, with Count Agusta finally accepting the Honda threat to the larger capacity classes, MV returned with full works' support for road racing.

No longer would Hailwood have to fight a lone battle against Honda. A young Italian champion by the name of Giacomo Agostini, who had been riding very successfully for Morini, had caught the Count's attention and with aspirations of an Italian World Champion on an Italian motorcycle, Count Agusta signed up the talented Agostini to ride for MV team alongside Mike Hailwood.

On the Island, it was the maestro teaching the pupil and Agostini learned quickly. He had to if he hoped to compete with experienced TT campaigners of the calibre of Redman, Read and Duff, because not only were Honda contesting the Junior TT but Yamaha also had their sights set on the race using over-bored versions of their extremely rapid 250 cc machines.

The pattern of TT week for 1965 remained unaltered from previous years, with three-lap races for the 50 cc, 125 cc and Sidecar events and six laps for the Lightweight 250, Junior and Senior races.

Max Deubel scored his second Sidecar TT victory in a row for BMW breaking his own existing lap record from 1962 with a speed of 91.80 mph. Second was his great rival in the World Championship stakes, Fritz Scheidegger (BMW),

and third, Georg Auerbacher (BMW). Deubel won the race by a mere 14 seconds and established the first over-90 mph race record for the Sidecar TT. His time for the three laps was 1 hour, 14 minutes and 59.8 seconds, to give an average of 90.57 mph.

The Lightweight 250 and Junior TT double had become something of a Jim Redman speciality; he had pulled off this result two years in succession and hoped to repeat the performance for Honda again in 1965. His practice times showed that he had every opportunity of completing the hat-trick, but the opposition from Yamaha and Suzuki in the Lightweight race was considerably stronger than in previous years. But Redman, the experienced professional that he was, promptly dispelled any doubts spectators or officials might have had by setting a scorching pace to clock the first-ever 100-mph lap on a 250 cc machine. Phil Read and Mike Duff on their rotary-valve Yamahas did their utmost to stay with the bright red Honda, but Read's machine failed in the attempt.

The square-four Suzuki two-strokes were no match for either the Yamahas or Hondas and the race was convincingly won by Redman, when he crossed the line 3 minutes, 41 seconds ahead of Mike Duff on the Yamaha. Frank Perris proved the best of the Suzuki riders by finishing third, 1 minute, 6 seconds behind Duff.

The fact that Yamaha had done their homework during the winter months was proved in the Lightweight 125 race on the Wednesday of TT week. On a scaled-down version of their 250 machine, Phil Read pinned the opposition to the ground, and in a fantastic ding-dong battle with Honda's Luigi Taveri and Suzuki's Hugh Anderson, Read raised the race record to 94.28 mph.

Anderson on his Suzuki lifted the lap record to 96.02 mph in his three-cornered struggle with the Honda and Yamaha riders, but the Suzuki could not stand the pressure and, after mechanical problems, Anderson limped home to finish fifth.

Read beat Taveri by a mere 5.8 seconds and Mike Duff took third place for Yamaha, 15.2 seconds down on the Swiss rider.

With the return of MV Agusta to full **Grand Prix** support and with two riders, Hailwood and Agostini, entered on new machines for the Junior TT, it appeared that Jim Redman's chances of winning yet another Junior were fairly slim. In the race, Hailwood demonstrated that MV had been working overtime on their new 350s by setting a lap record of 102.85 mph, but Hailwood still failed to reach the finishing line. Once again it was Redman who managed to keep his Honda all in one piece over six laps of the tortuous Mountain Circuit to win the Junior.

There was no doubt that the MV had the pace to match Redman's Honda, but the wily Rhodesian merely put sufficient pressure on Hailwood to make him work the bike to breaking point. And eventually it happened, allowing Redman to score his hat-trick with a winning average speed of 100.72 mph.

What of the newcomer Giacomo Agostini? In his first race on the Isle of Man, he averaged 98.52 mph to finish in third place behind Phil Read's Yamaha. It was a superb effort and an obvious forecast of a bright future for the young Italian rider.

Interest in the 50 cc TT dropped to an all-time low in 1965, when Kreidler dropped out of the event leaving only Honda and Suzuki to compete for race honours. Due to the vast difference in performance between the works' machines and the privateers, only 8 riders out of the 23 starters in the race won silver replicas. In other words, if you weren't on a works' Suzuki or Honda, you might just as well not have bothered to enter the race.

The event aroused very little enthusiasm among the spectators and most watched because there was little opportunity of reaching their vantage point for the Senior race after the roads had closed. The future of the 50 cc race looked very doubtful and, had it not been for the fact that it was still classified as a World Championship event, and the Japanese were keen on impressing the world with their 50 cc lightweights, the race would have been removed from the TT calendar.

Nevertheless, in spite of being a boring procession to watch, one could not help admiring the riders who piloted the spindly little tiddlers at such incredible speeds around the TT course. Luigi Taveri, without the chance of a Kreidler, had returned to ride the Honda 50 cc machine and, although weather conditions were far from satisfactory on the Friday of TT week, he still managed to set a fastest lap of 80.83 mph on his tiny machine, to regain Honda's prestige in the 50 cc event. The two Suzukis of Hugh Anderson and Ernst Degner finished second and third respectively behind Taveri.

Interest in the Senior had been aroused because there was an element of competition between the handsome, young Italian, Giacomo Agostini, and the established 'fire-engine' ace, Mike Hailwood. Nobody really doubted Hailwood's ability to win mainly because of the young Italian's inexperience

over the TT course, but it was interesting to see how the pupil would fare against the master.

The weather had deteriorated considerably by Friday afternoon, but, with the all-clear given by the stewards, racing started. Hailwood and the MV immediately took the lead, followed by his Italian team mate. Because of the weather, lap speeds were well down on previous years. In fact, the fastest lap recorded by Hailwood was 95.11 mph, slower than that set by Hugh Anderson on the 125 Suzuki in the Lightweight race earlier in the week.

Then came news that Agostini had fallen at Sarah's Cottage, rider okay but unable to proceed. It looked as though Hailwood would simply ride cautiously home to finish. But then came even more drama; Hailwood had also come off at Sarah's Cottage and literally landed at the feet of his Italian team mate.

However, Hailwood being Hailwood, he literally kicked his bike straight, turned it round in the road to take advantage of the downhill run, bump started the machine and proceeded on his way. When the MV came past the pits looking very much the worse for wear, with broken screen and flattened exhaust megaphones, everybody wondered whether Mike could maintain his lead over Joe Dunphy's Norton and the Matchless of third placeman, Mike Duff.

The records now show that he did with the slowest race speed since 1959 when Surtees also had the fickle Isle of Man weather to contend with. Hailwood's race speed was a lowly 91.69 mph, but it was sufficient to give him his fourth Senior TT victory and to lead Joe Dunphy over the line by 2 minutes, 19.8 seconds. Canadian Mike Duff finished third. It was a race that will be long remembered by spectators on the Island that year mainly because of the sheer courage and determination of Mike Hailwood, the kind of courage that places the Isle of Man champions head and shoulders above other riders in their will to overcome all obstacles and win.

Hailwood's need to win races was one of the many reasons for his decision to leave MV Agusta at the end of the 1965 season and rejoin Honda. Having established themselves as the greatest manufacturer of lightweight racing and roadster motorcycles in the world, Honda looked towards the 500 cc World Championship as their ultimate goal and the man to win it for them had to be the best, and the best at that time was without a doubt Stanley Michael Bailey Hailwood.

Honda's offer was too good to refuse. Not only would they build a 500-four to win the World

**Above** *There was a dramatic finish to the 1952 Senior when the winner, Reg Armstrong (Norton), just managed to coast over the line with a broken chain. If you look closely, you can just see it trailing below his left foot.*

**Right** *Les Graham was highly respected by TT competitors, officials and enthusiasts alike. After winning the 1953 Lightweight race, he was tragically killed in the Senior TT of the same year. A memorial was erected in his honour above Stone Bridge on the Mountain section, just before the Bungalow.*

**Right** *The Sidecar TT returned to the Isle of Man in 1954, after a break of almost 30 years. Racing was over the Clypse course and here competitors can be seen rounding Creg-ny-Baa in the reverse direction to the Mountain Circuit!*

C

**Above left** *While Norton struggled for supremacy against MV and Gilera in the Senior TTs of the early 1950s, AJS attempted to take the Junior title from the Bracebridge Street team. In 1954 they succeeded, when Rod Coleman rode the 'three-port' 350 AJS to victory at a record average speed of 91.51 mph.* **Above right** *Bob McIntyre the magnificent! The first man ever to lap the Isle of Man Mountain Circuit at over 100 mph.* **Below** *Golden Jubilee year meant a double victory for Bob McIntyre and Gilera in the Junior and Senior TTs: eight laps in the Senior at an average speed of 98.99 mph and seven laps in the Junior at 94.99 mph, plus the incredible, magic 'over-the-ton' record of 101.12 mph. Here is the 'flying Scotsman' in action at Ballaugh Bridge.*

**Above left** *John Surtees, MBE, began riding for MV Agusta in 1956 and scored his first Senior TT victory that year. He continued to ride for MV on the Island until 1960, during which period he scored six outright victories in the Junior and Senior TTs. He was enticed from motorcycle sport to the Grand Prix car racing scene and has the rare distinction of becoming World Champion in both these sports.* **Above right** *Surtees in action on a Norton. His fantastic success on Britain's short circuits, where he was virtually unbeatable, brought him the works' MV Agusta contract. Here he demonstrates his superb riding style on the approach to Kate's Cottage in the 1955 Junior TT.* **Below** *Surtees, riding the mighty MV 500-four, on his way to the first of many TT victories in the 1956 Senior.*

**Left** *Derek Minter was the first man to lap the Isle of Man at over 100 mph on a single-cylinder machine, a Steve Lancefield-tuned Manx Norton 500. 'King of Brands Hatch' and probably one of the most under-rated road racers, Minter showed his true determination and capability when he won the 1962 Lightweight 250 TT on a privately entered Honda-four against the opposition of the full Honda works' team.*

**Below** *The dice which brought Derek Minter that ton-plus lap. Here he is chased hard by Mike Hailwood at Signpost Corner during the 1960 Senior race. Minter retired and Hailwood went on to finish in third place.*

**Right** *The Japanese teams arrived in force on the Isle of Man in 1961 and Honda made a clean sweep in both Lightweight races. Bulbous fairings typified the Yamaha entry in the Lightweight 125 race and here Fumio Ito (Yamaha), who finished 11th in the race, rounds Cronk-ny-Mona.*

**Below** *Twin cylinders, double-overhead-camshaft, revving to 22,000 rpm and only 50 cc! Honda produced the ultimate in motor-cycles with egg-cup size engines and still hold the Ultra-Light-weight 50 cc lap record for the Mountain Circuit of 86.49 mph! Here Luigi Taveri, winner of the 50 cc race in 1965, accelerates away from Governor's Bridge. Note the calliper front brake which operates on the wheel rim!*

**Left** Mike 'the bike' Hailwood, MBE, GM, could be placed as number one among the all-time great TT riders. With 12 TT victories to his credit on Norton, Honda and MV machines, he still holds both Senior and Junior lap records, dating back to his last appearance on the Island in 1967, when riding for Honda. He is also the only rider to have won three solo TT races in one week; this was in 1961 when he claimed the Lightweight 125 and 250 events as well as the Senior race.

**Below** Little bike but giant of a rider! Tucked cleanly away to accelerate out of Braddan Bridge, Mike Hailwood, riding the Honda 125, on his way to victory in the 1961 Lightweight 125 TT.

Championship from MV, but Mike would have bikes to contest both the 350 and 250 World Championships, plus a pile of money if he signed on the dotted line.

Mike Hailwood and Jim Redman were to contest the Grands Prix with the established Honda teamsters, Luigi Taveri and Ralph Bryans. A newcomer to the Honda team was Stuart Graham, son of the late, great Les Graham.

Yamaha also took on another rider to strengthen their team of Mike Duff and Phil Read on their new four-cylinder two-strokes. His name? A fiery youngster from Maidstone in Kent, Bill Ivy.

And so the pattern was set for some of the most exciting racing ever to be seen on the Island. Honda, Suzuki, Yamaha and MV, all works' teams hotly contesting the World Championships and spending a fortune on developing the fastest motorcycles ever seen on the world's road-racing circuits.

To combat the Suzuki 50 cc water-cooled two-stroke, Honda developed the incredible twin-cylinder, double-overhead camshaft four-stroke which revved to 22,000 rpm and incorporated a 12-speed gearbox to cope with the extremely narrow power band.

In order to match the V-four Yamaha and Suzuki 125 cc square-four two-strokes, Honda produced the remarkable five-cylinder 125 cc four-stroke. And to compete with the fantastically fast V-four Yamaha 250 two-stroke, Honda quickly designed a brand-new six-cylinder 250 machine, which was over-bored to 296 cc to contest the 350 World Championship.

Meanwhile, only in the sidecar events were there less dramatic changes and these were not so much in engine design (the BMW twin still reigned supreme) but in the profile of the actual outfits. The racing kneeler outfit had long since ousted from popularity the normal motorcycle with sidecar attached and, with the purpose of achieving better adhesion for cornering the low-slung outfits, riders were beginning to consider fitting car racing tyres on small, wide wheels. It was more through the improvements in chassis design and construction that the Sidecar TT lap records were broken each year than because of any exciting improvement in the BMW power units.

The sidecar event which opened TT week in 1966 was an absolutely fantastic race. Admittedly the machines were the same, well almost, but the pilots were different and when you had two riders of the calibre of Fritz Scheidegger and Max Deubel on the TT course, then the sparks were bound to fly. Both of their BMW outfits performed perfectly and after a race-long, neck-and-neck duel, when both broke the existing race record, Fritz Scheidegger just managed to beat his great rival, Max Deubel, by eight-tenths of a second. Fritz averaged 90.76 mph for the $113\frac{1}{4}$-mile race and Max, 90.75 mph, to provide one of the closest finishes in a Sidecar TT. Georg Auerbacher came third for the third year in succession.

All the promise shown by the Yamaha 250s in 1965 completely misled the pundits the following year. One by one the works' team of Duff, Read and Ivy dropped out of the running in the Lightweight 250 race which was completely dominated by the flying six-cylinder Hondas of Hailwood and Stuart Graham. All opposition wilted away as Mike turned on the pressure and set a new lap record of 104.29 mph.

Hailwood had taken over where Jim Redman left off and for Honda he claimed their sixth Lightweight 250 TT victory in succession. Such was the performance of the new Honda that Hailwood not only set a brilliant new lap record for a 250 cc machine, but also achieved a race record of 101.79 mph, which was faster than Redman's existing lap record! All Stuart Graham could do was follow in the wake of the champion to finish second, some 5 minutes, 54 seconds later. And the gap between Graham and the third placeman, Peter Inchley on a Villiers 250 single-cylinder two-stroke, was even more pronounced at 9 minutes, 14.4 seconds.

Honda were still top of the tree in the Lightweight 250 class, but it was a different story in the 125 race. There the high-revving, ear-shattering two-strokes ruled the roost. The four-cylinder Yamahas and Suzukis were more than a match for the Honda team and, with lightweight Bill Ivy at the controls, Yamaha scored their second win in the 125 TT race.

Little Bill's race average of 97.66 mph was faster than that of Stuart Graham's Honda in the 250 race earlier in the week and, to the knowledgeable TT enthusiasts, it seemed absolutely incredible that the 125s were getting so close to the 100-mph lap. Bill Ivy had taken the screaming Yamaha two-stroke around the course at 98.55 mph and beat teamster Phil Read by 28.4 seconds. The battle for second place was in the balance right up to the end of the event, but was decided when Hugh Anderson brought his Suzuki home six seconds behind Read. Mike Duff finished fourth on the other works' Yamaha; Perris came fifth on another Suzuki; then Hailwood, Bryans and Taveri on their Hondas filled the next three places.

In the Junior TT, a titanic battle was expected

between Agostini on his new MV and Hailwood on the Honda, but everybody was disappointed to see the Honda drop out of the race before Hailwood had the chance to get to grips with the young Italian. So, on his second visit to the Isle of Man, Giacomo Agostini won his first TT without any opposition, but he did it so convincingly by breaking Hailwood's existing lap record of 102.85 mph, that very few spectators could wait to see the duel between Hailwood and Agostini in the big race, the Senior, at the end of the week. Second and third places in the Junior had been taken by Peter Williams on his 7R AJS and Chris Conn on a Norton. Agostini averaged 100.87 mph for the six laps and led Peter Williams over the finishing line by 10 minutes, 6.2 seconds.

Seventeen machines started in the three-lap Ultra-lightweight 50 cc race in 1966, the lowest number since the race had been introduced four years earlier. There were 11 Hondas and six Suzukis, which included the half-dozen pukka works' racing machines.

In one way the race was literally dying on its feet, but in another it demonstrated to the world the outstanding progress that had been made in the field of motorcycle engineering. The reason was obvious because, if anybody had said ten years earlier that a 50 cc motorcycle would lap the Isle of Man Mountain Circuit at 86.49 mph, he would have been considered more than a little eccentric, possibly verging on insane. But that remarkable lap speed is precisely the record set by Ralph Bryans on the twin-cylinder Honda 50, when he won the race at an average speed of 85.66 mph!

The record still stands to this day and it is unlikely that it will ever be surpassed, because a 50 cc TT is now no longer held on the Island.

Honda took first and second places in the race with Luigi Taveri finishing second at an average speed of 84.74 mph, while Hugh Anderson on the Suzuki was third at 83.14 mph. It was a race to be remembered not for its boredom for the spectators, but for the absolute sheer mechanical genius of the designers of the remarkable race-winning motorcycles.

The Honda 50 was clocked at a speed in the region of 110 mph and the brakes used to stop the bike were little more than giant calliper appliances, similar to those on a push-bike, which operated directly on to the wheel rim. The aim was to achieve minimum weight for maximum performance and in this the designers succeeded to very good effect.

The classic race of 1966 TT week had to be the Senior. Hailwood versus Agostini, Honda versus MV. Agostini had won the Junior event earlier in the week and by Friday it was accepted that he had learned a great deal about the circuit from his ex-team mate Mike Hailwood. There was also some considerable doubt about the handling qualities of the very powerful Honda 500-four.

Hailwood had constantly criticised Hondas for their bad handling and even went so far as to have a special frame built by Renolds Tube Company to house the Honda 500 power unit. But, the bike he used in the Senior was the unadulterated factory frame version and, as he hurtled away from the start line to do battle with the MV of Agostini, which handled superbly, officials and spectators alike prayed that Hailwood would master the wild, snaking machine. It was said at the time that if anybody could control such a machine, Hailwood was probably the only rider capable of doing so.

To this day, spectators at the 1966 Senior TT talk of Hailwood's epic ride. He slid, snaked and weaved around the TT circuit as though the Honda had broken its frame, but his riding skill was such that he was able to fight the Honda to a new lap record of 107.07 mph. Hailwood won his battle with the machine and rode to a clear-cut victory over Agostini and the MV by crossing the finishing line 2 minutes, 37.8 seconds ahead of the Italian. A corporal in the Royal Air Force, Chris Conn repeated his success in the Junior race, by finishing third behind the two works' machines.

The Diamond Jubilee of the TT races was celebrated in 1967 and, for the first time for some years, road-going production motorcycles were wheeled out to line up for a Le Mans-type start on the Glencrutchery Road. The Tourist Trophy races had literally turned full circle, because, having originated for the purpose of racing touring machines some 60 years earlier, there on the start line were 60 sports touring motorcycles, any one of which was perfectly and properly equipped for use on public roads.

The Production Machine Race took place on the Saturday preceding TT week and was run with three classes for 750 cc, 500 cc and 250 cc machines, being started at three-minute intervals, with the larger machines first away on the massed start three-lap event.

One of the interesting points about the race was that, for the first time since Norton and AJS had withdrawn from road racing, a British manufacturer, Triumph, officially supported a race on the Isle of Man. In the 750 cc class, Triumph had entered a Bonneville 650 ridden by the ex-MV and Gilera teamster, John Hartle and, with his superb knowledge of the TT circuit, their choice proved very wise.

On the first lap he led Steve Spencer, riding another Bonneville, by 44.8 seconds, with Paul Smart on a Dunstall Norton Dominator lying third. When Spencer dropped out on the second lap, Paul Smart took up the chase after Hartle, but there was no catching the works-prepared Bonnie. Hartle steamed home to win the 750 class by 1 minute, 51.2 seconds from Paul Smart, with Tony Smith on a BSA Spitfire finishing third. Hartle's average speed for the three laps was 97.10 mph and he set a record lap of 97.87 mph.

In the 500 cc class, Manxman Neil Kelly riding a Velocette Thruxton led from start to finish to win by 37.8 seconds from Keith Heckles on another Velocette, while David Nixon on a Triumph Tiger 100 finished third. Kelly's winning average speed was 89.89 mph and he also set the record lap of 91.01 mph.

Perhaps the most surprising race of all was the 250 cc class, where the speed of the two leading bikes ridden by Bill Smith and Tommy Robb was greater than all but the first two riders in the 500 cc class. On two Bultaco Metralla machines, Smith and Robb had a most fantastic dice throughout the entire three laps, with first Smith leading Robb over the line at the end of lap one and then Robb taking the lead by a fraction of a second on the second lap. The final outcome was a four-tenths-of-a-second win for Bill Smith, who averaged 88.63 mph and also set the record lap of 89.41 mph. The Suzuki 250 of Barry Smith finished in third place over two minutes behind the two Bultacos. At the time, there was some controversy about the winning bike, because it was claimed that it was virtually an out-and-out racing machine equipped with expansion box silencer and roadster electrics to enable it to qualify as a production machine. This, in fact, could explain the phenomenal performance of the winning 250 when compared with the bikes in the 500 cc production class. However, because the regulations for machines in the production race were loosely phrased, the Bultacos were accepted as the winners in the 250 class.

The first of the International TT races on Monday June 12 was the 500 cc Sidecar event and, as usual, it was a BMW benefit. Initially, on the first lap, it was a three-cornered fight between Klaus Enders, Georg Auerbacher and Seigfried Schauzu, with Enders holding a marginal 1.6-second lead over Auerbacher and Schauzu filling third place on the leader board only 6.4 seconds behind the leader. On the second lap, it was

Auerbacher who took over with a lead of almost 16 seconds and, in his attempt to pull away from Enders and Schauzu, established the fastest lap at a speed of 91.70 mph. Schauzu had also caught and passed Enders on the second lap and held a mere six-tenths of a second advantage over his fellow countryman.

But then on the last lap came drama as Auerbacher, looking all set to win the race, dropped out of the running with mechanical trouble. He had pushed his BMW too hard and, with victory almost in his grasp, Auerbacher saw Enders and Schauzu go hurtling past in their neck-and-neck battle on the roads. Schauzu had picked up Enders' 20-second starting advantage and all he had to do was keep his opponent in sight and he knew he was the winner.

Enders crossed the finishing line first, just 1.6 seconds ahead of Schauzu, but on corrected time Schauzu was the winner at an average speed of 90.96 mph. Colin Seeley riding another BMW finished third, with the best British machine being the Kirby-BSA ridden by Terry Vinicombe, who came sixth.

The first six-lap TT of the week was the Lightweight 250 race in which the Honda six-cylinder 250s of Mike Hailwood and Ralph Bryans had the four-cylinder Yamahas of Bill Ivy, Phil Read and Motohashi as the major opposition. The works' MZs of Heinz Rosner and Derek Woodman had also proved reasonably fast in practice, but were not considered a serious threat to the fantastically fast Honda and Yamaha works' bikes.

Bryans and Woodman were the first two away at the start of the race, followed by Motohashi, then Rosner and Gilberto Milani on his Aermacchi. Hailwood started alongside Alberto Pagani on another Aermacchi works' bike, some 30 seconds after Bryans.

However, the pace set by Hailwood on the Honda was such that, by the end of the first lap, he had caught up and passed every rider who started ahead of him and, as he flew past the pits, he not only led the race on the road but also on corrected time with a 1.8-second lead over Phil Read's Yamaha. Bill Ivy lay third a mere eight-tenths of a second behind Read.

But there was no stopping Hailwood, the TT ace. Having received signals to tell him of his precarious lead over the Yamaha riders, Mike wound the Honda as hard as it would go and on his second lap set the lap record at 104.50 mph. Nobody, not even the experienced Phil Read, could match Mike's performance as the gap widened to just over 12 seconds at the end of lap two. And when Mike equalled the newly established record on lap three, everybody knew that if the Honda kept going Mike had the race in the bag. Even after stopping at the end of lap three to refuel, as did Phil Read, Mike continued to increase his lead over the Yamaha works' riders.

By the end of lap four, both MZ riders were out of the race with machine failure and little Bill Ivy, who had put up such a gallant fight on his Yamaha, toured in to retire at the pits with engine trouble. This allowed Ralph Bryans on the other Honda works' bike up into third spot and that is how the race ended, with Phil Read on the Yamaha sandwiched between the incomparable Mike Hailwood and team mate Ralph Bryans on their very special Honda six-cylinder machines.

Mike's average speed for the six-lap race was 103.07 mph and he beat Read by 1 minute, 18.8 seconds.

Had Honda entered Hailwood in the Lightweight 125 race, which took place on the Wednesday morning of TT week, he might well have become the first rider ever to have won four solo TTs in one year. Unfortunately, Honda had dropped out of both the 50 cc and 125 cc events, leaving the battle to be fought between the works' Yamaha and Suzuki teams in the 125 class and a walkover victory for Suzuki in the 50 cc race.

In the 125 TT, it was Read, Ivy and Motohashi for Yamaha against Stuart Graham and Katayama on works' Suzukis. The other Suzuki rider, Itoh, had had a spill in practice and was a non-starter.

Without Hailwood as his mentor, Read soon established a lead on his Yamaha, but was pushed extremely hard by Stuart Graham on the Suzuki. Bill Ivy unfortunately was nowhere in the hunt because of machine trouble and only managed to complete one lap of the Mountain Circuit before dropping out of the race.

Meanwhile, by the end of the second lap, Stuart Graham had ousted Read from number-one place on the leader board, when he picked up 1.6 seconds on Read's lap time to gain a two-tenths of a second advantage over the Yamaha rider. But Read accepted the challenge and, with a superb last lap of 23 minutes 0.8 seconds, Read stole a 3.4-second victory from Stuart Graham. Motohashi on the other Yamaha finished third, Dave Simmonds on a Kawasaki fourth, while the unfortunate Katayama failed to complete even one lap on the other works' Suzuki. Read's fastest lap for the race was 98.36 mph.

Hailwood, who had destroyed all opposition and

completely dominated the Lightweight 250 TT, did the same in the Junior race. His opposition was, of course, Agostini and the MV, and with Yamaha's team being registered as non-starters for the race, it was a straight duel between the two TT aces.

Hailwood began the race alongside Derek Woodman on the MZ works' bike and Agostini started 10 seconds later. By the time Hailwood had reached Union Mills on the first lap, he led on the roads as well as on time. With the course ahead of him absolutely clear and no other riders there to hinder his progress, Hailwood set about showing the spectators and the rest of the competitors just who was master of the TT course.

On absolutely shattering form, Mike hurled the Honda around the 37¾-mile course in 21 minutes, 0.8 seconds to clock 107.73 mph from a standing start! In just one lap, he picked up a lead of 48.6 seconds over Agostini and set a new lap record in the Junior TT, which was faster than he had set in the Senior TT the previous year. Behind the record-breaking Hailwood and MV rider, Agostini, could be heard the yowl of another four-cylinder machine, the Benelli of Renzo Pasolini. His lap of 22 minutes, 58.2 seconds placed him in a secure third spot on the leader board, but it was a position he was only to hold for three laps, when the Benelli retired with mechanical trouble.

Meanwhile, Hailwood continued to increase his lead over the MV and, with pit signals telling him to slow the pace, Mike cruised home an easy winner some 3 minutes, 3.2 seconds ahead of Agostini. With a race time of 2 hours, 9 minutes, and 45.6 seconds, Mike averaged 104.68 mph for the six laps! MZ finished third with Derek Woodman bringing the East German two-stroke home ahead of Pagani on the works' Aermacchi. It was an incredible race which made everybody even more keen to witness the return match in the Senior TT two days later.

With only 28 entries in the 50 cc TT, it seemed somewhat pointless to run the event, but run it was and the only works' team competing in the race finished first and second. The Suzukis of Stuart Graham, Georg Anscheidt and Katayama simply walked away from the rest of the field by about five minutes per lap. However, Katayama's machine only completed one lap before expiring out on the course, allowing Tommy Robb up into third place on his Suzuki production racer.

Stuart Graham steamed round on his third lap in 26 minutes, 34.4 seconds to set the fastest lap and beat Anscheidt by 1 minute, 1.2 seconds, to average 82.89 mph. Tommy Robb finished over 15 minutes later to claim third place and give Suzuki their 1–2–3 victory.

The race that has been talked about ever since it was run was the Senior TT of Diamond Jubilee year, when Hailwood, for the second time in his racing career, won three TTs in a week. Mike started the race some 30 seconds ahead of Agostini and, as in the Junior, within a few miles Mike was out in the lead on the roads being chased hard by Agostini. With nobody to pace him, Mike was in a difficult situation because the huge, powerful Honda 500-four was handling like a camel and he was not very happy with having to set the pace on a bike that was likely to cast him up the road at anything up to 160 mph.

The result was that Agostini picked up 11.8 seconds on Mike on the first lap to take the lead away from the Honda rider. The moment Hailwood realised what had happened, the fight was on. Like a man possessed, Hailwood threw himself into the task of recapturing those vital seconds. Spectators around the course could only gasp in amazement at the incredible antics of the leaping, bucking Honda and the even more amazing performance of Hailwood, who wrestled the bike back under control every time it tried to throw him off. In a demonstration of riding skill, the like of which has yet to be equalled, Hailwood completed his second lap in 20 minutes, 48.8 seconds, to set the fantastic lap record of 108.77 mph!

But still he could not regain the lead from Agostini, because the fiery Italian, too, had lapped at over 108 mph and held an 8.6 second advantage at the end of lap two. But Hailwood continued to pile on the pressure to regain a further 6.6 seconds on the third lap. This meant that, as the two machines pulled into refuel at the end of lap three, Agostini still held a two-second advantage over Hailwood.

The atmosphere in the grandstand and pits on the Glencrutchery Road was electric as first Hailwood and then Agostini hurtled in to fill their racing mounts with petrol. The seconds ticked by as nervous-fingered pit attendants slammed the filler caps shut and first Hailwood and then Agostini heaved their machines into life.

Still there was only a couple of seconds dividing them on corrected time and the battle for supremacy over the Mountain Circuit continued. Agostini increased his advantage over Hailwood by another 9.6 seconds on the fourth lap and, as Mike flashed past the pits, he knew he had to make up 11.6 seconds in two laps if he hoped to climb on to the winner's rostrum at the end of the race.

Nobody envied Hailwood's task on the ill-mannered brute of a Honda. The MV was much easier to handle and it looked as though Agostini would win the race. But then it happened; on the fifth lap the Italian was reported as touring. The MV had broken under the pressure and a very dejected Agostini coasted in to the pits, leaving Hailwood to cruise home at a much more sedate and safe pace on the final lap, to average 105.62 mph.

Second place went to Peter Williams on the Arter-Matchless G50, who finished 7 minutes, 43.8 seconds behind Hailwood, while Steve Spencer claimed third place on the Lancefield Norton.

It was a truly tremendous race, packed with tension and drama, in which records were set that still stand to this very day. Nobody as yet has beaten the 108.77 mph set by Hailwood on the second lap of the 1967 Senior TT.

Honda, of course, withdrew from Grand Prix racing at the end of the 1967 season, leaving Mike Hailwood without any race machinery for the World Championship events. In fact, Honda paid Mike *not* to race for any other manufacturer in the Grands Prix of 1968 and, consequently, 1967 was the last year Isle of Man spectators were to be thrilled by the sight of Mike 'the bike' Hailwood fighting the big Honda 500-four around the Mountain Circuit. Mike's decision to retire from motorcycle racing to take up car racing was a sad day for the sport, and he was awarded the MBE for his outstanding contribution to road racing. A fitting tribute to probably the greatest-ever Isle of Man TT competitor!

# CHAPTER SEVEN

# The shape of things to come

WITH HONDA AND SUZUKI withdrawing from Grand Prix racing at the end of 1967, because of the impending FIM ban on multi-cylinder machines in the Lightweight classes, it meant that two manufacturers, MV and Yamaha, had things very much their own way. Yamaha completely dominated the Lightweight events and MV, the 350 and 500 classes. Benelli made a spirited attempt with Pasolini in the Lightweight 250 and Junior 350 Grands Prix to tackle the established champions. But on the Isle of Man in 1968 it was not so much the rivalry between manufacturers that aroused spectators' interest as the bitter struggle between the two Yamaha team riders, Read and Ivy.

Yamaha had decreed that Ivy should win the 250 cc World Championship and that Read would have the honour of becoming 125 World Champion. Such was the domination by Yamaha of road racing at that time. However, realising that it would probably be Yamaha's last Grand Prix season, Read presumably decided to go for both 125 and 250 World Championships and promptly set about beating Ivy. Bill soon became aware of Read's intentions and so developed a tense battle between the two Yamaha riders, which began initially on the Isle of Man.

Race week opened with the addition of the 750 cc sidecar race to the programme, making eight events in all; the largest number of races so far in the history of the TT.

On Saturday, June 8, there were two, three-lap sidecar events, one for 500 cc machines counting towards the World Championship and the other for the 750 cc class. The 750 entry list comprised mainly all-British-built outfits, the vast majority of which used roadster-derived power units.

In the World Championship 500 cc Sidecar TT, it was exactly the same old story, with BMWs ridden by Schauzu, Enders, Attenberger, and Luthringshauser dominating the race. Only the lone four-cylinder URS, designed by Helmut Fath, could compete successfully against the Munich twins. In the race, it was Klaus Enders who started number one, and for the first two laps he demonstrated precisely how a racing outfit should be driven around the TT circuit. He established a new lap record of 94.32 mph in his efforts to lose the opposition and at the end of lap two he was 1 minute, 22 seconds ahead of his nearest rival, Seigfried Schauzu. Third was Attenberger on another BMW, followed by Luthringshauser (BMW) and Fath on his home-brewed URS outfit.

But, as in the previous year, Enders was not to maintain his lead, because on the last lap the BMW outfit struck mechanical trouble and Enders could only limp home to the finishing line and claim eighth place. Schauzu took over the lead and finished the race as winner at an average speed of 91.09 mph. Attenberger was second, Luthringshauser third and Fath, on his URS, fourth.

The A-CU had unwisely run the second of the Sidecar TTs on the same day, allowing no time for the 500 cc class riders to change engines for the larger capacity event or vice versa. Thus there were no World Championship contenders in the race and it was a BSA-versus-Triumph confrontation, just as normally happened at the short circuit events of the period.

Chris Vincent was reigning British Sidecar Champion and to confirm his ability he stormed into the lead on the first lap, setting a record lap of 89.11 mph from a standing start! But the push-rod BSA twin could not stand the pace and Vincent went out of the running during the course of his second lap. The man who took over the lead was Terry Vinicombe on the Kirby-BSA and he was followed by Norman Hanks, passengered by Mrs Rose Arnold, on another BSA outfit.

In fact, at the finish, BSA outfits took the first three places with Vinicombe, Hanks and Peter

Brown piloting the British-built push-rod operated twins. Terry Vinicombe averaged 85.85 mph to finish 2 minutes, 36.6 seconds ahead of Norman Hanks.

The first race on Monday morning was the 50 cc TT which attracted a ridiculous line-up of only 21 starters for the three-lap event. With no Japanese works' teams on the line, Barry Smith on the works' Derbi had no opposition from the few, over-the-counter production Honda 50 racing machines.

The Derbi finished 7 minutes, 49.2 seconds ahead of the Honda of C. M. Walpole, which was second. Third place went to another Honda, this time ridden by E. L. Griffiths. Barry Smith's winning speed was 72.90 mph, considerably slower than the previous year's race speed and his fastest lap of 73.44 mph was over 12 mph slower than the existing lap record! After such a pitiful entry and such a boring race, it was no wonder that the A-CU finally let the 50 cc TT die that year.

With Suzuki and Honda out of contention for the Lightweight 250 TT, everybody expected the race to be a Yamaha benefit. The practice times had shown that both Read and Ivy were capable of winning and, with a little bit of needle creeping into the two riders' Championship races, most people expected to see a very hard-fought race.

Ivy knew that Read had the advantage on the TT course with the high-speed Yamahas, mainly because Ivy's lack of weight made it difficult for him to keep the leaping machine on the road. Read had more experience, was bigger and heavier and did not encounter such serious handling problems around the bumpy circuit.

Little Bill decided to go all out from the drop of the flag to gain enough of a lead to keep Phil Read at bay for the rest of the race. His plan was simple; just go as hard as he and the machine could and then see what happened. Similar to Hailwood's performance in the Senior TT the previous year, Ivy fought the Yamaha 250 over every inch of the course and from a standing start he lapped at 105.51 mph to break Hailwood's Honda 250 record.

The crowds could not believe their ears or their eyes as the diminutive Ivy screamed past the pits and the commentator announced a lap time of 21 minutes, 27.4 seconds for the Yamaha rider. Phil Read was 14.2 seconds down on his teamster and obviously intent on catching him because, at the end of lap two, he had reduced Ivy's lead to 9.6 seconds.

The question in everybody's mind was, could Bill Ivy maintain his lead or would the pounding he was taking from the machine tire him and give Read

the advantage? The answer came at the end of the third lap when Read came in to refuel with a 14.6 second lead over Ivy. The little champion had shot his bolt, or so it seemed, and all Read had to do was maintain his steady pace as Ivy's lap times became slower and slower.

But as has happened so many times to so many riders on the Island, fate plays cruel tricks and, although Read practically had the race sewn up, on the fourth lap his bike received a puncture in the back wheel, and Read could only coast home to retire leaving Ivy once more in the lead.

With the pressure off, Ivy's lap time slumped to over 24 minutes for the fifth lap, but Pasolini on the Benelli was closing the gap on the leader, so Ivy had to speed up a little on the last lap to win by 2 minutes, 12 seconds from the Italian rider. Heinz Rosner on the East German MZ was third.

Bill Ivy finished the race with his hands bleeding from the struggle he had had to control the four-cylinder Yamaha. Blisters across the palms of both hands had burst and the skin had been torn off in fighting the wild-handling bike. Even so, he still managed to average 99.58 mph for the six-lap race.

The three-lap Production Machine Race had been transferred from its previous Saturday date to the Wednesday of TT week and, with a strong entry of Triumph Bonnevilles for the 750 class, plus continued support from the Triumph factory, it looked as though there was a very good chance of their repeating the 750 class victory.

Unfortunately, mist on the Mountain caused Triumph's number-one runner, John Hartle, to have a spill which allowed Ray Pickrell on the Dunstall Norton Dominator into the lead, a lead he was to have throughout the entire race which he won at an average speed of 98.13 mph. Billy Nelson on a Norton Atlas was runner-up, followed by Tony Smith on a BSA Spitfire.

In the 500 class, journalist Ray Knight on a Triumph Daytona romped home the winner, at 90.09 mph, 1 minute, 17.6 seconds ahead of John Blanchard on a Velocette Thruxton. David Nixon on another Triumph Daytona finished third.

Both Pickrell and Knight set record laps for their respective classes; Pickrell at 99.39 mph and Knight at 91.03 mph.

The 250 Production Machine Race once again raised the question of expansion chamber exhaust systems being used as silencers in conjunction with a racing engine fitted with roadster electrics. Protests were made and heard but dismissed with a note to modify regulations for future events.

Trevor Burgess on a Spanish OSSA 250 won the

class at an average speed of 87.21 mph from George Leigh on a Bultaco, with Barry Smith finishing third on the Thompson-Suzuki. Burgess also set fastest lap with a speed of 87.89 mph.

With the challenge from Benelli in the Junior TT, MV did not intend taking any chances and had signed John Hartle to ride for them as number two to Agostini. But John's crash in the Production Machine Race earlier in the day had crocked him for the Junior and so he was among the list of non-starters.

This meant that Agostini had a straight duel with Pasolini on the Benelli, but the young World Champion had no trouble in establishing a commanding lead right from the first lap of the race.

Although never really pushed or challenged by Pasolini on the Benelli, Agostini still managed to establish a new race record of 104.78 mph, although he failed to beat Hailwood's Honda lap record. The fastest lap which Agostini made was 106.77 mph.

Up until his retirement on lap three, Kel Carruthers had been lying fourth on his Aermacchi behind the flying East German, Heinz Rosner (MZ), but when they dropped out, Bill Smith stepped into third place on his Honda 350-twin production racer. And that's how the race ended with Agostini, Pasolini and Smith, first, second and third. The highest-placed British machine was a Seeley, which was ridden into fifth place by John Cooper.

The three-lap Lightweight 125 TT which took place on the Friday prior to the Senior was a foregone conclusion as far as forecasting the winners was concerned. Yamaha had said that Phil Read should win but, just to prove that he was more adept at riding the 125 than Read, Bill Ivy set the pace for the first two laps. He led Read over the line by four seconds at the end of lap one and, with a flying start to lap two, Ivy hurtled around the course to clock the first ever 100-mph lap on a 125 cc motorcycle! His lead over Read had increased to 16.4 seconds, but then, strictly to factory orders, Ivy rolled off the power to allow Read to pass him and take the 125 TT win. It was even said that Ivy stopped at Creg-ny-Baa to ask who was leading the race on the last lap.

This was to be the last race for Ivy on the Isle of Man, because the courageous little rider retired at the end of the season, completely disillusioned by not winning the 250 World Championship as had been planned for him by the factory. Ivy did take up Formula 2 car racing but, after a couple of costly prangs, he was tempted back into motorcycle racing by the offer of a Jawa works' ride on a new, four-cylinder two-stroke. Unfortunately, while practising for the East German Grand Prix at the Sachsenring, the Jawa seized and little Bill Ivy was killed in the resulting crash. A very sad loss to the sport.

The Senior TT of 1968 saw John Hartle back on MV to support Giacomo Agostini. He had recovered sufficiently from his Wednesday Production Machine crash and everybody was hoping Hartle would be able to challenge his Italian team mate and thereby make a race out of the Senior rather than the expected walk-away win for Agostini. Unfortunately, Hartle crashed on the first lap of the race and left Agostini to take an unchallenged victory by 8 minutes, 29 seconds from Brian Ball on his Seeley, with Barry Randle on the Petty-Norton, third.

Agostini's fastest lap was 104.91 mph and this was from a standing start. With no opposition, he simply cruised home to average 101.63 mph for the race, considerably slower than his winning speed in the Junior race.

Having realised the error of running two sidecar races on the same day, and with the dropping of the 50 cc event, in 1969 the A-CU were able to re-allocate the races so that the 750 cc Sidecar TT was run on the Saturday. The 500 cc Sidecar and Lightweight 250 cc races took place on the following Monday, with the Production Machine Race and the Junior on the Wednesday and, finally, the Lightweight 125 and Senior TTs on the Friday.

This improved planning allowed the 750 Sidecar riders to swop engines in their outfits and race again in the 500 TT on the Monday, making for a much more interesting pair of sidecar events.

Surprisingly, in the 750 cc race, the German BMW machines proved unreliable and two of the favourites to win the race, Georg Auerbacher and Klaus Enders, dropped out with mechanical trouble without even completing the first of the three laps. This, plus the fact that Helmut Fath was a non-starter, meant that the British push-rod twins were in with a reasonable chance.

Chris Vincent was a leading contender for the race but, after chasing hard after Schauzu for two laps, Vincent's BSA ground to a halt. Peter Brown on another BSA took over second place from Vincent, but he stood no chance of catching Schauzu and his BMW outfit. The final result was a win for Schauzu at an average speed of 89.83 mph, with Peter Brown finishing second, 3 minutes, 41.4 seconds behind the BMW rider. Bill Currie on his home-built LWC special finished third.

The second of the Sidecar TTs on Monday morning saw basically the same groups of riders entered for the race as had appeared in Saturday's event. The favourites to win were also the same, but this time Klaus Enders' machine did not fail him and, by the end of the first lap, he not only led the race on the roads but also had a 10.4-second lead over Helmut Fath and his four-cylinder URS. In third place lay Georg Auerbacher (BMW), followed closely by 750 Sidecar race winner, Schauzu.

On the second lap, Auerbacher dropped out with mechanical trouble, while Enders increased his lead to 24.6 seconds over Fath, who in turn led Schauzu by 28 seconds.

The race was won by Enders on his BMW but, unfortunately for Fath, he ran into mechanical trouble which cost him precious seconds in his climb over the Mountain, allowing Schauzu to beat him to second place by 20.6 seconds. Enders averaged 92.48 mph for the race and also set the fastest lap at 92.54 mph.

Without works' teams from Honda, Suzuki or Yamaha, it appeared that the Lightweight 250 cc race would not create a great deal of interest for spectators but, although the race speeds were somewhat slower than when the works' specials were on the Island, a new pattern of racing was established. Only the works' Benellis with Kel Carruthers and Phil Read aboard, the Jawa of Franta Stastny, the MZ of Derek Woodman and the OSSA of Santiago Herrero could be considered one-off specials. All the remainder were production racing Yamaha TD1C or Suzuki TR250 machines, plus the odd Kawasaki, Bultaco or Greeves.

Phil Read had been signed up to ride the Benelli 250-four along with Kel Carruthers and, with Carruthers setting the pace on the first lap, only Rodney Gould on his Yamaha could split the two works' machines. On the second lap, the story was the same, with Gould holding a precarious 5.4-second lead over Read. Neither could make any impression on the leader, the flying Aussie Carruthers, who set the fastest lap of the race at 99.01 mph. But on lap three, Gould struck trouble and lost 18 minutes correcting the fault before continuing on his way well at the bottom of the field.

This left the two Benellis lying first and second, with Frank Perris, who had come back out of retirement to ride the Crooks-Suzuki TR250, lying third ahead of Herrero on the OSSA.

Just as it looked as though Benelli had a fairly safe one-two for the first time in a Lightweight TT, on the last lap Phil Read's machine failed allowing Frank Perris to finish second behind Carruthers, with Santiago Herrero third. Carruthers' average

speed for the race was 95.95 mph, way down on the record set by Hailwood on the Honda.

The three-lap Production Machine Race on Wednesday morning was of growing importance and interest to spectators, particularly as all the machines entered were the same as those which many of the visitors to the TT used as their own personal transport. Triumph were making a tremendous effort around this period to win as many Production Machine events as possible and their chief development engineer, Doug Hele, worked wonders with the road-going Bonneville to gain the first-ever 100-mph lap by a production push-rod engined motorcycle.

The rider who achieved this was Welshman Malcolm Uphill, when he won the 750 cc class at an average speed of 99.99 mph. His fastest lap, which was a new record, was 100.37 mph. Second to Uphill was Paul Smart on a Norton Commando and third was Darryl Pendlebury on another Triumph. Uphill led the three-lap race from start to finish and crossed the line 25.8 seconds ahead of Paul Smart's Norton.

In the 500 cc class, Tony Dunnell buzzed off into the lead on his three-cylinder Kawasaki to set the fastest lap from a standing start at 90.84 mph. But on his second lap, Dunnell crashed and allowed Graham Penny, riding a Honda CB450, into the lead. This Penny held to the end of the race, winning from Ray Knight on his Triumph Daytona and Ron Baylie, also on a Triumph. Penny's winning average speed was 88.18 mph.

With regulations regarding expansion chamber/silencers tightened up to keep out disguised raceware from production machine racing, the two-strokes lost out in the 250 class of the race. Speeds also dropped noticeably, although it did not spoil the actual racing.

Alan Rogers on a Ducati Mach 1 averaged 83.79 mph to win the race from Frank Whiteway on his Suzuki T20. A second Ducati in the hands of Charles Mortimer took third place and he also set the fastest lap at 85.13 mph.

The Junior TT of 1969 was not so much interesting for the way in which Agostini dominated the event from beginning to end, as he did in every Junior and Senior TT until 1972, but more for the fantastic racing which took place behind Agostini. Everybody accepted that, with the total withdrawal of all works' teams capable of competing with MV Agusta, road racing in the larger capacity classes had begun to stagnate. The racing behind Agostini's MV was close and hard fought, but the speeds were down and Agostini simply went along certain in the knowledge that, unless his bike failed, he would win. And with no machinery capable of pushing the MV hard enough to make it fail, Agostini always did win!

This was certainly the case in the Junior TT of 1969, where he crossed the line 10 minutes, 11 seconds ahead of the second placeman, Brian Steenson on an Aermacchi.

Perhaps the gap would not have appeared so enormous if many top runners had not dropped out of the running. But the battle for second place was so closely fought over the six laps that at least five of the top contestants, including Phil Read, Rod Gould, Kel Carruthers, Malcolm Uphill and Bergamonti, failed to complete the race. Had they kept going only the second to seventh place names would have changed because, even with Read chasing Agostini, the Italian and his MV led Phil by 1 minute, 12.8 seconds at the end of the first lap.

When Read's Padgett-Yamaha expired from overwork, Kel Carruthers took up the chase on his single-cylinder Aermacchi, but even he dropped back to 1 minute, 49.4 seconds behind Agostini at the end of lap two. He lost a further 1 minute, 8.6 seconds on the third lap to Agostini, while at the same time pulling away from Bergamonti on another Aermacchi. There was not a single motorcycle in the race that could get within sniffing distance of the big, red MV Agusta; most, if not all, failed in the attempt.

In fact, on the last lap, when it looked as though Kel Carruthers had a safe second place to Agostini, his Aermacchi and that of Bergamonti gave up the ghost, allowing Brian Steenson to pip Jack Findlay at the post for second spot.

Agostini's average speed for the six laps was 101.81 mph and he set a fastest lap of precisely 104 mph from a standing start. Unfortunately, Agostini has been criticised sometimes for taking easy wins at the TT races, particularly when there was no opposition from either riders of the calibre of Hailwood or machines with the performance of the Honda. But when one stops to consider Agostini's individual performance, like this 104 mph standing start lap on a 350 machine without pressure from any other rider, then he must still be considered among the best of the TT exponents. He is also one of only two men who have lapped the Mountain Circuit at over 108 mph; the other was Mike Hailwood.

With the withdrawal of the works' Yamahas and Suzukis from the Lightweight 125 race, it suffered almost as severely as the 50 cc event. From the 100 mph-plus lap of Bill Ivy the previous year, the speeds dropped to a fastest lap of 92.46 mph by Dave Simmonds on his twin-cylinder Kawasaki.

From the start of the race, Dave Simmonds led all the way. At the end of the first lap, John Ringwood on the ex-works MZ held second place followed by Charles Mortimer on his Villa. Tommy Robb lay fourth on his production racing Honda twin with Kel Carruthers fifth on a 125 Aermacchi.

Ringwood's MZ packed up on the second lap, letting Mortimer into second place behind Simmonds and his Kawasaki twin. Third was Kel Carruthers and in fourth place came Gary Dickinson on another Honda production racer. On the last lap, Charles Mortimer also dropped out of the running on his Villa and the finishing order was Simmonds, Carruthers and Dickinson. Only 26 riders completed the course and, with a gap of almost six minutes between the winner and the runner-up, the spectators had to watch quite a boring procession of machines, with long intervals of neither sight nor sound of the competitors.

The Senior TT was almost a repeat of the Junior race as far as the spectators were concerned, with Agostini proving yet again that there was no opposition for the MV Agusta 'fire engine'. He started 1 minute, 20 seconds behind first man away from the start line, Derek Woodman, but, by the end of the first of six laps, Agostini was first on the road and way out in the lead on time. On his second lap, Agostini established the fastest lap of the race with a speed of 106.25 mph, once again without being pressed by any other rider in the race. His ride was a solo demonstration of his own racing ability and the outstanding development of the MV Agusta four-cylinder racing motorcycle.

Behind Agostini, Alan Barnett on the Kirby-Metisse established himself in second place, while Tom Dickie and Derek Woodman fought for third spot on the leader board. The final outcome of the race was that Agostini won at an average speed of 104.75 mph to finish 8 minutes, 32.4 seconds ahead of Alan Barnett, who in turn beat Tom Dickie by 31.6 seconds. The most incredible thing about the race was the high casualty rate amongst the machinery, with only 33 of the 97 starters in the race actually completing the course.

Another reshuffle of race days heralded the competitors in the 1970 TT races, with the Production Machine Race earning its 'International' status by being extended to five laps of the Mountain Circuit.

Triumph had changed their racing policy to support the new three-cylinder 750 cc Trident machine, which was a natural progression from the twin-cylinder Bonneville. For the first time, they also had official opposition from the Norton-Villiers organisation with works' rider and development engineer Peter Williams contesting the Production Machine Race 750 cc class on a Norton Commando.

Malcolm Uphill was the Triumph number-one rider with Tom Dickie, on another Trident, giving support against the Nortons of Peter Williams and Ray Pickrell. Right from the Le Mans start, Malcolm Uphill roared off into the lead, chased hard by Peter Williams on the Commando. At the end of the first lap, Uphill led by 36 seconds from Peter Williams and he increased his lead to 46.8 seconds by the end of the second lap.

Uphill could afford to lift the pressure a little on the third lap and this he did, allowing Williams to pull back 4.8 seconds. But Triumph and Uphill had not reckoned on the determination of the be-spectacled Peter Williams, who promptly axed another 28 seconds from Uphill's lead on the next lap and had the Triumph Trident in his sights.

The last lap and the race over the Mountain were absolutely unnerving for the spectators as they listened to the tense, round-the-circuit commentary. On the drop down to Creg-ny-Baa it was still neck and neck between Uphill and Williams. On the last dash out of Governor's Bridge dip to the finishing line, Uphill just managed to keep the lead and win by 1.6 seconds at an average speed of 97.71, but it was Williams who set the fastest lap at a speed of 99.99 mph. Ray Pickrell on another Norton finished third, just over two minutes after the winner.

In the 500 class, there was not a single rider or machine that could live with the performance of Frank Whiteway on Eddie Crooks' Suzuki T500 two-stroke twin. On the first lap he was able to pull out a 27-second lead over Gordon Pantall on a Triumph Daytona and, when Frank Whiteway increased this lead by another 16.8 seconds on the second lap, it was obvious to all that he was on his way to a runaway victory in the class.

With a substantial lead on his refuelling stop at the end of lap three, Whiteway was able to cruise home for an easy victory, 1 minute, 28 seconds ahead of Gordon Pantall, who in turn just managed to scrape home only four-tenths of a second in front of Ray Knight on another Triumph Daytona machine. Whiteway averaged 89.94 mph for the five-lap race and set the fastest lap at a speed of 90.75 mph.

Charles Mortimer on a Ducati 250 had come extremely close to winning the 250 Production Machine TT in 1969, and he made certain of taking first place in 1970, but it was far from an easy victory. In fact, there was a tremendous dice between the first four riders, Mortimer, John Williams, Woods and Hunter, on the first lap with only 4.8 seconds separating them as they crossed the finishing line at the end of the lap. John Williams was marginally in the lead with his Honda CB250, followed by Mortimer on his Ducati and Stan Woods on his Suzuki. Mortimer led by two-tenths of a second at the end of lap two and so the battle for the lead raged back and forth with first Mortimer, then Williams and Woods heading the race.

This changing of the leading positions continued throughout the duration of the race and was finally resolved in Charles Mortimer's favour, when he beat John Williams over the line by 5.6 seconds at an average speed of 84.87 mph. Stan Woods finished third, while Mortimer set the fastest lap with a speed of 86.71 mph.

With the transfer of the International Production Machine Race to the Saturday, the Sidecar TT 750 event was moved to the Monday morning spot and the Sidecar 500 race was scheduled for the Wednesday morning.

In both races, two names stood out above all others, Enders and Schauzu. Their personal duels, as well as the speed of their BMW outfits, carried them way out in front of any other opposition and this proved to be the case in the 750 Sidecar race. From a standing start Enders smashed the existing lap record with a speed of 92.37 mph and led Schauzu over the finishing line at the end of lap one by 19.4 seconds. Both of the other fancied German sidecar aces, Luthringshauser and Auerbacher, failed on their first lap in the chase after Enders, but it was Klaus Enders turn on the next lap. While leading on the roads and on time from his great rival, Schauzu, Enders once again ran into mechanical problems with the BMW, leaving Schauzu to cruise home the winner, 3 minutes, 41.6 seconds ahead of Peter Brown (BSA) and E. Leece (LMS) who was surprised to find himself in third spot after Bill Currie had stopped on the last lap. Schauzu averaged 90.20 mph for the three-lap race.

If you didn't have a Yamaha, then you didn't stand much chance of winning lightweight races. This had become an accepted fact, because the twin-cylinder two-stroke produced by this Japanese company as an over-the-counter racing machine was considerably faster than anything else available to the racing enthusiast. Of the 24 finishers to receive silver replicas in the Lightweight 250 TT in 1970, 22 of the riders were Yamaha-mounted. The other two machines were the works' MZ ridden by

Gunter Bartusch and the Crooks Suzuki of Peter Berwick.

The Lightweight TT, in fact, reflected what had been happening at Europe's short circuit meetings, where quite often the entire line-up on the starting grid comprised nothing more than Yamaha production racers. Although Yamaha had officially withdrawn from road racing, the company was shrewd enough to produce a series of racers based on their ordinary roadsters which were to dominate the racing scene throughout the world.

Being mounted on much the same sort of raceware, riders of similar capability produced exciting, very close racing for the spectators. The Lightweight 250 TT might have lost the prestige of works' teams, but it had lost none of its spectacular attraction for the riders and the Isle of Man visitors who went to watch the racing.

New names, too, were beginning to be recognised as up-and-coming riders who might well be the TT stars of the future: Stanley Woods (not the original making a comeback, just the same name and no relation), Paul Smart, Paul Cott, Tony Jefferies, Mick Grant, Tony Rutter, Barry Randle and many more besides.

In the Lightweight 250 race, it was the established and very experienced Kel Carruthers who set the pace on his Yamaha twin, with Paul Smart chasing hard after him, followed by Rodney Gould and Stanley Woods, all Yamaha-mounted. But there was no catching the wily Australian Carruthers; his machine ran faultlessly for the entire six laps of the race. This was not so for either Paul Smart, who dropped out on the third lap while in second place, or for Stanley Woods, whose Yamaha failed while he was also lying second to Carruthers.

The leader board behind Kel Carruthers changed constantly, but at the finish it was Rodney Gould who came home in second place, 3 minutes, 34.8 seconds behind Carruthers. Third was the MZ of Gunter Bartusch.

The fastest lap of the race was set by Kel Carruthers at a speed of 98.04 mph and he averaged 96.13 mph for the six laps. When one considers that just two years earlier Bill Ivy had lapped in the same race at over 105 mph from a standing start, it does demonstrate the startling difference in performance between pukka works' racers and over-the-counter production racing bikes.

The Sidecar 500 cc TT on Wednesday morning proved a far more successful race for Klaus Enders than the 750 event. It was obvious Enders was in a class of his own when he scorched around the TT circuit from a standing start at 93.79 mph, to leave every other competitor, including Schauzu, way behind. At the end of the first lap, Enders had a 44-second lead over Auerbacher who had started 10 seconds after him and had done his best to keep him in sight. But as soon as Enders had disappeared from view, Georg Auerbacher slowed the pace and it was Schauzu who took over in second spot, followed soon after in third place by Heinz Luthringshauser. And this was the finishing order at the end of the three laps with Enders winning at an average speed of 92.93 mph.

BMW took six out of the first seven places, with the URS driven by Horst Owesle splitting them by finishing in fifth spot. The highest placed British machine was the Norton of the veteran campaigner Charlie Freeman, which finished eighth.

Although Pasolini was entered on the Benelli 350-four in the Junior TT, from the start of the race there was never any question of his challenging Agostini for his third consecutive Junior victory and sixth TT win. Almost nonchantly and to the same pattern established over the previous two years, Agostini destroyed all opposition on the opening lap with a speed of 104.56 mph. Then, with more than half-a-minute in hand over his nearest rival, Paul Smart on the Padgett-Yamaha, Agostini was able to ease off and cruise to the finishing line 4 minutes, 55.2 seconds ahead of the second man to finish, Alan Barnett on the single-cylinder Aermacchi.

There had been a tremendous dice for second place between Paul Smart and Alan Barnett on the opening three laps of the race, but the Aermacchi rider, using the superb handling and braking of the low, light Italian machine to its best advantage, was able to pull away from Smart and lead him at the finish by 1 minute, 45 seconds. Pasolini and the Benelli were never even in the hunt and dropped out of the race on the fifth lap.

The interesting point at this time was that the simple, push-rod operated, single-cylinder four-stroke Aermacchis were a match for the Yamaha 350 two-stroke twins and out of the first eight places, four went to Aermacchi, three to Yamaha and, of course, number one to Agostini and MV, who won at an average speed of 101.77 mph.

Favourites to win the Lightweight 125 TT in 1970 were Dave Simmonds on his Kawasaki, Dieter Braun on the ex-works' Suzuki and possibly Gunter Bartusch on the works' MZ two-stroke. When Simmonds came through in the lead by 49.8 seconds at the end of lap one, it looked as though he was going to repeat his victory of the previous year. Dieter Braun lay second with Bo Jansson on the Maico, third.

But unfortunately for Simmonds, his standing-start lap of 90.90 mph was too much for the little Kawasaki twin and on the second lap the motor seized allowing Dieter Braun to take over the race. The ex-works Suzuki was far too fast for the single-cylinder Maico of Bo Jansson and Braun claimed the victory by 2 minutes, 23.4 seconds at an average speed of 89.27 mph. Bartusch finished third on the MZ from East Germany. Twenty-six riders in all finished the race and, with gaps of anything up to three minutes between solitary machines, spectators around the 37¾-mile course were more than delighted when the Senior TT began an hour or so later.

The race itself was, of course, another high-speed demonstration by Agostini and his MV Agusta. Behind came a parade of good, old British single-cylinder racing machines: Matchlesses, Nortons, Seeleys with the occasional Triumph twin or Aermacchi single entered to add a little variety to the mix. But wait! Entered for the first time were two, three-cylinder Kawasaki two-strokes, one to be ridden by Martin Carney, the other by Bill Smith, the motorcycle dealer from Chester.

The Kawasakis were reputed to be incredibly quick but, like other large-capacity Japanese racers, they were something of a problem when it came to cornering on bumpy circuits such as the Isle of Man.

The race behind Agostini for places on the leader board was epic. Peter Williams on the Arter-Matchless was the man to beat and, with Alan Barnett full of confidence from his Junior ride, the two men battled for second spot behind Agostini. On the first lap, Williams led Barnett by two seconds, but on the second lap Barnett reversed the position with a 9.6-second lead over Williams.

Barnett increased his lead over Williams to 28.2 seconds on the third lap and it looked as though he was going to repeat his success of the Junior TT by finishing second to Agostini. Barnett's second lap was recorded at just over 101 mph and he was riding superbly. Meanwhile, the Kawasaki of Bill Smith lay fifth and was living up to its reputation for poor handling. Unfortunately, Carney had retired on his Kawasaki on lap three. Then, on lap four Barnett's Seeley failed and Peter Williams stepped into second place behind the MV and that was how the race ended, with Agostini winning by 5 minutes, 9.4 seconds from Peter Williams, with Bill Smith coming through into third place.

Agostini averaged 101.52 mph to win his seventh TT and set a fastest lap of 105.29 mph.

The very sad thing about the 1970 TT races was that six riders died during the course of practice and racing, including the promising young rider, Brian Steenson from Ireland and the OSSA works' rider, Santiago Herrero. The very serious question of safety for riders in the TT was raised and, the following year, all efforts were made to improve certain sections of the circuit, as well as liaise with the riders regarding the positioning of straw bales, etc.

With the development of Formula 750 racing in the United States, the A-CU decided to take the initiative in Europe and run a three-lap Formula 750 race in conjunction with the 1971 TT events. Triumph, BSA and Norton had raced their new superbikes at Daytona with motors developed from their 750 roadster machines. The racing had been a tremendous success, and with the declining interest among spectators, who were becoming bored with lack of challenge to Agostini and the MV, the A-CU rightly decided to attract the superbikes to the Isle of Man.

Any motorcycle having an engine capacity over 250 cc and under 750 cc and based on a production roadster machine was eligible, which meant that the entry for the first Isle of Man Formula 750 race comprised the works' BSA and Triumph machines ridden by Ray Pickrell and Tony Jefferies, the works' Norton ridden by Peter Williams, plus an assortment of private entries on Yamaha 350 racers, Kawasaki 500s, as well as a fair entry of ordinary production roadster machines.

From a standing clutch start, Tony Jefferies lapped at over 100 mph on the works' Triumph to lead Charlie Sanby on the Kuhn-Norton by 6.2 seconds and Ray Pickrell by 7.6 seconds at the end of the first lap, with Peter Williams a further 10.4 seconds behind on the Norton. On the second lap, Jefferies gained a further 3.6 seconds over Sanby, who was riding like a demon to stay ahead of Jefferies on the road. But Sanby pushed the Kuhn-Norton too hard and dropped out of the running on the last lap. Pickrell moved up into second place and there he stayed to finish 26 seconds behind Jefferies, who averaged 102.85 mph and set the fastest lap and record at 103.21 mph. Peter Williams finished 1 minute, 4 seconds behind Jefferies to bring his Norton home in third place.

The 750 cc Sidecar TT could almost be described as the most explosive race in the 1971 series, mainly because of the large number of top riders' machines which disintegrated before reaching the finish! Georg Auerbacher won the race, but the runner-up, Alan Sansum, was amazed to find that he had been raised from tenth place on the first lap to second on

109

the third and final one because of the number of retirements.

Thirteen machines failed to complete the first lap; 21 more failed on their second lap, including the race leader Siegfried Schauzu, and a further seven dropped out on the last lap.

With Schauzu's main rival, Klaus Enders, out of the 1971 TTs, everybody expected to see Siefgried Schauzu have a runaway victory in both sidecar events. In fact, when he broke the lap record from a standing start in the 750 race, with a speed of 93.44 mph, it appeared that he would be able to win with ease. Schauzu led Auerbacher by 42.6 seconds at the end of the first lap, while behind them came a whole gaggle of BSAs ridden by Hanks, Vincent, Barker and Windle. The BMWs of Luthringshauser and Butscher were tying for sixth position on the leader board.

Then four runners out of the top six, including Schauzu, Luthringshauser, Butscher and Roy Hanks, dropped out of the race, leaving a very confused field of riders and lap scorers. Vincent and Barker moved up to second and third places on their BSA twins, with D. Wood on his Norton outfit taking fourth position at the end of lap two. But to add to the confusion, Vincent and Barker retired on the last lap and, with Wood limping home with mechanical problems, Sansum on his Triumph and Williamson on the WHB Weslake moved into second and third places behind the winner, Georg Auerbacher. It was an eventful race to say the least, with the lone BMW finally taking the honours at an average speed of 86.86 mph.

With motors swopped and fairings cleaned, the charioteers wheeled out their outfits on Monday, June 7, for the 500 cc International Sidecar TT. In this event, there was no motor capable of beating the BMW and the point was proven when the first five places were won by the Bavarian twins. The first British machine home was a BSA twin in sixth place ridden by Chris Vincent.

The race itself was a fairy tale start-to-finish victory for Schauzu, who scored his fifth Sidecar TT victory at an average speed of 86.21 mph. However, Schauzu did not make the fastest lap; it was his opponent Georg Auerbacher, who on the last lap picked up 5.6 seconds on the leader to finish a mere 5.4 seconds down at the finish. A. Butscher finished in third place.

With the Junior TT moved from Wednesday to Monday and reduced in length from six to five laps, everybody expected the quite normal MV win to give Agostini his eighth TT victory. But the impossible happened; the MV Agusta actually broke

down on the first lap and a cheer went up around the course as it was announced that Agostini had retired from the race. At last, for the first time in four years, the spectators were to see a race for a TT win and not a second place.

Phil Read set the pace on his Yamaha 350 with a standing start lap of 100.37 mph; 29.8 seconds behind him came Alan Barnett on his Yamsel, followed by Rod Gould on another Yamaha. The pressure was on Read, but his Yamaha only stood the pace for three laps before expiring and allowing Gould to take over at the front of the pack of howling Yamahas. Barnett's Yamsel had quit on lap three.

At the end of lap four, Gould, too, had relinquished the lead as his Yamaha went sick and he finally retired from the race. On the last lap, it was a neck-and-neck struggle between Dudley Robinson and Tony Jefferies, but Robinson nervously over-braked and took a spill which cost him the race.

Jefferies played it cool to finish the race on his Yamsel 36.4 seconds ahead of Gordon Pantall on the Padgett-Yamaha, while veteran TT rider Bill Smith paced himself perfectly to finish third on his Honda twin. Tony Jefferies' average speed was 89.98 mph and it was a popular win with the crowds, and was Tony's second victory of the week.

Jefferies was out again the same day riding the works' Triumph Trident in the Production Machine Race. The event had been extended to four laps and both Norton and Triumph were looking for a victory.

Peter Williams was Norton's number-one rider and it was he and Ray Pickrell, the other Triumph rider, who diced neck and neck for the entire $37\frac{3}{4}$ miles of the first lap, with Pickrell leading Williams by two-tenths of a second at the start of lap two. Williams' vast knowledge and experience of the TT circuit, as well as the lighter weight of the Norton compared with the Trident, helped him take the lead by 2.6 seconds at the end of the second lap.

Unfortunately for Norton, the one item which had given them so much trouble in practice, the gearbox, failed yet again before the end of the third lap and Williams coasted to a halt to watch Pickrell go rushing on to his second Production TT victory. Tony Jefferies on the other works' Trident followed him home in second place, with Bob Heath filling the number three spot on the leader board with his BSA Rocket-3. It was a superb victory for Pickrell, who averaged 100.07 mph on the Triumph roadster, but Williams had the consolation of setting a new record lap at 101.06 mph on the Norton.

In the 500 cc class of the race, Honda chalked up another one-two victory with John Williams and Graham Penny on their CB450 twins, with Suzuki T500 twins filling the next five places at the finish of the race. But the Hondas did not have things all their own way because, although John Williams led from start to finish, Roger Bowler on a Triumph Daytona and Gordon Pantall on a Suzuki 500 separated the two Hondas for three out of the four laps. But then both Pantall and Bowler went out with machine trouble, leaving Graham Penny to finish 2 minutes, 11.2 seconds behind Williams, with Adrian Cooper finishing third on his T500 Suzuki.

John Williams, no relative of Peter, set a new race record of 91.04 mph and lap record of 91.45 mph.

Honda also scored a victory in the 250 cc class of the Production Machine Race when Bill Smith led from start to finish on the CB250 twin-cylinder machine. Charlie Williams, still no relative of the other two TT riders, finished second on a Yamaha YDS7 and Tommy Robb on a Honda CB250 came third. It was a straight race for Bill Smith and he won by a mere 6.2 seconds at an average speed of 84.14 mph, after Charlie Williams had made a last-lap effort to catch the Honda rider. This gave Williams the fastest lap of 84.64 mph.

Reducing the Lightweight 250 TT from six to four laps meant that the mortality rate of the high-revving two-strokes was greatly reduced but, with almost 80 per cent of the entries riding Yamaha TD2s, it was a foregone conclusion that one of these Japanese-built bikes would win.

Phil Read was the obvious favourite and, although initially he was chased for the lead on lap one by Peter Williams riding the works' MZ, the fragile East German machine could not stand the pace and failed, giving Read over a minute's lead ahead of third placeman, Charles Mortimer, whose Yamaha also rapidly ground to a halt. A mere 25 seconds covered fourth to eighth places, and soon Barry Randle, Alan Barnett and Rod Gould moved up to fill the three places behind Read.

However, being the cunning campaigner that he is, Read kept a very close eye on his signal positions around the circuit and reduced the pace sufficiently to retain the lead without stressing the motor of his Yamaha. The result was that he won from Barry Randle by 2 minutes, 4 seconds at an average speed of 98.02 mph. Alan Barnett and his Yamsel finished third.

Read's race psychology had paid off because his cracking first lap speed of 100.08 mph had pushed his main opposition to breaking point and he was then able to dictate his own pace sufficient to keep ahead of the rest of the field.

The weather for the Lightweight 125 TT on Friday, June 11, could only be described as diabolical. The race had twice been postponed and, when it did eventually start, heavy, black rain clouds hung sullenly in the sky. Charles Mortimer was favourite to win the race and it was obvious why when he completed the first lap 1 minute, 12 seconds ahead of Bo Jansson. Mortimer gained another 46.2 seconds on his second lap on his Yamaha. When mist closed in on the Mountain and it began to rain heavily on the last lap, Mortimer was able to slow the pace and cruise to a clear cut victory by 2 minutes 49.6 seconds over Bo Jansson and his Maico. Third place went to John Kiddie on his Honda 125 twin production racer. Some indication of the bad weather conditions was shown in Mortimer's average speed of 83.96 mph and his fastest lap of 87.05 mph, which were considerably slower than previous year's speeds.

In fact, because of the weather, the Senior TT was postponed until the last Saturday of TT week, but this made very little difference to a completely predictable result.

Agostini may have lost out in the Junior TT at the beginning of the week, but the MV mechanics had left nothing to chance for the Senior. With no real need to hurry through corners because of his machine's vastly superior speed on the straights, Agostini cruised to TT victory number eight. In the race behind Agostini and his MV, there were some very interesting developments with the two Williamses, Peter and John, battling it out for second place, both on Arter-Matchlesses. Frank Perris, the ex-Suzuki works' rider, was also in the hunt riding one of the twin-cylinder, 500 cc 'Daytona' Suzuki two-strokes.

John Williams' Matchless went sick on the fifth lap while he was still in with a good chance of a high finishing place and John retired allowing Frank Perris to fill the vacant third position behind Peter Williams and Agostini. At this point the race was won and the first three places decided; at an average speed of 102.59 mph and setting the fastest lap of 104.86 mph, it was Agostini again.

Peter Williams, too, was beginning to set a tradition by always finishing second to the MVs on the Arter-tuned machines.

And so into 1972, possibly one of the most critical years in the history of the TT, when a number of the world's top road racers decided they would no longer ride on the Isle of Man! However, there was no indication of the discontent that was to arise at the end of the week when the International Production Machine Race started on the first Saturday.

Tony Jefferies had joined Peter Williams in the Norton team in an attempt to beat the all-conquering Triumph Trident, but the chances of a great race between Williams and Pickrell virtually ended before the race began, when Williams lost 35 seconds in trying to start the big Norton twin. Meanwhile, Pickrell had rocketed off into the lead, being chased hard by Jefferies on the other works' Norton.

Using all his skill and knowledge of the TT course, Williams carved his way through the field in an attempt to get back on level terms with Pickrell but, before the first lap was completed, the old Norton gearbox trouble had struck and Williams lost fourth gear on his machine. At the end of the lap, Pickrell pulled into refuel, and rejoined the race still in the lead, while Tony Jefferies pulled into his pit to retire with gearbox trouble on his Norton.

Without fourth gear, Williams was at a distinct disadvantage to Pickrell and stood no chance of catching the Triumph rider who won the race at an average speed of precisely 100 mph to gain his third Production TT victory. Williams was able to nurse the Norton Commando home into second place to finish 3 minutes, 14.8 seconds behind Pickrell, who had set a new record lap of 101.61 mph. This was the sixth time that Peter Williams had finished second in a TT race. David Nixon on the Boyer Trident finished third.

If the 750 class was a runaway win for Ray Pickrell, the opposite was the case for Stan Woods (Suzuki) in the 500 class of the Production Race. On the first of the four laps, there was a tremendous ding-dong battle for the lead with first Roger Bowler (Triumph) and then Woods in front. In fact, at the end of lap one, only nine seconds separated Woods, Bowler, Hugh Evans on a Kawasaki, Bill Smith on a Honda and the Tomkinson BSAs of Clive Brown and Nigel Rollason.

At the end of the second lap, Woods still held the lead but by only two seconds from Evans, who had displaced Bowler. However, Evans pulled into refuel and was never able to rejoin the Woods-versus-Bowler fight for the lead.

At the start of the last lap, Bowler had pulled out a seven-second lead on Woods, but the Suzuki rider had no intention of giving in and fought back to take the lead, and won by 6.8 seconds from Bowler on the Triumph twin.

It was a fantastic race, with both race and lap records being broken by the leading two riders, but

it was Woods' final lap that set a new record of 93.61 mph and he averaged 92.20 mph for the four laps. Bill Smith on his Honda 500-four finished exactly one minute behind Bowler to claim third place.

The first four places in the 250 class went to four different makes of machine. First was the Honda CB250 of John Williams; second, the Yamaha YDS7 of Charlie Williams; third, the Suzuki T250 of Eddie Roberts; and fourth, the Ducati Mach 3 of Dave Arnold. Initially, it looked as though the racing was going to be as close as the 500 class because, at Ballacraine, the two Williamses were literally neck-and-neck but, by the time they had arrived back at the grandstand at the end of lap one, John Williams had pulled out an 11-second lead on his Honda, and from then on he never looked like being caught.

Local rider Danny Shimmin moved up into third place on the third lap to displace Eddie Roberts (Ducati), but his position was restored when Shimmin dropped out on the last lap.

John Williams beat Charlie Williams by 1 minute, 41.4 seconds at an average speed of 85.32 mph and also set the fastest lap of 85.73 mph on the 250 Honda. Eddie Roberts was third.

The 750 cc Sidecar TT had all the ingredients for a fantastic battle between the three West Germans, Enders, Schauzu and Luthringshauser. However, it all came to nought on the first lap when Enders pulled out of the race at Ballaugh Bridge and Luthringshauser stopped a few miles further along the course at Ginger Hall.

With his main opposition out of the running, Schauzu completed the first lap just over a minute in the lead from Alan Sansum on the Quaife Triumph. Schauzu picked up another 49 seconds on the second lap and finished 2 minutes, 44 seconds ahead of Sansum on the last lap to win his sixth Sidecar TT at a new race record of 90.97 mph. Schauzu also set the fastest lap at 91.33 mph. Jack Barker on the Devimead BSA finished third, and once again all but one of the larger capacity BMWs, which were favoured to win, failed to finish in the 750 race.

MV Agusta first, Yamahas for the next nine places. That basically was the result of the Junior TT when Agostini scored his ninth TT win for the Italian factory. Up to this point, there was still not a single machine capable of challenging the MV and, although Agostini won the race by almost five minutes, the battle for second place was what interested the crowds.

Phil Read had been signed up to ride for MV,

but his TT debut was far from successful when, after lying second to Agostini at the end of lap one, his machine failed on the second lap. And so began the struggle between Tony Rutter, Mick Grant and Jack Findlay to see who would finish first *behind* Agostini, second in the race!

Grant was in second place at the end of the second lap when he stopped to refuel and this dropped him back to fourth behind Rutter and Findlay, but they still had to make their fuel stops. This they did on their third lap and, with only one lap to go, the advantage was back with Grant. Then Rutter made a really tough, all-out effort to lap at over 100 mph and take the second place away from Mick Grant, who slowed on the last lap because of fuel shortage. In fact, he coasted over the line in third place with a dry fuel tank and a dead engine.

Agostini, who was never pushed or harried in the race, won at an average speed of 102.03 mph and established the fastest lap at 103.34 mph, proving yet again the invincibility of the MV Agusta.

The second race on Monday, June 5 1972, was the International Sidecar 500 cc TT and Siegfried Schauzu became the first man ever to win both Sidecar races in the same year.

It was a race packed with action because, apart from the BMW ex-World and World Champions all competing in the event, Britain's Chris Vincent at last had a competitive 500 cc machine, the ex-Helmut Fath, four-cylinder Munch-URS.

On the first lap, Klaus Enders as usual set a tremendous pace leaving all in his wake, except Chris Vincent on the Munch. Only three seconds separated Enders and Vincent at the end of the lap and the crowds were on their toes urging Vincent on to victory. But then there were sighs of disappointment as Vincent went out of the race, leaving Enders way out in the lead and all set for victory. He had a lead of 25 seconds over Schauzu and there appeared to be nothing that the BMW ace could do to close the gap.

Also, not far behind Schauzu was the veteran Heinz Luthringshauser waiting to pounce should anything go wrong, and for Enders it did; because at Ballaugh it was obvious he was having machine trouble and eventually he stopped at Ramsey to retire from the race.

This put Schauzu in the lead, but an inspired effort by Luthringshauser on the last lap, which gained him the fastest lap of the race, almost snatched victory from Schauzu. He won by a mere 6.6 seconds from Luthringshauser, while the British

Boret brothers, Nick and Gerry, took third place in their unusually shaped Renwick wedge outfit.

Generally speaking, the weather for the 1972 TT races was appalling and the Lightweight 250 race was postponed for 24 hours in the hope that conditions would improve the following day. Fortunately they did and with 46 Yamahas lined up to do battle, along with three Suzukis, a Bultaco, an OSSA and a Kawasaki, it appeared that with so many top riders of similar ability the battle would be very closely fought.

As it worked out, there was one rider who stood head and shoulders above all others and that was Phil Read who rode to his second successive Lightweight TT victory. His high-speed navigation of the circuit took him straight into the lead and, although starting 30 seconds down on time to Rodney Gould, by Ramsey, Read was not only leading the race on time but also way out in front on the roads. His first two laps, including the standing start, were clocked at over the 'ton'.

In fact, with a 1 minute, 11.6 second lead at the end of lap two he pulled in to refuel and had departed again before Gould had appeared along the Glencrutchery Road. On the third lap, Read's lead had dropped back to 53.4 seconds because of his fuel stop, but he opened up the advantage again to finish the four-lap race 1 minute, 28.4 seconds ahead of Gould.

Read's fastest lap was at a speed of 100.61 mph and he averaged 99.68 mph for the four laps. Early in the race, there was a close-fought battle for second place between Gould and John Williams but, when Williams had to stop for fuel and Gould went straight through, Williams was relegated to a certain third place.

There was also a similar battle for fourth place between Charlie Williams and the Swiss rider, Werner Pfirter. On the last lap at the Bungalow they were level-pegging on time, but an all-out effort by Williams on the drop down the Mountain to the finishing line gave him a 2.8-second advantage to claim fourth place. Yamaha machines filled all the first 22 places, with a lone Suzuki finishing 23rd.

Similar to the Lightweight 250 TT, the Formula 750 race had also been postoned for 24 hours. Extended from three to five laps, the Formula 750 event had attracted a bigger entry, with the main interest centered on the John Player Norton team and their choice of John Cooper, Phil Read and Peter Williams to ride against the Triumphs of Ray Pickrell and Tony Jefferies. Jack Findlay added a dash more interest with his very special, three-cylinder works' Suzuki 750 two-stroke.

Norton had trouble in practice with gearboxes, but were fairly sure that they had cured the fault in time for the race. But to everybody's disappointment, not one of the three machines completed more than two laps. Read stopped at Ramsey on the first lap and then toured in to the pits, while John Cooper also came in at the end of lap one.

Peter Williams steamed through on his first lap 17.4 seconds down on Pickrell and only 2.6 seconds behind Jefferies, but the Norton got no further than Ballaugh. The two Triumphs were out on their own with Jefferies doing his best to catch Pickrell. But, although Jefferies passed Pickrell when the leader came into refuel, the reverse happened on the third lap when Jefferies had to stop to take on petrol. Meanwhile, Aussie Jack Findlay was really flying on his heavyweight Suzuki to hold third place ahead of Dave Nixon on a Seeley-Triumph and Charlie Williams on a Yamaha. In spite of having to stop twice to top up the tank of his giant fuel-gobbler, Findlay managed to keep his third place behind the winner, Ray Pickrell and second placeman, Tony Jefferies.

Pickrell won his second TT of the week at an average speed of 104.23 mph and set a new lap record of 105.68 mph after his race-long duel with team mate, Tony Jefferies.

The Lightweight 125 TT was held in pouring rain on Friday and for Yamaha rider, Charles Mortimer, it was an easy victory. At the start of the race, he had to contend with the challenge of Italian Gilberto Parlotti on the Morbidelli works' machine and, at the end of lap one, Mortimer was 15 seconds down on Parlotti in spite of leading on the roads.

Sadly, on the second lap, Parlotti crashed on the Verandah section of the course and was fatally injured. Mortimer went on to win the race by 6 minutes, 44.8 seconds from Charlie Williams (Yamaha) and Bill Rae (Maico). Mortimer's race average was 87.49 mph and his fastest lap 90.58 mph.

The final race of the week was the Senior TT which, because of bad weather, had to be postponed until late in the afternoon. But, by the start of the race, the roads had dried all round the course and conditions looked set fair for some high-speed laps by Agostini and his team-mate Alberto Pagani on the MV Agustas.

The first surprise of the race came at the end of lap one when it was learned that John Williams on the Arter-Matchless was splitting the two MVs and leading Pagani by 2.4 seconds. But the Italian managed to gain second place behind Agostini on the next lap, only to be slowed by an oil leak which was causing some hair-raising slides.

John Williams took over 2nd spot at the Bungalow on lap 3 and Pagani lost precious seconds when he pulled into his pit to make adjustments to his machine. Williams still separated the two MVs at the start of the last lap, with a 1 minute, 30 second advantage over Pagani. But then came drama, because on the Verandah, just a few miles from the finish line, Williams ran out of fuel and Pagani repassed him to give MV Agusta a one-two victory.

With Williams out of the race, the vast amount of chopping and changing which had been happening on the leader board was resolved when Mick Grant, riding a Kawasaki, came home to finish third.

Agostini had completed the race with all of his six laps at over the 'ton' to average 104.02 mph. He also established the fastest lap of 105.39 mph.

To date, this was Agostini's last appearance on the Isle of Man, where he has scored ten TT wins and recorded a total of 53 laps at over 100 mph, a record which has yet to be beaten. The reason given by Agostini for refusing to ride in the TT again was the death of his friend and fellow countryman Gilberto Parlotti. Agostini has blamed the TT Mountain Circuit for Parlotti's fatal accident and, together with a number of other leading Grand Prix riders, including Phil Read, has vowed never to race again on the Isle of Man.

It has been said that the TT circuit is dangerous bearing in mind the performance of present-day racing machines and it is true that over 100 competitors have lost their lives during the 67 years in which the races have been held on the Isle of Man. But racing of any kind on any circuit is dangerous; witness the untimely and unfortunate deaths of little Bill Ivy in the East German Grand Prix, Bob McIntyre at Oulton Park, Florian Camathias at Brands Hatch, Renzo Pasolini and Jarno Saarinen at Monza, and Kim Newcombe at Silverstone.

Racing is dangerous. It requires great courage, skill and determination and the Isle of Man Mountain Circuit has since 1911 been regarded as the toughest and most demanding course for road racing in the world. Manufacturers have built their reputations from success in the TT; riders have won world-wide acclaim and, in spite of personal protests from a number of riders, the TT races continue to attract even larger numbers of entries, all of whom are prepared to demonstrate and test their skill in this, the greatest road race in the world.

With the departure of Agostini, Read and Pagani from the TT scene, the 1973 races took on an air of mystery. Who would be the new TT stars? There were many riders capable of winning the races on their privately owned or sponsored machines and many, such as Peter Williams, Jack Findlay, Tony Rutter, Barry Randle, John Williams, Mick Grant, Tommy Robb, Stan Woods and Charlie Williams, were already established as competent TT riders. With the ultra-fast MV Agusta out of the running, both the Junior and Senior TTs were now a possible goal for any one of a dozen extremely good riders.

The three-lap 750 Sidecar race opened the TT action and all Europe's top three-wheeler exponents were after victory, including Klaus Enders, Siegfried Schauzu, Heinz Luthringshauser and Willi Klenk, the West German BMW experts who fought so hard for TT honours.

From practice times it was obvious that Klaus Enders was the man to beat and in the first lap of the race he proved the point by taking a 2.8-second lead from his great rival Siegfried Schauzu. On his second lap, Enders piled on the pressure; he was leading on the roads and with a clear course ahead pulled out another 4.4-second lead over Schauzu. On the final lap, there was absolutely nothing that anyone, including Schauzu, could do to overcome Enders' devastating form because, with a lap time of 23 minutes, 22.2 seconds, Enders shattered the record with an incredible lap of 96.86 mph. The 100-mph lap for a sidecar outfit was in sight!

Enders avenged his failures of 1972 with a superb race win at an average speed of 93.01 mph and beat his friendly rival, Siegfried Schauzu, by 1 minute, 1.2 seconds.

With Luthringshauser, Klenk and Bill Currie dropping out of the race before the end of the first lap, plus Roy Hanks and Jack Barker retiring before the start of the last lap, the battle for third place behind the two flying BMWs had to be decided between John Brandon with his four-cylinder Honda outfit and Mick Boddice with his three-cylinder Kawasaki. The honours went to Brandon, who beat Boddice to the line by 12 seconds.

In the 750 Production Machine Race, the challenge to the John Player Norton team of Dave Croxford and Peter Williams came mainly from Triumph Trident riders Tony Jefferies, John Williams and David Nixon. Peter Williams made an immaculate start on his Norton Commando and roared off into the lead, being hard chased by Tony Jefferies on his Trident.

In the hands of the experienced Williams, the lighter, more manageable Norton soon began to pull away from the field and, at the end of the first lap, Williams crossed the line 4.4 seconds ahead of Jefferies, followed by John Williams some 35 seconds later.

Peter Williams continued to extend his lead on the second lap and in the process set the fastest lap of the race at 100.52 mph. At the start of the third lap, he had 8.2 seconds in hand over Jefferies and looked all set to take the 750 Production Race win for John Player Norton, but then, as had happened before, the Norton TT jinx struck and Williams was out of the race. This left Jefferies with more than 57 seconds in hand over second placeman John Williams and David Nixon moved up into third spot on the leader board.

However, torrential rain on the last lap caused spectators to scramble for cover and riders to reduce speed considerably. In Jefferies' case he almost slowed down too much because John Williams picked up over 15 seconds on the run in to the finish, but fortunately Jefferies had sufficient time in hand to take the win at an average speed of 95.62 mph.

In the 500 cc class, the race was a fierce struggle between Bill Smith on a Honda CB500 and Stan Woods on a Suzuki T500. On the first lap Stan Woods led by 4 seconds and, at the start of the third lap, Smith had reversed the order to lead by 4.8 seconds. Woods had pulled in to refuel at the end of lap one as had Keith Martin in third place on his Kawasaki. But Bill Smith on the four-stroke Honda was able to go straight through without having to stop for petrol.

At the start of the last lap, Woods had caught up and passed Smith to gain a very comfortable lead of over 25 seconds, but then the rains came and, on the climb over the Mountain in a torrential downpour, both the leading machines cut out. Smith was staggering along on two out of four cylinders and Woods stopped completely at the Bungalow. Third-place rider, Keith Martin passed Woods but did not see him stuck at the side of the road and came within 12 seconds of catching the leader, Bill Smith, whose Honda had dried out and chimed back on to four cylinders.

Stan Woods, too, got his Suzuki going again as the heat of the motor dried out the sparking plugs and, riding on the limit, he chased after, caught up and passed Martin about two miles from the finish, but just failed to catch Smith and his Honda. The result was a win for Bill Smith at an average speed of 88.10 mph, with a record lap by Stan Woods of 94.44 mph.

In the 250 Production Race, there was an unbelievable scrap for first place on the opening laps.

115

The initial leader was Charlie Williams on a Yamaha, with Tommy Robb lying second on a Honda. In third place, and you could have thrown a blanket over the two riders as they went past the pits, was Eddie Roberts, slip-streamed by Peter Courtney. At the end of the second lap, Charlie Williams still led the race and Eddie Roberts had managed to pass Tommy Robb, leaving Peter Courtney far behind in fourth place. At the end of the third lap, Roberts had picked up a 16-second deficit on Williams and briefly took the lead. But the up-and-coming TT ace, Williams, pulled out all the stops on the last lap to take a well-earned victory, 41 seconds ahead of Roberts. Tommy Robb finished third.

Williams' average speed for the race was 81.76 mph and the fastest lap went to Eddie Roberts at 84.06 mph.

The three-lap 500 cc Sidecar TT on Monday, June 4, was another absolutely superb victory for Klaus Enders. The West German led from start to finish on his BMW and set a remarkable new lap record of 95.52 mph as well as establishing a new race record of 94.93 mph. Out in a class of his own, Enders rode the opposition into the ground and even the experienced TT campaigner Schauzu did not see the going of his arch rival.

Enders finished the race 2 minutes, 45.8 seconds ahead of Schauzu, who in turn led third placeman, Rolf Steinhausen on his Konig-powered outfit, by 1 minute, 17.2 seconds. The racing could never have been considered close, but it was extremely spectacular for the crowds who were stunned by the unbelievable speed of Klaus Enders' beautifully prepared outfit.

With the absence of Agostini, Read and Gould in the Junior TT, it seemed as though the riders who, up to that time had not received much of the limelight, went 'ton'-lap crazy. If the spectators thought they would not see much action, then they were very much mistakened because, in perfect weather conditions, the first four to finish in the race, Tony Rutter, Ken Hugget, John Williams and Barry Randle, all averaged over 100 mph for the five laps of the race!

Mick Grant set the ball rolling when, as number one away at the start of the race, he completed his first lap at over 103 mph to lead Tony Rutter by 25.8 seconds but, with Grant having mechanical problems at the end of the second lap and retiring at the pits, it was Tony Rutter who made all the running. On his second lap he clocked 104.22 mph to set the fastest lap of the race.

Behind Rutter, Ken Hugget and John Williams

tried hard to catch him but did no more than maintain their places ahead of a constantly changing leader board, as Barry Randle, Phil Carpenter and Derek Chatterton scrapped hard to improve their positions in the race. But there was no way they could catch Rutter and he stormed home winner of the Junior TT at a speed of 101.99 mph, with Ken Hugget second and John Williams in third place. It was an exciting, fast race with closely fought battles but, with Yamaha taking the first 21 places, it lacked that different sound, that sparkle which one or two other makes of machine would have given to the race.

In the Formula 750 event on the Wednesday of TT week, John Player Norton at last fulfilled all of their promise. With a new monocoque designed frame, which gave greater rigidity to the gearbox mounting and obviated the flexing which had caused the previous year's failures, Peter Williams was confident of success. As back-up rider for the TT, Norton had signed on Mick Grant to ride the new powerbike.

By past results and practice times, the main opposition to the Nortons was obviously to come from Tony Jefferies on his Triumph 750-three and Jack Findlay on the big Suzuki triple two-stroke. Through the speed traps, Findlay had clocked over 160 mph on the unwieldy Japanese machine but, with that sort of straight-line performance, he could afford to take it easy through the corners.

Right from the engines-running, clutch start, Peter Williams roared into the lead on the Norton with a lap of over 106 mph. At the end of the first lap, Williams led Findlay on the Suzuki by 23.8 seconds, with a tremendous dice for third spot between Grant and Jefferies, with the Triumph rider holding under a second advantage.

At the end of the second lap, Williams had increased his lead still further over the Suzuki and Findlay had over 40 seconds in hand over Grant and Jefferies, who were still battling neck and neck for third place.

The pattern of the race was set and, with Mick Grant finally getting the better of Jefferies on the third lap, it looked like a Norton, Suzuki, Norton finish. But then, to the disappointment of many spectators around the course, Jack Findlay and his flying Suzuki dropped out of the race on the last lap.

John Player Norton were jubilant. Peter Williams came first at an average speed of 105.47 mph and also set a new record lap at 107.27 mph, and Mick Grant gave them a one-two victory. Tony Jefferies finished third on his Triumph, but only by the skin of his teeth. Charlie Williams (Yamaha) had made a flying last lap and lost out to Jefferies by only eight-tenths of a second.

The name Williams confused many people during the week, because all three, Peter, John and Charlie, constantly appeared in the results. Almost as if to compensate for his disappointment in fractionally missing third place in the F750 event, Charlie Williams made certain of success in the Lightweight 250 race.

There was never any question or doubt about it; right from the start the young rider took the lead from John Williams, who in turn held a comfortable second place ahead of Bill Rae. (They were all mounted on Yamahas.) On his second lap, Charlie Williams set the fastest lap of the race at 102.24 mph, to pull even further ahead of his namesake, who increased his lead over Rae. And that is how the race progressed for the entire four laps, with Charlie Williams winning by 24.6 seconds from John at an average speed of 100.05 mph. Bill Rae finished third.

Perhaps the most interesting and hardest-fought scrap in the race was between Derek Chatterton, Alex George and Tony Rutter, who constantly changed positions on the leader board in their fight to gain fourth place. It finally went to Chatterton, with George fifth and Rutter sixth. Yet again the race was entirely a Yamaha production racing machine benefit, with the first 29 riders mounted on these incredibly quick two-strokes which were originally derived from an ordinary roadster motorcycle.

Yamaha also dominated the Lightweight 125 TT by taking the first four places in the three-lap race with that great, little veteran Tommy Robb scoring his first TT victory since he began racing on the Island in 1958. Ex-works' rider for Honda and Suzuki, Ulsterman Tommy Robb had finished in practically every position on the leader board except number one. But, in the last TT ride of his racing career, he took over Charlie Mortimer's Yamaha to score what was probably the most popular win of the week.

Robb led the race from start to finish ahead of Jan Kostwinder and Neil Tuxworth and, although the event proved to be the usual rather boring procession, the crowds were eager to see Tommy Robb ride to victory and this he did at an average of 88.90 mph and in the process set the fastest lap of the race at 89.24 mph.

The big question in everyone's mind before the start of the Senior TT was, now that Agostini was out of the running, could Peter Williams, who had finished second to Agostini so many times on the Arter-Matchless, actually win the race?

The answer, after almost two and a quarter hours' racing, was no, because it was Jack Findlay on his water-cooled, twin-cylinder Suzuki who beat Williams by 1 minute, 14.2 seconds to gain his first-ever Isle of Man TT win. The crowd were disappointed to see Williams lose out yet again in the Senior but, if there was any other rider they would rather have seen take the win, it was the Aussie, Jack Findlay, who had been campaigning on the Island since 1959 without a solitary win to his credit.

At the start of the race, it looked as though neither Williams nor Findlay would win, because it was Yorkshireman Mick Grant, who rushed into the lead on his 354 cc Yamaha with a standing start lap of over 104 mph. This gave him a 33-second lead over Findlay at the start of lap two and, when this lap was complete, Grant had extended his lead to 53.2 seconds. Meanwhile, Findlay and Williams were having a tremendous struggle for second place, with Findlay leading by two-tenths of a second on the first lap and 1.2 seconds on the second.

Grant was absolutely flying on his Yamaha and he appeared to have the race sewn up, that is until he hit a patch of oil entering Parliament Square in Ramsey and crashed. Although unhurt, the damage to his machine was sufficient to put him out of the race and allow Jack Findlay to take the lead.

However, Findlay had to work hard all the way to keep his lead because Williams did not give any quarter and grudgingly fought for every fraction of a second that he gave to the faster, twin-cylinder Suzuki. At the end of the fourth lap, Findlay led Williams by a mere 8.6 seconds and it was still anybody's race. Behind the two leaders, there was also a battle royal to decide who was going to claim third spot. Tony Rutter had held fourth place on the first lap, until he crashed at Ramsey depositing the fuel on the road which was to bring down Grant a lap later. With Rutter out of the running, Charlie Sanby on the Hi-tac Suzuki, Alex George on a Yamaha and Roger Nicholls on another Suzuki swopped places up until the fourth lap.

At this point the pattern was set and Jack Findlay romped home the winner, after Peter Williams' Matchless had begun to slow on the last two laps, by 1 minute, 14.2 seconds at an average speed of 101.55 mph. Charlie Sanby finished third.

The fastest lap of the race was established by Mick Grant at 104.41 mph and, with the Senior TT

117

bringing the week's racing on the Isle of Man to its conclusion, most spectators agreed that the few riders who had decided not to race there had not really been missed. The racing had been improved by the absence of a runaway winner and the close-fought competition of practically all of the 1973 events.

With the tremendous boom in motorcycling in Europe, as well as the world-wide publicity the TT races had received early in the year, a record crowd of over 38,000 visitors flew or sailed to the Isle of Man from all corners of the world to see the 1974 races.

Unfortunately, the temperamental Manx climate was at its worst on the Saturday when both the Sidecar 750 race and the Production Machine event were to be held, and both were postponed until the following week.

In order to save many of the sidecar riders having to swop engines, the 750 Sidecar TT was postponed until Monday and the 500 Sidecar race was in turn transferred to the Tuesday.

Although the weather was bad, the racing was absolutely great. In the first event of the week, the 750 Sidecar, most people expected to see Schauzu provide his usual, faultless performance to claim his seventh TT victory. But they forgot Rolf Steinhausen and his incredibly quick Konig outfit.

From a standing start he shattered Klaus Enders' lap record with a fantastic lap of 98.18 mph and Schauzu, who had started 10 seconds behind Steinhausen, did not see him again until he passed Steinhausen's silent outfit which had broken down on the second lap. From then on, Schauzu was out on his own with only veteran rider Heinz Luthringshauser to worry about.

However, with 3 minutes, 33.8 seconds in hand over Luthringshauser at the finish, it was obvious that Schauzu was never in any danger of being caught, and he established a new race record of 96.59 mph, only a fraction slower than Enders' previous lap record.

The dice for third place was considerably closer, but at the finish the decision went to John Bingham on his Weslake-powered outfit when he beat John Barker on the Devimead BSA by 22 seconds.

The first solo race of the week was the Junior TT and, even without the super-fast works' machines, Chas Mortimer came close to equalling Hailwood's lap record with a lap of 106.39 mph. Also, the eventual winner of the race, Tony Rutter, established a new five-lap race record of 104.44 mph, which compared very favourably with Agostini's 1968 race record of 104.78 mph.

The racing was extremely fast and furious and it seemed amazing that standard, over-the-counter production racing machines should be capable of performances equalling those of the highly developed works' racers of just a few years before.

Chas Mortimer, who had spent the start of the season riding in the Continental GPs, came to the Island confident in his knowledge of the circuit. From the drop of the starting flag, Mortimer set the pace and Rutter tried his level best to keep him in sight and within beating distance but, as Mortimer piled on the pressure on the third lap to set fastest lap of the race, he pulled away from Rutter and looked all set for victory.

But as so often happens, it is not always the fastest rider that wins and Rutter was waiting to take over the lead when Mortimer's Yamaha failed. The disappointed Mortimer could only stand and watch as Rutter hurtled past on his way to take the chequered flag 1 minute, 44 seconds ahead of Mick Grant. The battle for third place, which had been a fierce struggle between Paul Cott and Tom Herron, was resolved in the finishers' enclosure when it was announced that Cott's last-lap effort had given him third place by a mere 3 seconds.

The Production Machine Race, which had originally been removed from the TT programme but had been saved by the combined sponsorship of Marlboro cigarettes and *Motor Cycle*, was the first race on Tuesday, June 4. Because of the decision by John Player Norton not to enter works' machines in the event, Peter Williams had opted to ride a Gus Kuhn Norton Commando and Mick Grant, the other favourite for the race, rode 'Slippery Sam', the Triumph Trident which had won the event for the previous three years.

The larger capacity class had been raised from 750 to 1,000 cc, allowing the big BMW 900 cc machines to enter the race, along with 850 Nortons, and one very standard 900 cc four-cylinder Kawasaki.

From the start it looked as though Peter Williams and the bigger-capacity Norton had a chance of beating the ageing Triumph, but Norton were again out of luck because, while lying second to Grant and trying to keep the Triumph's of Darryl Pendlebury and David Nixon at bay, plus the BMWs of Butenuth and Dahne, the hard-pressed Norton twin failed yet again. After setting the fastest lap at 100.74 mph, Mick Grant maintained the pressure to win by 1 minute, 53 seconds from Butenuth, with Dahne finishing third. Grant's average speed for the four-lap race was 99.72 mph.

In the 500 class, Keith Martin on a Kawasaki led

from start to finish breaking both race and lap records for the event. He was chased fairly hard by second placeman, Alan Rogers on a Triumph Daytona, but the superior speed of the three-cylinder two-stroke over the four-stroke twin gave Martin a distinct advantage on the climb over the Mountain and he won the race from Rogers by 29.4 seconds, setting a new race record of 93.85 mph and a lap record of 95.21 mph. Phil Gurner on a BSA 500 single finished third, 1 minute, 16.4 seconds behind Rogers.

The hardest-fought contest in the Production Machine Race was in the 250 class, where Martin Sharpe and Eddie Roberts spent the last of the four laps passing and repassing one another almost down to the last corner of the circuit. Initially, Sharpe had pulled out a 30-second-plus lead from the rest of the field, but little by little Roberts pegged back Sharpe's advantage and passed him on the climb up the Mountain on the final lap. Then followed the most exciting wheel-to-wheel duel from Kate's Cottage down to Signpost Corner, where Sharpe managed to outbrake Roberts, and gain a sufficient lead to carry him over the line 2.3 seconds ahead of the other Yamaha rider. Third place went to Bill Rae on a Suzuki GT250.

Sharpe's average speed for the race was 86.94 mph and he was extremely pleased with the result as it was his first race on the Isle of Man. The only consolation for Roberts was that he set the fastest lap with a speed of 88.48 mph.

For some time, the BMW 500s had been considered invincible in the Isle of Man Sidecar TT races, but in 1974 there was a machine to challenge their supremacy – the Konig-powered outfit ridden by Jeff Gawley.

Siegfried Schauzu, as usual, set the pace, but it was not quick enough for Gawley and he steamed into the lead on the first lap with his flat-four-cylinder two-stroke engined outfit. In fact, so rapid was his progress that he set the fastest lap of the race at 93.36 mph. Completely aware of what had happened, Schauzu stepped up the pace to catch Gawley and his flying Konig, but Schauzu did not have to try all that hard because on the second lap Gawley's expensive motor disintegrated, leaving Schauzu out in the lead, being chased hard by Luthringshauser on the other BMW outfit.

At the start of the third lap, it looked as though Schauzu would do the Sidecar TT double. But on the climb up the Mountain things started to go wrong with the machine and, by the time Schauzu reached the Bungalow, Luthringshauser had passed him to capture the lead on the road and in the race.

Trevor Ireson, who was one of the fastest in practice on his Konig outfit, also passed Schauzu to take second place, but promptly ran out of fuel on the home stretch from Signpost Corner. This allowed George O'Dell on another Konig into second place and Mac Hobson with his Yamaha-powered outfit into third.

Ireson managed to push home into fifth place after being passed literally on the finishing line by Dick Hawes, while the unfortunate Schauzu toured home to finish ninth.

Luthringshauser's average speed for the three laps was 92.97 mph.

The fickle Manx weather changed yet again for the Wednesday and, with rain, drizzle and mist on the Mountain, the Lightweight 250 race was twice delayed, causing the afternoon's Senior TT to be postponed to the following day.

None of the competitors were very happy about the cold, damp conditions, especially the wet roads around the course.

Probably because of conditions, racing was extremely close, with Chas Mortimer, Mick Grant, Charlie Williams and Tom Herron, all riding Yamahas, mixing it for places on the leader board. Close behind came the winner of the Junior TT, Tony Rutter. On the fourth and last lap, Mick Grant made a supreme effort to catch the leader, Charlie Williams, and set the fastest lap speed of the race at 97.85 mph. But the effort was to no avail, because Williams finished 59.4 seconds ahead of Grant, who in turn ousted Mortimer from second place by 22 seconds. Williams' average speed for the race was 94.16 mph.

One of the changes from tradition in the 1974 TT week was the moving of the Senior race day from Friday to Wednesday but, with the event having to be postponed until Thursday, it meant that there was racing on every single day. The reason for the change-round was that the A-CU now considered the 'Open Formula 750 Classic International TT Race' to be the major attraction of the week. However, it was the Senior that had the attraction of the works' Suzuki 500-fours ridden by Paul Smart and Jack Findlay. In practice, Findlay had lapped at 106 mph, but Smart, who had to fly off to race in America in between practising for the TT and the Senior race day, was unhappy with the handling of his machine and had no time to solve the problem.

The main opposition to the works' Suzukis was the vast number of privateers on their 'stroked' Yamaha twins and, with riders of the calibre of Tony Rutter, Mick Grant, Charlie Williams, Barry

Randle and more besides, both Smart and Findlay were promised no easy victory.

The weather for the race was not much better than that of the previous day when the event had to be postponed. But shortly before the start, strong winds lifted the cloud and, after only a short delay, the competitors lined up on the starting grid.

On drying roads, Jack Findlay got away to a flying start and was soon involved in a scrap for leader board positions with a whole gaggle of Yamaha riders including Williams and Rutter. But Paul Smart, who was very unhappy with the performance of his machine, was almost touring on the first lap.

The high winds, that made riding over the Mountain extremely difficult, also brought back the rain at the end of the lap and Jack Findlay, who had fitted 'dry' tyres to his Suzuki just five minutes before the start of the race, found the high-speed, four-cylinder two-stroke almost unmanageable on the wet roads. He had to slow the pace and could do nothing to stay with the lighter, more manageable Yamaha twins.

At the end of the first lap Paul Smart pulled into retire leaving Jack Findlay to battle on against the weather and the flying Yamahas of Williams and Rutter.

On the second lap of the race, Williams established his lead by setting the fastest lap at a speed of 101.92 mph but, as weather conditions worsened, so Findlay dropped down to sixth place and finally retired. Because of the weather, the race length had been cut to five laps and, although Williams had set the fastest lap, it was Phil Carpenter who came storming through the rain to catch the leader and build up a 50-second advantage over the last lap to take the chequered flag at an average speed of 96.99 mph. Junior winner, Tony Rutter finished in third place, 2 minutes, 25.8 seconds behind Williams.

What was incredible about the result of the Senior TT was that the first full-sized 500 cc machine to finish the race was the Cowles-Matchless ridden by Selwyn Griffiths. Ahead of him were eight twin-cylinder Yamahas varying in capacity from 351 to 395 cc, indicating precisely how this Japanese manufacturer completely dominates the road-racing scene.

Yamaha machines also dominated the Lightweight 125 race, when they took the first four places in the Friday morning event which preceded the F750 'Classic'.

Austin Hockley was the rider to catch on the first lap because he rode his Granby-Yamaha to such good effect that, from a standing start, he set the fastest lap of the race at 88.78 mph. But both Clive Horton and Ivan Hodgkinson had Hockley in their sights on the second lap and, when Hockley's Yamaha failed, Horton took over the lead and promptly equalled Hockley's lap speed on his second circuit of the Mountain course.

Horton finished 40 seconds ahead of Hodgkinson to average 88.44 mph for the race. Third rider home was Tom Herron on another of the miniature Yamaha twins, 41.6 seconds behind Hodgkinson.

The final race of the week, and the one that everybody considered *the* 'Classic', was the Formula 750 race. The entry list looked formidable with Peter Williams and Dave Croxford riding the works' John Player Nortons, Jack Findlay on the works' Suzuki, Mick Grant on the Boyer Team Kawasaki, plus Chas Mortimer, Charlie Williams, Tony Rutter on their Yamahas and Percy Tait on the ex-works' Triumph triple.

Norton had scored a 1-2 victory in the previous year's F750 race and, although the event had been extended to six laps for this year, nobody really thought that the Nortons would have any problem lasting the distance. But nothing could have been further from the truth, because both machines failed before Ramsey with piston trouble.

This left Percy Tait on the Triumph 750 and Mick Grant on the Kawasaki to take on yet another swarm of 350 Yamahas, with Chas Mortimer and Charlie Williams leading the pack, followed by Tony Rutter and Billy Guthrie. Throughout the race the leader board constantly changed as riders pulled into refuel and lost vital seconds in the pits.

But on this day, it was Chas Mortimer's race. The difficult-to-handle Kawasaki 750 was no match for the lighter Yamahas over the tortuous $37\frac{3}{4}$-mile circuit and, when it started to rain, Mick Grant, who was riding with his right arm in plaster, found the super-powerful Kawasaki far too much to handle.

Meanwhile, Percy Tait was having a race-long dice with Tony Rutter for third spot and Charlie Williams was intent on catching Chas Mortimer. On the last lap, Williams got a pit signal that Mortimer was less than half a minute in the lead and, in a superb effort which gave him the fastest lap of the race at 106.61 mph, Williams came within 8.6 seconds of catching the winner. Tony Rutter was also able to pull sufficient out on the last lap over Percy Tait to take third place by 34.2 seconds. In fact, Billy Guthrie almost pipped Percy Tait at the post when he finished only one second behind the veteran road racer.

And so ended the 1974 Isle of Man TT week, with Chas Mortimer averaging 100.52 mph over the six laps of the Formula 750 Classic International TT Race, to earn a £1,000 for his efforts.

In spite of the atrocious weather, the racing proved a tremendous success and offered entertainment second to none for the thousands of visitors who made their annual pilgrimage to see the greatest road racing in the world.

The Isle of Man is steeped in racing tradition. It is an Island full of memories, some sad, some glad, some of complete disappointment, but above all it is an Island of sweet jubilation for the victors and those who have conquered the Mountain Circuit.

# CHAPTER EIGHT
# All-time greats

WINNING A TT is to the majority of racing motor-cyclists the supreme ambition in their career. In the long history of the races, only about 120 men have had the skill, ability and occasionally the good fortune to win one or more of the TT races.

By its very nature, the TT circuit demands the utmost from both competitors and their racing machines. There is no easy road to victory and even to win a TT replica or a finisher's award requires a thorough knowledge of the circuit, superb riding ability and, of course, a well-prepared and reliable machine.

Races have been won and lost by a slight mis-judgment in braking or the failure of a sparking plug or chain. Indeed, many of the men who have won a TT would admit that, but for the mis-fortunes of one or two other competitors, they would never have had the honour of wearing the winner's garland.

It would, of course, be quite wrong to say that TT victories are more a matter of luck than skill, because there are a number of men who have com-peted on the Isle of Man and scored such out-standing successes that their achievements raise them head and shoulders above all others. Choosing just a handful of men from all the great riders and World Champions who have raced on the Island is extremely difficult, but fortunately each era seems to produce a 'natural', a rider of such remarkable ability that, so far as all other competitors are concerned, he is the man to beat, the rider with an in-born talent for extracting 100 per cent-plus from his machine, no matter what the circumstances or conditions.

## Charlie Collier

Probably the first of these naturally talented riders was Charles Richard Collier who, with his elder brother Harry, was responsible for the development and tremendous success of Matchless motorcycles. With their father Harry A. Collier, they had begun manufacturing motorcycles as early as 1899 at Plumstead in London.

Almost immediately, the brothers saw the value of motorcycle sport and competition, not only as a means of developing and testing any new designs, but also as the best way of promoting their com-pany's products. Even prior to the first TT races in 1907, Charlie Collier competed in events for touring motorcycles and had represented Great Britain for three successive years in the International Cup races run in Europe. In fact, it was also partly due to his instigation that the Marquis de Mouzilly St Mars donated the magnificent trophy for the Isle of Man TT races and it was only fitting that, in 1907, Charlie Collier should have been the first-ever recipient of the trophy, for winning the single-cylinder class, riding his 431 cc Matchless.

Charlie Collier's achievements in TT racing on the Isle of Man span a relatively brief seven-year period from 1907 to 1914, when the First World War interrupted proceedings, but his prowess as an engineer and rider made him the first of the all-time great TT exponents.

After winning in 1907, Collier finished second to Jack Marshall (Triumph) the following year. Then, after retiring in the 1909 event, which his brother Harry won for Matchless, Charlie came storming back to win the 1910 event at the record speed of 50.63 mph.

In his first race 'over the Mountain' in 1911, Charlie Collier had what was probably the most disappointing ride in his Isle of Man career. Riding his belt-driven Matchless, he displayed his outstanding ability by splitting the far superior Indian chain-driven machines to finish second in the Senior; but he was disqualified for 'unofficially' taking on fuel.

The following year, Charlie finished fourth on his Matchless and this was to be his last successful ride in a TT, because in 1913 and 1914 he retired with machine failure in both events. However, the lessons both he and his brother Harry (who died in 1944) learned on the Isle of Man enabled them to establish Matchless as one of the truly great motor-cycles in British history.

Apart from being one of the pioneers who put

the TT on the map, so far as the world of motor-cycle sport was concerned, Charlie Collier never lost his interest in motorcycles nor his sympathy with motorcyclists, and was a keen rider all his life. In August 1954 he died suddenly, aged 69, in his managing director's office in the Matchless/AJS factory at Plumstead.

## Howard Davies

Although the First World War interrupted the Isle of Man races from 1914 to 1920, Howard R. Davies was among a considerable brigade of riders who competed both before and after the hostilities. Like Charlie Collier, Davies was an outstanding motorcycle engineer and, although he initially rode for Sunbeam in 1914, when he was 18, and A. J. Stevens (AJS) in 1920, he also produced the famous range of HRD motorcycles.

In his very first ride over the Mountain Circuit in 1914, Howard Davies proved his ability by finishing second in the Senior TT, tying with O. C. Godfrey at a speed of 48.50 mph. After the First World War, Howard joined AJS as competitions manager and team rider, but retired in both Junior and Senior TTs in 1920. He thereupon redesigned the frames.

However, 1921 was perhaps the most out-standing year in his Isle of Man career, because he became the first and only man ever to win the Senior TT riding a 350 cc machine! In fact, using the same engine in a different frame, he had also finished second in the Junior event behind his AJS team-mate, Eric Williams.

Davies learned a great deal about motorcycle design during his stay with the A. J. Stevens factory and, after retiring in every race from 1922 to 1924, he appeared on the Island with his own HRD machines. It was a fantastic debut for Howard, because not only did he finish second in the Junior, but he also won the Senior at the first attempt on a machine of his own design. A lapse of only eight months from production launching to Island victory must surely be a record!

Howard Davies continued to manufacture and race his own machines up until 1927 and, although he had no further success on the Isle of Man, due to mechanical trouble, another rider, Freddie Dixon, won the 1927 Junior and was sixth in the Senior on the HRD marque. At this point, Howard gave up building motorcycles, although he did remain in close contact with the motorcycle industry. In fact, in the mid-1930s, there was a revival of the HRD name when Philip Vincent began production of the now world-famous Phil Irving-designed HRD

500 cc single-cylinder and 1,000 cc V-twin machines. It was a Vincent-HRD 500 cc bike that gave John Surtees his first road-racing successes in the early 1950s, but that's another story.

## Freddie Dixon

A contemporary of Howard Davies who really set the TT circuit alight with his fiery riding style in both solo and sidecar events was 'Fearless' Freddie Dixon. He first raced on the Island in 1912, when he retired on his Cleveland machine with mechanical trouble. In fact, his next appearance on the Mountain Circuit was not until 1920, when he returned to ride a single-cylinder Indian machine into 12th place.

The following year, still riding for Indian, he was runner-up to Howard Davies' 350 AJS. However, Freddie continued campaigning Indian mounts until 1923, when he not only finished third in the Senior TT, but also won the first-ever Sidecar race with his famous 'banking' Douglas outfit. The machine was banked by the passenger raising or lowering the sidecar wheel axle and, because the officials were a little dubious about its handling capabilities, they demanded that Freddie should give them a demonstration on the Glencrutchery Road.

The observers, who had taken up a vantage point in the middle of the road so as to get a good view of the outfit, did not expect Dixon to hurtle towards them at almost race speed. Then, as they were leaping for their lives, Freddie calmly braked to about 20 mph and promptly did a U-turn in the road. Needless to say, the outfit was declared controllable and fit for racing.

Freddie Dixon was, of course, the only TT rider to have the unique distinction of winning both solo and sidecar races on the Isle of Man, and he con-tinued to race in both classes until the first Sidecar TT series was disbanded in 1925.

Riding a 350 HRD, developed and built by his old racing rival, Howard Davies, Freddie won the 1927 Junior TT and also finished sixth in the Senior on a 500 cc version. He returned to Douglas raceware for 1928, but it was to be his last season on bikes because, after finishing 18th in the Junior and retiring in the Senior, he approached Riley cars and convinced them that he was the greatest driver they had ever encountered. Unable to offer him a works' drive, they sold him a 'sports racer' which he promptly set to work on, determined to beat the factory's cars, which he did on many occasions.

Because his home for many years was in Middles-brough, Freddie Dixon was frequently claimed by

Yorkshiremen as one of their own folk. In fact, he was born in Stockton-on-Tees, Co Durham, where his first TT mount, the Cleveland, was built.

Outwardly an extrovert with a sometimes almost alarming zest for life, Freddie had a highly developed mechanical mind and his prime interest in racing was really with the technical aspects of the game. As he was wont to observe, it was just a bit of luck that he could also ride and drive!

## Jimmie Simpson

Another individual who earned tremendous respect as a rider on the Isle of Man was Jimmie Simpson and this was in spite of his winning only one TT, the 1934 Lightweight event on a Rudge.

His career began in 1922 and he rode in 26 Isle of Man races but only managed to finish in 11. He was one of the unluckiest riders because, although he made eight fastest laps, while leading the races he repeatedly struck mechanical trouble and failed to finish. In his first TT he rode a Scott in the Senior but had to retire at the end of the first lap due to a split petrol tank. From 1923 to 1928, Jimmie Simpson rode AJS machines in the Senior, Junior and Sidecar TTs; he was third in the Junior and fifth in the Sidecar races of 1925, second in the Junior of 1926, third in the Junior of 1927, but all his other rides for AJS in the Senior and Junior races up to and including 1928 ended in retirements.

In 1929 Jimmie transferred his allegiance to Norton and rode for them until his retirement from road racing in 1934. Even with a change of machinery his record was still blighted with Island ill-luck and his first reasonable result for Norton was a third place in the 1930 Senior. In 1931 he finished eighth in the Junior but retired in the Senior; then in 1932 he was third in the Senior but retired in the Junior!

His overseas Grand Prix record, however, was not plagued with the same amount of misfortune and he won many international road races on the Continent.

In 1933 Simpson scored his highest TT placing to date, a second spot in the Senior race, but once again he failed to finish in the Junior. Then, in 1934, he had his most outstanding season of all, winning six International Grands Prix, the Lightweight 250 TT on a Rudge, plus second places in both Junior and Senior races on Nortons.

Jimmie Simpson will always be remembered as the first rider to lap the Mountain Circuit at over 60 mph (the 1924 Junior), at over 70 mph (the 1926 Senior) and at over 80 mph (the 1931 Senior). Like many riders of his day, Jimmie was a completely versatile competitor who raced a sidecar outfit, rode solos and was also very successful in hill-climbs and sprints. In fact he also successfully competed in reliability trials.

When he retired from racing, Jimmie Simpson became motorcycle competitions manager for Shell-Mex and BP. A founder-member of the TT Riders' Association, he now lives in Cornwall.

## Stanley Woods

Whereas Jimmie Simpson never gained the number of wins he deserved on the Isle of Man, one of his contemporaries, and often a team-mate, strung up no fewer than ten in a career that spanned 17 years.

His name is Stanley Woods, a soft-spoken Irishman from Dublin, who competed in his first TT at 17 years of age, riding a Cotton in the Junior race. Had his machine not caught fire at a pit stop, Woods might well have won his first TT race; as it was, he continued without brakes to finish fifth!

Stanley Woods raced a variety of machines throughout his Isle of Man career. During 1924 and 1925 he rode Cotton, New Imperial, Scott and Royal Enfield models; then, in 1926, he was offered works' machines by Norton. This was perfectly understandable when one considers that he had won the Junior TT at his second attempt in 1923.

In his first race for the Bracebridge Street factory, he won the 1926 Senior but was not to score another victory for them until six years later. However, Woods' true potential was magnificently demonstrated in the TT races of 1932 and 1933. In what must be considered as one of the highlights of his racing career, he became the first rider ever to score a double 'double'! The incredible Irishman roared to victory in both Junior and Senior TTs in two consecutive years! Thus began a run of success which has only been bettered by one TT rider, the great Mike Hailwood.

Stanley Woods was practically invincible and only through machine failure did it appear that anyone could hope to beat him to the chequered flag. Surprisingly, after such tremendous success with Norton, Stanley went 'foreign' in 1934 when he rode an Italian Guzzi into fourth place in the Lightweight TT and retired while leading the Senior on the Swedish Husqvarna V-twin. His machine ran out of fuel on the last lap.

Woods scored another double in 1935, this time in the Lightweight and Senior TTs while riding for Moto Guzzi. Then, in 1936, he transferred to the Velocette factory team and finished second in the

**Right** *Aviating at Ballaugh. Hailwood gave MV Agusta four TT victories on the Island and taught team-mate Agostini almost everything he knew about the tricky TT circuit.*

**Below** *Probably the ultimate in man and machinery on the Island: Mike Hailwood aboard the Honda 250 six-cylinder Grand Prix machine on which he won the 1967 Lightweight 250 TT. Here Mike accelerates out of the Gooseneck on the climb up the Mountain.*

D

**Left** *Phil Read, World Champion for MV Agusta in 1973 and 1974, made his name on the Isle of Man where, after winning the Manx Grand Prix in 1960, he rode to victory in the Junior TT the following year. He then joined the Yamaha works' team and gained TT victories in the Lightweight 125 class in 1965, 1967 and 1968, with further victories on his own privately entered machines in the Lightweight 250 TTs of 1971 and 1972.*

**Below** *Phil Read rounding Ballacraine on the 350 MV.*

**Right** *Giacomo Agostini proved a very apt pupil as team-mate to Hailwood in the MV Agusta camp. Also, with the exception of Hailwood, he is the only man to have lapped the Mountain Circuit at over 108 mph! Ten TT successes came his way when Hailwood went car racing, all of them on MV Agustas. Now he no longer rides on the Island, where he earned much of his fame, but continues on the GP circuits for Yamaha.*

**Below** *A lap of 108.49 mph on his MV 500-three in the Senior TT of 1967 almost brought Giacomo Agostini victory against the Honda of Mike Hailwood, but a broken rear chain put him out of the running!*

**Left** *Five feet of sheer guts and determination, Bill Ivy, as a Yamaha teamster in 1968, achieved the incredible Lightweight lap record of 100.32 mph for a 125 cc machine, and 105.51 mph from a standing start on the 250 Yamaha four-cylinder two-stroke! Both records still stand to date and it was a great loss to road racing when little Bill was killed in the East German Grand Prix the following year.*

**Below** *High-speed action with Bill Ivy aboard the Yamaha 250-four in 1968. On this machine, Ivy literally kicked himself off walls and banks to hurtle around the TT circuit from a standing start at over 105 mph and gain his second TT victory.*

**Above** *The wheel turned full circle when production machine racing returned to the Island in 1967. On basically fully equipped roadsters, competitors astounded critics by lapping at nearly 100 mph in the 750 class, over 90 mph in the 500 class and almost 90 mph with the Lightweight 250 cc machines, not much slower than the tuned GP racers! Here is Keith Heckles (Velocette Thruxton) in action.*

**Right** *End of an era! Giacomo Agostini pushes off his MV Agusta in the Senior TT of 1972, the last race on the Island in which MV and Agostini were to compete, because of Agostini's claims that the circuit was too dangerous. Pushing alongside Agostini is long-time supporter of the TT, Bill Smith and his Kawasaki. Look closely and in the background you may see Reg Armstrong, Geoff Duke and ex-Shell competitions manager, Lou Ellis.*

Present-day TT heroes!

**Above** *Chas Mortimer set fastest lap of 106.39 mph on his Yamaha two-stroke twin in the 1974 Junior.*

**Left** *Charlie Williams won the 1974 Lightweight 250 TT on a Dugdale-Yamaha two-stroke twin. Here he rounds Quarter Bridge.*

**Above** *Stanley Woods (Suzuki) and Tony Rutter (Yamaha), both TT winners on the Island, push off at the start of the 1973 Senior.*

**Right** *Mick Grant finished second in both Junior and Lightweight 250 races in 1974 and won the 1,000 cc class of the Production TT.*

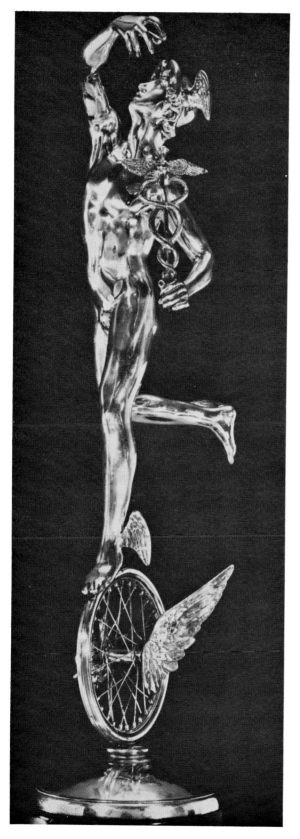

**Above** *Peter Williams, Norton works' rider and development engineer, is probably one of the most outstanding TT exponents today.*

**Left** *The trophy presented by the Marquis de Mouzilly St Mars. It is awarded to the winner of the Senior TT.*

Senior TT after retiring in the Junior. He also rode the German DKW two-stroke in the Lightweight race, but failed to finish.

He remained faithful to Velocette until his retirement from road racing in 1939 and he brought great success to the Hall Green, Birmingham, factory in their constant struggle with the Nortons from Bracebridge Street.

Although he did not contest another TT after his 1939 Junior victory and Senior fourth place, Stanley has never really given up motorcycling. Post war, he rode in trials and scrambles in Ireland, Scotland and England, and those who witnessed the occasion will never forget the surprise he sprang in the 1957 Golden Jubilee TT practising period, when he appeared without warning as a Guzzi reserve rider. Although he had not ridden the circuit for 18 years, and at the age of 51, he turned in laps at over 80 mph!

There has never been a more popular rider with TT fans than Stanley. From the very start of his career he was the special idol of the Scouts who manned the scoreboard. He presented them with tins of toffee; his father, who encouraged him to go racing, was a traveller for Mackintosh.

## Jimmy Guthrie

One of the few contemporaries of Woods who was capable of challenging, and occasionally beating, him was the superb and determined rider, Jimmy Guthrie. A native of Hawick in Scotland, Jimmy G first competed on the Island in 1923, riding a Matchless, but he failed to finish the race. In fact, he did not return to race again until 1927, when he retired in the Junior TT, but gave ample proof of his ability by finishing second in the Senior on the larger of his brace of New Hudsons.

In 1928 and 1929, Guthrie rode Nortons but without success, failing to finish in any of the three races he entered. Indeed, he had to wait until 1930 for his first TT win, and this was in the Lightweight 250 race, riding for AJS. Unfortunately, Jimmy G still failed to finish in either the Junior or Senior events.

The following year, Guthrie became a Norton teamster, with the opportunity of riding an OK-Supreme in the Lightweight event. Still the elusive win in the larger capacity classes did not materialise, because in 1932 it was Stanley Woods who beat him into second place in the Senior, which was disappointing after Guthrie had been forced to retire with mechanical trouble in the Junior. But still he persevered with Norton and, in fact, continued to ride for the Bracebridge Street factory

until his fatal crash while leading the 1937 German Grand Prix.

As a team rider, Jimmy G was second to none and, with a third place in the Junior of 1933 and a fourth position in the Senior, it was obvious that even greater TT success was not far away. He had been producing outstanding performances in the Continental Grands Prix and when he returned to the Island in 1934 it all happened for the superb Scottish road racer; he scored his first TT double by winning both Junior and Senior races!

He almost repeated the performance the following year when he won the Junior and was cheered in as winner of the Senior race, only to be told later that Stanley Woods had pipped him at the post by a mere four seconds!

The racing between Woods and Guthrie was marvellous and in 1936 Jimmy reversed the Senior result of the previous year, when he beat Woods by only eight seconds. Unfortunately, due to chain trouble, the best Jimmy could manage in the Junior was a fifth place.

However, Jimmy Guthrie won the Junior of 1937, but in the Senior he retired at The Cutting, just before the Mountain Mile, and this is the spot where, as a tribute to a really fabulous motorcyclist, the Guthrie Memorial was erected. As a Norton team rider in 14 TTs, Jimmy never finished in lower than fifth place and retired only twice. So high was his reputation as a rider and a sportsman that his death was lamented in newspapers all around the world.

## Freddie Frith

The link-man in the story of the all-time greats must be that classically stylish rider, Freddie Frith of Grimsby. Following the untimely death of Jimmy Guthrie, it was he who had the monumental task of competing against the almost invincible Stanley Woods.

Freddie Frith was one of the Manx Grand Prix 'school' of riders and, after winning the Junior and finishing second in the Senior MGP of 1935, he was snapped up by Norton to support Jimmy G. The outcome was that, if and when Guthrie failed, it was Frith who succeeded. This proved to be the case in Freddie's first TT in 1936, when he won the Junior for Norton.

Then, in 1937, after finishing second to Guthrie in the Junior, Frith rose to the occasion in the Senior when the Scot retired with engine trouble and, in a meteoric last-lap challenge to the leader of the race, Stanley Woods, Freddie clocked the first-ever over-90 mph lap of the Mountain Circuit at 90.27 mph, to beat Woods by 15 seconds. This gave Frith his first Senior TT victory and, quite surprisingly, his last, because in 1938 the best he could manage was third place in both Junior and Senior races. Then, in 1939, just prior to the beginning of the war, Freddie retired with machine trouble in the Junior and finished third in the Senior. He and Harold Daniell were using the 1938 mounts without works' support.

It was to be another nine years before Frith was to compete in the TT races again. A practice crash kept him out of the 1947 events and in 1948 he rode for the Mansell-Spring équipe on Velocette and Triumph machines. Freddie had lost none of his old skill and won the Junior on the Velocette, though he failed to finish on the Triumph in the Senior.

The seal of success to Freddie Frith's racing career came in 1949 when, after yet again winning the Junior TT on a Velocette but failing to finish on the 500 cc version, he went on to win the World 350 cc Road Racing Championship. At the end of the season, he decided to retire and as an appreciation for his services to the sport, and upholding British prestige overseas, he was awarded the OBE (Order of the British Empire), becoming the first motorcyclist to be so honoured.

Hanging up his helmet was not the end of TT interest for Freddie Frith. Over the years this one-time stonemason's apprentice has given invaluable help and advice to the A-CU and the Isle of Man authorities and he rarely misses a visit to Douglas in June.

## Geoff Duke

The next brilliant, natural rider and superb stylist to arrive on the TT scene was Geoffrey Duke. Like all the 'aces' who had gone before, Duke had that magic something which was patently obvious even in his first race on the Island, the 1948 Manx Grand Prix. He had entered the GP on a Norton for 'a bit of fun' and, although it was his first road race, he led right up until the last lap when a split oil tank caused his motor to seize.

Geoff Duke learned to ride a motorcycle as a despatch rider with the Royal Signals and, on his demob after the Second World War, had taken up trials riding with outstanding success. But a hankering for speed led him into road racing and, after that near-success in his first race, he decided to return in 1949, determined to win the Manx Grand Prix. However, there was another race on the Island which he could enter before the Grand Prix in September; this was the Clubman's TT and

Geoff proved that he was 'a natural' by storming to victory in the Clubman's Senior race on a 500 cc International Norton.

Winning the Clubman's TT in 1949 gave Duke an automatic entry into the Manx Grand Prix of that year and, with meticulous care, he rode around the Mountain Circuit on his trials bike, studying each and every section of the course in preparation for the races.

Geoff started among the favourites to win the September races and, on his second appearance in the MGP, he almost did the 'double', finishing second in the Junior and first in the Senior. That was good enough so far as the Norton team was concerned and Duke was immediately signed up to ride works' mounts the following season.

In 1950, on the new Featherbed Nortons, Duke had a fantastically successful year, including winning the Senior TT, and in this event, which brought him his third Senior trophy in one year, he became the first rider to average over 90 mph for seven laps of the Mountain Circuit. In the Junior TT, he finished second.

The most outstanding year in Geoff Duke's career was 1951, in which he won both the 500 cc and 350 cc World Road Racing Championships, was elected Sportsman of the Year and, in recognition of his outstanding ability, was presented with the Segrave Trophy. He also became the second racing motorcyclist to be awarded the OBE.

On his way to winning the World Championships in 1951, Duke accomplished the TT double, winning both Senior and Junior events at race and lap record speeds. His success with Norton continued in 1952 when yet again he won the Junior TT and went on to win the 350 cc World Championship. However, in the Senior race of that year he had retired with clutch trouble.

At the end of 1952, Geoff was approached by the Gilera factory to ride their works' 500 cc four-cylinder machine and, realising that it was the only way he could continue winning Grands Prix, he signed for the Italian team for the 1953 season. However, while leading the Senior TT that year, on the fourth lap he was brought down by a patch of oil on the road at Quarter Bridge, and retired from the race.

In 1954 Norton works' rider Ray Amm was ahead of Duke and his Gilera in the Senior TT when the race was curtailed because of the atrocious weather conditions. Yet there was no disputing Geoff's superiority in 1955, when he roared to victory in the Senior and came within a fraction of being the first to lap the Mountain Circuit at 100 mph.

134

Unfortunately, later in the year at the Dutch Grand Prix, Duke was involved in a dispute with the organisers and was eventually suspended from racing. The result was that he missed the TTs of 1956 and also again in 1957, this time due to injury. In fact, 1955 was the last year that motorcycle enthusiasts were to see Geoff Duke aboard the Gilera 500-four on the Isle of Man, because the Italian company pulled out of racing at the end of 1957, leaving Duke without competitive machinery for the following season.

Geoff rode a works' BMW 500 in the 1958 Senior and a Reg Dearden Norton in the Junior, but without any success. In 1959 he had a final fling in the Junior TT, finishing fourth riding a Norton with a frame and suspension which he had developed himself. For Geoff Duke it was the end of a fabulous racing career. 'When racing stops being a challenge and it's no longer fun, then that's the time to give up', said Geoff, and that is precisely what he did!

But, like his fellow OBE holder, Freddie Frith, Geoff continued to give his services to the sport, a memorable example of his achievements being the selection of one of the toughest International Six Days Trial courses ever known, when the event was held on the Isle of Man, where Geoff now lives.

## John Surtees

Some people consider that, because Gilera and Moto Guzzi pulled out of Grand Prix racing in 1957, MV Agusta, and John Surtees in particular, had things very much their own way. But it should be remembered that South Londoner Surtees started his racing career at the age of 17, first on a Vincent 'Grey Flash' 500 and later transferring to Nortons. He was virtually unbeatable on Britain's short circuits and in 1954 he decided to tackle the TT Mountain Circuit.

Surtees earned two silver replicas in his first TTs by finishing 11th in the Junior and 15th in the Senior. It was not an unpromising start to his Isle of Man career, and his short circuit record showed he could be a winner; all that was needed was more experience on the Isle of Man.

Norton were prepared to take the gamble and, with works' machines for the 1955 races, the young Surtees rode splendidly against very strong competition in the Junior TT to finish fourth. Unfortunately, he struck trouble in the Senior and limped home a lowly 29th.

In 1956 John Surtees was approached by MV Agusta to race both 350 cc and 500 cc four-cylinder machines and immediately he proved his worth by

winning the Senior TT, but was disqualified from the Junior after accepting petrol from a spectator while leading on the last lap. The following year, John encountered the Isle of Man expertise of Bob McIntyre (Gilera) and had to be content with second place in the Senior behind the 'flying Scotsman'. In the Junior, the best Surtees could achieve was a fourth place.

But for John, better things were to come. After two years' experience of the big MV 'fire engines', 1958 was to prove his year. He won the Senior and Junior TTs and also claimed both the 350 cc and 500 cc World Championships. He repeated the process in 1959 and, to emphasise how popular this young rider was, he was voted 'Sportsman of the Year' by the Sports Writers' Association and by ballots organised by the *Daily Express* and BBC's *Sportsview*.

Surtees was the second man in the history of the TT to do the 'double-double' – winning both Senior and Junior races in two consecutive years. In fact, had he not struck mechanical trouble in the Junior TT of 1960, he would have been the first rider to do the hat-trick.

At the end of the 1960 season and at the height of his motorcycling reign, John Surtees decided to make the break from two wheels and accept the offer of a career in Grand Prix car racing. And, to stress his versatility and brilliance, he went on to win the Formula One World Championship; the only man to have won the premier titles in both car and motorcycle racing!

## Mike Hailwood

In 1958, the year when Surtees claimed his first TT double, there was a young, upcoming lad from Oxfordshire, by the name of Stanley Michael Bailey Hailwood, hoping to do well in his very first TT races on the Island. He was entered in all four solo classes and for him it was the start of a glorious Isle of Man career, unexcelled in the history of the races.

On his debut in 1958, he gained four TT replicas for finishing 13th in the Senior, 12th in the Junior, third in the Lightweight 250 and seventh in the Lightweight 125 races. At the age of 19, and with only two years' road-racing experience behind him, Mike Hailwood won all four solo A-CU Road Racing Stars (the equivalent of the British Championships). However, his return to the Island in 1959 was not so successful as in the previous year. He had entered in five solo races, including the new Formula 1 Junior event. But misfortune and machine failure dogged him and, apart from a third place in the Formula 1 350 race and a third spot in the Lightweight 125 TT, all other TTs that year brought retirements for Hailwood.

Meanwhile, back on the mainland, Mike was almost unbeatable on the short circuits. His 'Ecurie Sportive' Nortons were the pacemakers at practically every race meeting he attended and in 1960 he again scooped all four solo A-CU Road Racing Stars.

However, it was a bad year for Mike on the Island because he retired in three out of four TTs, with only the consolation of finishing third, behind the two MVs, in the Senior on the last race day of the week. But Hailwood's fame had spread far afield. The Japanese Honda factory were seeking likely lads in the Lightweight classes to ride their new and very fast Grand Prix racers, and for the 1961 season they lent Mike a 125 twin and a 250-four, though he was not a member of the pukka works' team.

With three years' TT experience, Mike was confident that he was in with a chance of winning some of the races during the 1961 TT week, but little did he know just how well he would do over the Mountain Circuit.

When he won the Lightweight 250 TT on Monday, Hailwood was very pleased, but in the Junior on Wednesday he was disappointed when the motor of his AJS 7R blew up on the last lap, especially as he had quite a substantial lead. On Friday morning the smile returned to Mike's face when he achieved his Lightweight TT double. He pipped Honda works' rider, Luigi Taveri, by 7.4 seconds to win the Lightweight 125 race.

But then the incredible, the historic happened; riding his Manx Norton in the afternoon's Senior, Hailwood romped home to win at an average speed of 100.60 mph, the first time that any British single-cylinder bike had averaged over the 'ton' in a TT race. Three victories in one week, and that same year Mike was to end the season as the 250 cc World Road Racing Champion and runner-up to Gary Hocking (MV) in the 500 cc World Championship!

Hailwood's rise to fame was nothing short of meteoric and Count Agusta, boss of the MV factory in Italy, decided that Mike was the big threat to MV's domination of the 500 and 350 World Championships. The Count offered Hailwood a very tempting contract to ride solely for MV in 1962, and the opportunity of winning the World 500 cc Road Racing Championship was something he could not disregard.

Mike teamed-up with Gary Hocking on the 350 and 500 cc MV Agusta-fours and there followed a battle on the world's Grand Prix circuits which dispelled anyone's ideas that the two MV men were riding to orders.

On the Island, Hailwood won the Junior TT and could well have ridden to victory in the Senior, except that he lost 12 minutes repairing a broken clutch. However, in spite of this, Mike still earned enough points at other GPs to realise his ambition – he became World 500 cc Road Racing Champion, a title he was to retain until he returned to the Honda team in 1966.

Throughout the 1963 and 1964 seasons, Mike was the lone MV works' rider and won practically every 350 and 500 cc race he entered. During this period, Hailwood won two Senior TTs and 500 cc World Championships but, with Honda making an entry into the 350 cc Grand Prix class, Jim Redman's machine proved lighter and faster than Mike's MV and he lost his claim to the 350 title.

In 1965 Mike was joined by a fast riding Italian named Giacomo Agostini. The Count saw a great future for his young protégé and, with Hailwood the master and Agostini the pupil, MV returned to the Island. As expected, Mike won the Senior easily, but broke down in the Junior.

When Honda offered to provide him with bikes for 250, 350 and 500 cc classes in the World Championships in 1966, Mike jumped at the chance. On the Isle of Man that year, he won the Senior TT and also the Lightweight 250 race, the latter at the incredible average speed of 101.79 mph. He almost completed the hat-trick, but his Honda failed in the Junior.

But, so far as TT history is concerned, 1967 must be considered Mike Hailwood's finest year, a year when he surely earned the title 'the fastest TT rider in the world'.

In the Lightweight 250 race it was Hailwood on Honda versus Phil Read on Yamaha; in the Junior it was Hailwood on Honda versus Agostini on MV; and in the Senior it was Hailwood versus his own ill-mannered, brutish Honda against Agostini and his smooth-handling MV Agusta!

In the 250 TT, Mike disposed of all opposition and romped home to win at an average speed of 103.07 mph. The story was the same in the Junior where he showed Agostini a clean set of meggas and put up a yet-to-be-broken lap record, from a standing start, of 107.73 mph!

But his finest hour came on the Friday of that TT week when he fought the wild-handling Honda 500-four over every yard of the 226.4-mile race to win at an average speed of 105.62 mph and set the still-standing lap record of 108.77 mph! It was Hailwood's second TT hat-trick and his 12th TT victory, and also his last ride on the Isle of Man.

At the end of 1967 Honda dropped out of Grand Prix racing and paid Hailwood *not* to ride any other machine in the World Championships in 1968. And, with Japanese factories leaving the GP scene, the Isle of Man TT lost this great rider to the world of motor racing.

## Giacomo Agostini

Where Mike Hailwood left off in the Junior and Senior TTs, Giacomo Agostini took over. Whether the Italian would have remained supreme until his last race on the Island in 1972 had Mike Hailwood continued racing is debatable. But Agostini is without a doubt the greatest Italian rider ever to have mastered the TT circuit and the only man apart from Hailwood to have lapped the Mountain Circuit at over 108 mph.

The Italian MV 'ace' finished third in his first-ever TT in 1965 and the following year won the Junior race at an average speed of over 100 mph, setting a new lap record of 103.09 mph – certainly a remarkable achievement for a rider competing for only his second time on the Isle of Man!

Agostini was, of course, no newcomer to the two-wheeler world when he was signed up by Count Agusta. In 1963, he won the Italian 175 cc Road Racing Championship, and in 1964 he captured the 250 cc Italian Championship. Then, in 1965, when he clinched the 500 cc Championship, the Count knew that he had found the man to achieve his

great ambition – an Italian rider on an Italian motorcycle winning the premier title in Grand Prix motorcycle racing.

Without opposition from Hailwood and Honda, the Junior and Senior TTs became very much a procession of victories for the handsome Italian. Indeed, from 1968 until his withdrawal from racing on the Island in 1972, Ago won all Senior and Junior TTs with the exception of the 1971 Junior, when his MV failed to complete the course.

In 1968 Agostini cracked Hailwood's race record for the Junior TT with a six-lap average of 104.78 mph, and that was without pressure from any other competitors. In the Senior TT of 1969, he 'cruised' the MV home at an average of 104.75 mph for the six-lap race. And so it went on for five years with Ago and MV picking up the Junior and Senior TT laurels with not a challenger in sight.

Then, in 1972, tragedy once again struck the Isle of Man. In the Lightweight 125 TT a fellow-Italian and friend of Agostini's, Angello Parlotti, was fatally injured whilst leading the race. After the Senior TT, which he won, Agostini vowed that he would never ride on the Isle of Man again. His courage and ability were never in question; Ago had proved to the world that he was as great as any other TT exponent. His decision to quit Island racing was purely personal. When you have won ten TTs and clocked up 65 racing laps of the TT course at over 100 mph, you must be good – and that is how Giacomo Agostini's Isle of Man record stands today.

# CHAPTER NINE

# It's a fact...

## Bookies at the TT races!

In the 1920s and early 1930s, on the green behind the grandstand on the Glencrutchery Road, there were a number of bookmakers prepared to take bets on the outcome of the races. Among the more notorious present were Long John Silver of Brooklands fame and Albert Milner, an ex-Levis TT rider. However, the bookies' experiment was short-lived because, unlike horse racing, the TT results were much easier to predict and the cash flowed the wrong way, as far as the bookies were concerned.

## The only woman

Women are now banned from holding International Competition Licences for solo road racing and, consequently, only one woman has ever competed in a race for solo machines on the Isle of Man. Her name was Beryl Swain and in 1962 she rode an Itom into 22nd place in the 50 cc TT over two laps of the Mountain Circuit. The following year, the FIM barred women from racing in solo International events and, because of her unique entry in the Isle of Man TTs, Beryl attracted almost as much attention from radio and press as the great Mike Hailwood.

## Men on the map

Six men and six men alone, all of whom earned the undying respect of their fellow TT riders, are rightly and justly honoured by having sections on the Mountain Circuit named after them. Walter Brandish is commemorated at Brandish Corner, Archie Birkin at Birkin's Bend, Walter Handley at Handley's Cottage, Bill Doran at Doran's Bend, and both Jimmy Guthrie and Les Graham have course-side memorials erected in their honour.

Brandish Corner, which is the fairly fast left-hander between Creg-ny-Baa and Hillberry, acquired its name when Walter Brandish, who had finished second in the 1922 Senior, crashed there during practice for the 1923 event and broke his leg.

Birkin's Bend, a fast, sweeping right- and left-hand section of the course about a mile beyond Kirkmichael, also earned its name following an accident during practice. This time it was between Archie Birkin and a fish lorry travelling the opposite way around the TT circuit. It was in 1927 and the roads at that time were not officially closed for practice, only for the racing itself.

Unfortunately, Archie Birkin could not see the tradesman's vehicle coming towards him as he negotiated the high-speed swervery on the racing line, and he was fatally injured in a head-on collision. Because of this tragic accident, it was decided that in future the roads would also be closed during all practice periods. The decision came too late to save Archie Birkin, but it has since benefited all other TT riders.

Except in the case of the Guthrie and Graham memorials, accidents or spills during practice or racing have led to these sections of the course being named after the poor unfortunates who came to grief there. Doran's Bend, the fast left-hander after Ballig Bridge, is another of these renowned course markers.

It was near here that the highly respected works' AJS rider, Bill Doran, crashed his machine during an evening practice session for the 1952 TT races. Actually, it was reported that Bill had crashed nearer Glen Helen than on the actual bend which bears his name. However, the spill, which sidelined him from both Junior and Senior races that year, was of sufficient notoriety for the press and public alike to acclaim the fast left-hander, which may have caused him to lose control of his machine, as 'Doran's Bend'!

Handley's Cottage is, of course, named after the all-time great TT exponent, Walter Handley. During 13 years' racing on the Island, competing in 28 races and winning four of them, Walter had more than his fair share of spills. His Isle of Man career began in 1922 when, in his very first race, he broke the Lightweight lap record from a standing start. Walter went on to break numerous lap records on OK Supreme, Rex-Acme and Rudge machines in all classes, but his twistgrip hand always seemed far stronger than the motorcycles it controlled. They often broke down.

Walter Handley's TT exploits were considerable and for this reason it is difficult to trace exactly what date and what machine he was riding when he came a purler at the tricky S-bend about a hundred yards short of the 12th Milestone, and now named Handley's Cottage. Knowing Walter Handley's fiery riding style, the spill must have been a beauty and many riders have since learned to respect this difficult spot on the course.

Six TT victories earned Scotsman Jimmy Guthrie a highly respected place among the greatest of Isle of Man riders. He made his debut in the Lightweight TT of 1923 but, with what was probably the fiercest ever competition from riders of the calibre of Stanley Woods, Alec Bennett, Walter Handley, Jimmie Simpson and Freddie Dixon, he had to persevere until 1930 before he claimed his first victory. In 1934, he accomplished the Senior-Junior 'double' and continued to win TTs right up until his untimely death at the German Grand Prix in 1937.

Because of his dedication to the sport, Guthrie's death shook the motorcycle world and, in remembrance of a truly great sportsman, it was decided to erect a memorial on the course to the brave Scot who gave everything, including his life, to motorcycling. What was once The Cutting, where Guthrie retired in the 1937 Senior TT, is now known as Guthrie's Memorial and on a clear day from this spot on the Mountain it is possible to see Guthrie's native Scotland.

A short distance from the Bungalow, nestling in the mountainside above Stone Bridge, is the Graham Memorial Hut. The sixth and most recent point around the TT circuit to earn its title from a famous Isle of Man road racer, the Graham Memorial honours Leslie Robert Graham, ex-RAF bomber pilot, ex-AJS works' rider and World Champion and, in 1953, works' rider of the MV Agusta four-cylinder 'fire engines'.

Chosen by the Italian factory to develop their high-speed racing machines, because of his Grand Prix success and outstanding ability on the Isle of Man, Les Graham poured all of his experience and knowledge into the MV racing department. In 1952, his efforts began to show effect when he finished second in the Senior TT but, after his one and only TT victory in the 125 event of 1953, he was tragically killed when he lost control of the big, four-cylinder 500 MV on the high-speed plunge down Bray Hill.

Six men, six names, all mapped on the TT circuit with pride. It isn't every season or even every generation that produces riders and sportsmen of their quality!

## Eight times around the mountain

To celebrate the Golden Jubilee of the TT races, in 1957 the Senior TT was run over eight laps of the Mountain Circuit. Some 302 miles had to be completed by the competitors and the race winner, Bob McIntyre, covered the distance in 3 hours, 2 minutes and 57 seconds to average 98.99 mph. He also set the first 100-mph lap with a new lap record of 101.12 mph on his 500 cc, four-cylinder Gilera.

## Five hours in the saddle

Time-wise, the longest race in the TT record book is the 1913 Senior which was held over six laps of the Mountain Circuit, three laps on one day and three the next. Tim Wood, the Scott works' rider, completed the 262½-mile race in 5 hours, 26 minutes and 18 seconds. However, it was not unusual around this time to have riders spending anything up to five non-stop hours in the saddle, riding over four or five laps of the Mountain Circuit, when it was little more than rutted, hard-packed mud roads and sheep tracks. The men had to be tough and their machines even tougher to complete the races.

## 67 years not out!

Norton is the only make of machine to have competed on the Island every year since the TT races began in 1907. They have also won more TTs than any other marque and have a record total of 36 wins to their credit. Next and very close to the Norton record comes the MV factory with 34 wins. However, MV only began their racing career on the Island in 1951 and gained their victories over a far shorter period of time.

## Mike the bike

The record for the greatest number of TT wins by one man is held by Stanley Michael Bailey Hailwood. His illustrious TT career began in 1958 and ended on his retirement from Grand Prix racing in 1967, during which period he scored 12 terrific Isle of Man victories. Mike 'the bike' Hailwood still holds the outright lap record of 108.77 mph for the Mountain Circuit. His closest rival in the TT wins stakes is Giacomo Agostini, who took the MV machines to ten Isle of Man victories to equal the great Stanley Woods' tally.

In the Sidecar TT, Siegfried Schauzu from West Germany has scored eight wins since he first appeared on the Island in 1966. Since 1967, except for two mechanical failures, Schauzu has finished either first or second in every TT he has entered. As both Hailwood and Agostini no longer race on the Island, there is a possibility that this outstanding sidecar driver could equal if not beat their number of wins!

## The only 350 Senior victory

Although the 1974 Senior TT was won by an 'over-stroked' 350 Yamaha two-stroke twin, the only genuine Junior machine to have won a Senior TT was the 348 cc AJS of Howard Davies. New for 1920, the overhead valve, push-rod AJS singles were way ahead of the opposition at that time and, apart from scooping five out of the first six places in the Junior TT, AJS also won the Senior race with Davies riding his Junior bike to a record-breaking victory at an average speed of 54.50 mph! It is the only time in the history of the TTs that a Junior machine has won the Senior race.

## Long-standing records

There are two solo class lap records on the Isle of Man that may never be broken; these are for the 50 cc and 125 cc races which have now been removed from the TT calendar. The first is held by Irishman Ralph Bryans, who in 1966 established the lap record for the 50 cc TT at an unbelievable 86.49 mph. The machine he rode was a marvel of mechanical engineering, being the double-overhead-camshaft, twin-cylinder Honda, which had a top speed approaching 110 mph! Even more incredible was the fact that the motor spun at anything up to 22,000 rpm.

The second record, and one which is just as outstanding, was that set in 1968 by little Billy Ivy on the works' four-cylinder, water-cooled Yamaha 125 two-stroke. His record lap of 100.32 mph was the first-ever 'over-the-ton' circuit of the TT course by a 125 cc machine, and nobody has achieved anywhere near the same speed since the withdrawal of the Japanese works' teams in 1968.

## The fastest single

Although in 1960 Derek Minter became the first rider ever to lap the Mountain Circuit at 'over-the-ton' on a single-cylinder motorcycle, it is Mike Hailwood who has set the fastest lap for a single. This was in 1961, when on a Manx Norton he lapped at 101.65 mph. The next fastest on a single is Peter Williams who, in 1967, lapped at 101.32 mph on the Arter-Matchless.

## The spikey Porcupine

Ever wondered how the AJS 'Porcupine' earned its nickname? In fact, if you ever see one of the original 1947 models on display, you will immediately know the reasons. The DOHC flat, parallel-twin, four-stroke 500 AJS had its cylinders both lying horizontal to the ground and, in order to aid cooling of the cylinder heads, dozens of sharp, spikey little radiating fins, or quills, poked forward from the cylinder heads. Consequently, it soon earned its nickname, 'porcupine'.

## Fuel for thought

With modern, racing two-strokes of 500 and 750 cc only covering between eight and 18 miles-per-gallon, it seems ridiculous that in 1907 the A-CU limited TT competitors to 75 miles-per-gallon for twin-cylinder machines and 90 miles-per-gallon for singles. Believe it or not, Charlie Collier won the first TT at an average speed of 38.23 mph with the remarkable fuel consumption of 94.5 miles-per-gallon. In fact, the following year, Jack Marshall on his Triumph went even better, to average 40.4 mph at an incredible 117.6 miles-per-gallon! The reason for this amazing economy from machines of that period was that tuning knowledge, including things such as valve overlap, was very limited and, consequently, the motors were extremely low-revving; 2,000 to 2,500 rpm was about their maximum. The result? Low revs, low fuel consumption!

# TT race results, 1907-1974

## 1907
**Twins 158½ miles**
1st H. Rem Fowler/Norton
4hr 21m 53s/36.22 mph
2nd W. H. Wells/Vindec
4hr 53m 4s/32.21 mph
3rd W. M. Heaton/Rex
5hr 11m 4s/28.50 mph
Fastest lap H. Rem Fowler/Norton
22m 6s/42.91 mph

**Singles 158½ miles**
1st C. R. Collier/Matchless
4hr 8m 8s/38.22 mph
2nd J. Marshall/Triumph
4hr 19m 47s/37.11 mph
3rd F. Hulbert/Triumph
4hr 27m 50s/35.89 mph
Fastest lap H. A. Collier/Matchless
23m 5s/41.81 mph

## 1908
**Twins 158½ miles**
1st H. Reed/DOT
4hr 5m 58s/38.59 mph
2nd W. H. Bashall/BAT
4hr 8m 15s/37.18 mph
3rd R. O. Clark/FN
4hr 11m 3s/36.19 mph
Fastest lap W. H. Bashall/BAT
22m 27s/42.25 mph

**Singles 158½ miles**
1st J. Marshall/Triumph
3hr 54m 50s/40.49 mph
2nd C. R. Collier/Matchless
3hr 57m 7s/40.01 mph
3rd Sir R. Arbuthnot/Triumph
4hr 7m 57s/38.22 mph
Fastest lap J. Marshall/Triumph
22m 20s/42.48 mph

## 1909
**158½ miles**
1st H. A. Collier/Matchless
3hr 13m 37s/49.01 mph
2nd G. L. Evans/Indian
3hr 17m 35s/47.28 mph
3rd W. F. Newsome/Triumph
3hr 31m 10s/45.88 mph
Fastest lap H. A. Collier/Matchless
18m 5s/52.27 mph

## 1910
**158½ miles**
1st C. R. Collier/Matchless
3hr 7m 24s/50.63 mph
2nd H. A. Collier/Matchless
3hr 12m 45s/48.61 mph
3rd W. Creyton/Triumph
3hr 17m 58s/46.28 mph

Fastest lap H. H. Bowen/BAT
17m 51s/53.15 mph

## 1911
**Senior 187½ miles**
1st O. C. Godfrey/Indian
3hr 56m 10s/47.63 mph
2nd C. B. Franklin/Indian
3hr 59m 52s/46.81 mph
3rd A. Moorhouse/Indian
4hr 5m 34s/45.39 mph
Fastest lap F. Philipp/Scott
44m 52s/50.11 mph

**Junior 150 miles**
1st P. J. Evans/Humber
3hr 37m 7s/41.45 mph
2nd H. A. Collier/Matchless
3hr 46m 20s/40.09 mph
3rd H. J. Cox/Forward
3hr 55m 56s/38.23 mph
Fastest lap P. J. Evans/Humber
53m 24s/42.00 mph

## 1912
**Senior 187½ miles**
1st F. A. Applebee/Scott
3hr 51m 8s/48.69 mph
2nd J. R. Haswell/Triumph
3hr 57m 57s/46.41 mph
3rd H. A. Collier/Matchless
4hr 1m 56s/44.89 mph
Fastest lap F. A. Applebee/Scott
45m 31s/49.44 mph

**Junior 150 miles**
1st W. H. Bashall/Douglas
3hr 46m 59s/39.65 mph
2nd E. Kickham/Douglas
3hr 51m 36s/37.58 mph
3rd H. J. Cox/Forward
4hr 6m 29s/34.27 mph
Fastest lap E. Kickham/Douglas
53m 53s/41.76 mph

## 1913
**Senior 262½ miles**
1st H. O. Wood/Scott
5hr 26m 18s/48.27 mph
2nd A. R. Abbott/Rudge
5hr 26m 23s/48.25 mph
3rd A. H. Alexander/Indian
5hr 30m 11s/46.10 mph
Fastest lap H. O. Wood/Scott
43m 10s/52.12 mph
**Junior 225 miles**
1st H. Mason/NUT
5hr 8m 34s/43.75 mph
2nd W. F. Newsome/Douglas
5hr 9m 30s/43.69 mph
3rd H. C. Newman/Ivy Green
5hr 23m 6s/41.57 mph
Fastest lap H. Mason/NUT
49m 32s/45.42 mph

## 1914
**Senior 225 miles**
1st C. G. Pullin/Rudge
4hr 32m 48s/49.49 mph
2nd= H. R. Davies/Sunbeam
4hr 39m 12s/48.50 mph
2nd= O. C. Godfrey/Indian
4hr 39m 12s/48.50 mph
Fastest lap H. O. Wood/Scott
42m 16s/53.50 mph

**Junior 187½ miles**
1st E. Williams/AJS
4hr 6m 50s/45.58 mph
2nd C. Williams/AJS
4hr 11m 34s/44.88 mph
3rd F. J. Walker/Royal Enfield
4hr 19m 55s/43.72 mph
Fastest lap E. Williams/AJS
47m 18s/47.57 mph

## 1920
**Senior 226½ miles**
1st T. C. De La Hay/Sunbeam
4hr 22m 23s/51.48 mph
2nd D. M. Brown/Norton
4hr 26m 15s/51 mph
3rd W. R. Brown/Sunbeam
4hr 32m 27s/49.68 mph
Fastest lap G. Dance/Sunbeam
40m 53s/55.62 mph

**Junior 350 cc 187½ miles**
1st C. Williams/AJS
4hr 37m 57s/40.74 mph
2nd J. Watson-Bourne/Blackburne
4hr 47m 7s/39.10 mph
3rd J. Holroyd/Blackburne
4hr 47m 37s/39.09 mph
Fastest lap E. Williams/AJS
44m 6s/51.36 mph

**Junior 250 cc 187½ miles**
1st R. O. Clark/Levis
4hr 55m 37s/38.30 mph
2nd G. Kuhn/Levis
35.61 mph
3rd F. W. Applebee/Levis
31.00 mph
Fastest lap R. O. Clark/Levis
52m 37s/43.00 mph

## 1921
**Senior 226½ miles**
1st H. R. Davies/AJS (350 cc)
4hr 9m 22s/54.50 mph
2nd F. W. Dixon/Indian
4hr 11m 35s/54.02 mph
3rd H. Le Vack/Indian
4hr 12m 6s/53.91 mph
Fastest lap F. G. Edmond/Triumph
40m 8s/56.40 mph

**Junior 350 cc 187½ miles**
**1st** E. Williams/AJS
3hr 37m 23s/52.11 mph
**2nd** H. R. Davies/AJS
3hr 41m 10s/51.20 mph
**3rd** T. M. Sheard/AJS
3hr 49m 9s/49.42 mph
**Fastest lap** H. R. Davies/AJS
41m 4s/55.15 mph

**Junior 250 cc 187½ miles**
**1st** D. G. Prentice/New Imperial
4hr 12m 37s/44.61 mph
**2nd** G. S. Davison/Levis
44.33 mph
**3rd** W. G. Harrison/Velocette
43.14 mph
**Fastest lap** B. Kershaw/New Imperial
49m 7s/46.11 mph

## 1922

**Senior 226½ miles**
**1st** A. Bennett/Sunbeam
3hr 53m 2s/58.31 mph
**2nd** W. Brandish/Triumph
4hr 0m 22s/56.52 mph
**3rd** H. Langman/Scott
4hr 2m 14s/56.09 mph
**Fastest lap** A. Bennett/Sunbeam
37m 46s/59.99 mph

**Junior 187½ miles**
**1st** T. M. Sheard/AJS
3hr 26m 38s/54.75 mph
**2nd** G. Grinton/AJS
3hr 37m 17s/53.00 mph
**3rd** J. Thomas/Sheffield-Henderson
3hr 47m 28s/50.00 mph
**Fastest lap** H. Le Vack/New Imperial
40m 7s/56.46 mph

**Lightweight 187½ miles**
**1st** G. S. Davison/Levis
3hr 46m 56s/49.89 mph
**2nd** D. Young/Rex-Acme
4hr 0m 17s/47.12 mph
**3rd** S. J. Jones/Velocette
4hr 1m 31s/46.90 mph
**Fastest lap** W. L. Handley/OK
44m 24s/51.00 mph

## 1923

**Senior 226½ miles**
**1st** T. M. Sheard/Douglas
4hr 4m 43s/55.55 mph
**2nd** G. M. Black/Norton
4hr 6m 26s/55.14 mph
**3rd** F. W. Dixon/Indian
4hr 7m 2s/55.00 mph
**Fastest lap** J. Whalley/Douglas
37m 54s/59.74 mph

**Junior 226½ miles**
**1st** S. Woods/Cotton
4hr 3m 47s/55.73 mph
**2nd** H. F. Harris/AJS
4hr 6m 16s/55.16 mph
**3rd** A. H. Alexander/Douglas
4hr 9m 35s/54.43 mph
**Fastest lap** J. H. Simpson/AJS
38m 0s/59.59 mph

**Lightweight 226½ miles**
**1st** J. A. Porter/New Gerrard
4hr 21m 37s/51.93 mph
**2nd** H. Le Vack/New Imperial

4hr 26m 19s/51.01 mph
**3rd** D. Hall/Rex-Acme
4hr 34m 20s/49.53 mph
**Fastest lap** W. L. Handley/OK
41m 58s/53.95 mph

**Sidecar 113½ miles**
**1st** F. W. Dixon/Douglas
2hr 7m 48s/53.15 mph
**2nd** G. W. Walker/Norton
2hr 9m 26s/52.50 mph
**3rd** G. H. Tucker/Norton
2hr 10m 27s/52.07 mph
**Fastest lap** H. Langman/Scott
41m 24s/54.69 mph

## 1924

**Senior 226½ miles**
**1st** A. Bennett/Norton
3hr 40m 24s/61.64 mph
**2nd** H. Langman/Scott
3hr 41m 51s/61.23 mph
**3rd** F. W. Dixon/Douglas
3hr 45m 46s/60.17 mph
**Fastest lap** F. W. Dixon/Douglas
35m 31s/63.75 mph

**Junior 226½ miles**
**1st** K. Twemlow/New Imperial
4hr 4m 21s/55.67 mph
**2nd** S. Ollerhead/DOT
4hr 7m 26s/54.91 mph
**3rd** H. R. Scott/AJS
4hr 9m 1s/54.55 mph
**Fastest lap** J. H. Simpson/AJS
35m 5s/64.54 mph

**Lightweight 226½ miles**
**1st** E. Twemlow/New Imperial
4hr 5m 3s/55.44 mph
**2nd** H. F. Brockbank/Cotton
4hr 17m 5s/52.85 mph
**3rd** J. Cooke/DOT
4hr 18m 33s/52.54 mph
**Fastest lap** E. Twemlow/New Imperial
38m 51s/58.28 mph

**Ultra-lightweight 113½ miles**
**1st** J. A. Porter/New Gerrard
2hr 12m 40s/51.20 mph
**2nd** F. G. Morgan/Cotton
2hr 17m 11s/49.51 mph
**3rd** C. Stead/Cotton
2hr 17m 39s/49.34 mph
**Fastest lap** J. A. Porter/New Gerrard
43m 2s/52.61 mph

**Sidecar 151 miles**
**1st** G. H. Tucker/Norton
2hr 56m 31s/51.31 mph
**2nd** H. Reed/DOT
3hr 26m 46s/43.80 mph
**3rd** A. Tinkler/Matador
3hr 33m 3s/42.49 mph
**Fastest lap** F. W. Dixon/Douglas
42m 32s/53.23 mph

## 1925

**Senior 226½ miles**
**1st** H. R. Davies/HRD
3hr 25m 25.8s/66.13 mph
**2nd** F. A. Longman/AJS
3hr 29m 10s/64.95 mph
**3rd** A. Bennett/Norton
3hr 30m 8s/64.65 mph
**Fastest lap** J. H. Simpson/AJS
32m 50s/68.97 mph

**Junior 226½ miles**
**1st** W. L. Handley/Rex-Acme
3hr 28m 56.4s/65.02 mph
**2nd** H. R. Davies/HRD
3hr 32m 42.2s/63.87 mph
**3rd** J. H. Simpson/AJS
3hr 33m 22.2s/63.67 mph
**Fastest lap** W. L. Handley/Rex-Acme
34m 23s/65.89 mph

**Lightweight 226½ miles**
**1st** E. Twemlow/New Imperial
3hr 55m 18s/57.74 mph
**2nd** C. W. Johnston/Cotton
3hr 58m 51s/56.88 mph
**3rd** K. Twemlow/New Imperial
4hr 3m 19s/55.83 mph
**Fastest lap** W. L. Handley/Rex-Acme
37m 36s/60.22 mph

**Ultra-lightweight 151 miles**
**1st** W. L. Handley/Rex-Acme
2hr 49m 27s/53.45 mph
**2nd** C. W. Johnston/Cotton
2hr 53m 54s/52.08 mph
**3rd** J. A. Porter/New Gerrard
2hr 57m 40s/50.98 mph
**Fastest lap** W. L. Handley/Rex-Acme
41m 52s/54.12 mph

**Sidecar 151 miles**
**1st** L. Parker/Douglas
2hr 44m 1.8s/55.22 mph
**2nd** A. E. Taylor/Norton
2hr 45m 58s/54.57 mph
**3rd** G. Grinton/Norton
2hr 46m 45s/54.31 mph
**Fastest lap** F. W. Dixon/Douglas
39m 36s/57.18 mph

## 1926

**Senior 264½ miles**
**1st** S. Woods/Norton
3hr 54m 39.8s/67.54 mph
**2nd** W. L. Handley/Rex-Acme
3hr 59m 0.4s/66.31 mph
**3rd** F. A. Longman/AJS
4hr 0m 3.4s/66.03 mph
**Fastest lap** J. H. Simpson/AJS
32m 9s/70.43 mph

**Junior 264½ miles**
**1st** A. Bennett/Velocette
3hr 57m 37s/66.70 mph
**2nd** J. H. Simpson/AJS
4hr 8m 2s/63.90 mph
**3rd** W. L. Handley/Rex-Acme
4hr 10m 6s/63.37 mph
**Fastest lap** A. Bennett/Velocette
32m 56s/68.75 mph

**Lightweight 264½ miles**
**1st** C. W. Johnston/Cotton
4hr 23m 16.4s/60.20 mph
**2nd** F. G. Morgan/Cotton
4hr 47m 30.4s/55.15 mph
**3rd** W. Colgan/Cotton
4hr 56m 5s/53.53 mph
**Fastest lap** P. Ghersi/Guzzi
35m 49s/63.12 mph

## 1927

**Senior 264½ miles**
**1st** A. Bennett/Norton
3hr 51m 42s/68.41 mph
**2nd** A. J. Guthrie/New Hudson
4hr 0m 4s/66.02 mph

**3rd** T. Simister/Triumph
4hr 1m 3s/65.75 mph
Fastest lap S. Woods/Norton
31m 54s/70.90 mph

**Junior 264¼ miles**
**1st** F. W. Dixon/HRD
3hr 55m 54s/67.19 mph
**2nd** H. J. Willis/Velocette
4hr 4m 39s/64.78 mph
**3rd** J. H. Simpson/AJS
4hr 4m 52s/64.33 mph
Fastest lap W. L. Handley/Rex-Acme
32m 44s/69.18 mph

**Lightweight 264¼ miles**
**1st** W. L. Handley/Rex-Acme
4hr 10m 22s/63.30 mph
**2nd** L. Archangeli/Guzzi
4hr 18m 52s/61.22 mph
**3rd** C. T. Ashby/OK-Supreme
4hr 19m 24s/61.10 mph
Fastest lap A. Bennett/OK-Supreme
35m 8s/64.45 mph

## 1928

**Senior 264¼ miles**
**1st** C. J. P. Dodson/Sunbeam
4hr 11m 40s/62.98 mph
**2nd** G. E. Rowley/AJS
4hr 18m 41s/61.27 mph
**3rd** T. L. Hatch/Scott
4hr 20m 18s/60.89 mph
Fastest lap J. H. Simpson/AJS
32m 20s/67.94 mph

**Junior 264¼ miles**
**1st** A. Bennett/Velocette
3hr 50m 52s/68.65 mph
**2nd** H. J. Willis/Velocette
3hr 56m 0s/67.16 mph
**3rd** K. Twemlow/DOT
4hr 8m 57s/63.67 mph
Fastest lap A. Bennett/Velocette
32m 13s/70.28 mph

**Lightweight 264¼ miles**
**1st** F. A. Longman/OK-Supreme
4hr 11m 59s/62.90 mph
**2nd** C. S. Barrow/Royal Enfield
4hr 29m 1s/58.92 mph
**3rd** E. Twemlow/DOT
4hr 29m 26s/58.83 mph
Fastest lap F. A. Longman/OK-Supreme
35m 8s/64.45 mph

## 1929

**Senior 264¼ miles**
**1st** C. J. P. Dodson/Sunbeam
3hr 39m 59s/72.05 mph
**2nd** A. Bennett/Sunbeam
3hr 44m 47s/70.51 mph
**3rd** H. G. Tyrell-Smith/Rudge
3hr 45m 37s/70.25 mph
Fastest lap C. J. P. Dodson/Sunbeam
30m 47s/73.55 mph

**Junior 264¼ miles**
**1st** F. G. Hicks/Velocette
3hr 47m 23s/69.71 mph
**2nd** W. L. Handley/AJS
3hr 48m 45s/69.29 mph
**3rd** A. Bennett/Velocette
3hr 49m 42s/68.97 mph
Fastest lap F. G. Hicks/Velocette
31m 55s/70.95 mph

**Lightweight 264¼ miles**
**1st** S. A. Crabtree/Excelsior
4hr 8m 10s/63.87 mph
**2nd** K. Twemlow/DOT
4hr 13m 25s/62.55 mph
**3rd** F. A. Longman/OK-Supreme
4hr 16m 33s/61.78 mph
Fastest lap P. Ghersi/Guzzi
35m 49s/63.12 mph

## 1930

**Senior 264¼ miles**
**1st** W. L. Handley/Rudge
3hr 33m 30s/74.24 mph
**2nd** G. W. Walker/Rudge
3hr 36m 49s/73.10 mph
**3rd** J. H. Simpson/Norton
3hr 38m 1s/72.70 mph
Fastest lap W. L. Handley/Rudge
29m 41s/76.28 mph

**Junior 264¼ miles**
**1st** H. G. Tyrell-Smith/Rudge
3hr 43m 0s/71.08 mph
**2nd** G. E. Nott/Rudge
3hr 43m 35s/70.89 mph
**3rd** G. W. Walker/Rudge
3hr 43m 58s/70.77 mph
Fastest lap G. E. Nott/Rudge
31m 21s/72.20 mph

**Lightweight 264¼ miles**
**1st** A. J. Guthrie/AJS
4hr 4m 56s/64.71 mph
**2nd** C. W. Johnston/OK-Supreme
4hr 7m 23s/64.07 mph
**3rd** C. S. Barrow/OK-Supreme
4hr 9m 27s/63.54 mph
Fastest lap W. L. Handley/Rex-Acme
33m 52s/66.86 mph

## 1931

**Senior 264¼ miles**
**1st** P. Hunt/Norton
3hr 23m 28s/77.90 mph
**2nd** A. J. Guthrie/Norton
3hr 24m 57s/77.34 mph
**3rd** S. Woods/Norton
3hr 27m 36s/76.35 mph
Fastest lap J. H. Simpson/Norton
28m 1s/80.82 mph

**Junior 264¼ miles**
**1st** P. Hunt/Norton
3hr 34m 21s/73.94 mph
**2nd** A. J. Guthrie/Norton
3hr 37m 26s/72.90 mph
**3rd** G. E. Nott/Rudge
3hr 39m 1s/72.37 mph
Fastest lap P. Hunt/Norton
30m 5s/75.27 mph

**Lightweight 264¼ miles**
**1st** G. W. Walker/Rudge
3hr 49m 47s/68.98 mph
**2nd** H. G. Tyrell-Smith/Rudge
3hr 52m 13s/68.26 mph
**3rd** E. A. Mellors/New Imperial
3hr 57m 8s/66.84 mph
Fastest lap G. E. Nott/Rudge
31m 34s/71.73 mph

## 1932

**Senior 264¼ miles**
**1st** S. Woods/Norton
3hr 19m 40s/79.38 mph

**2nd** A. J. Guthrie/Norton
3hr 21m 59s/78.47 mph
**3rd** J. H. Simpson/Norton
3hr 22m 13s/78.38 mph
Fastest lap J. H. Simpson/Norton
27m 47s/81.50 mph

**Junior 264¼ miles**
**1st** S. Woods/Norton
3hr 25m 25s/77.16 mph
**2nd** W. L. Handley/Rudge
3hr 27m 35s/76.36 mph
**3rd** H. G. Tyrell-Smith/Rudge
3hr 34m 8s/74.02 mph
Fastest lap S. Woods/Norton
28m 48s/78.62 mph

**Lightweight 264¼ miles**
**1st** L. H. Davenport/New Imperial
3hr 44m 53s/70.48 mph
**2nd** G. W. Walker/Rudge
3hr 46m 13s/70.07 mph
**3rd** W. L. Handley/Rudge
3hr 46m 53s/69.86 mph
Fastest lap W. L. Handley/Rudge
30m 34s/74.08 mph

## 1933

**Senior 264¼ miles**
**1st** S. Woods/Norton
3hr 15m 35s/81.04 mph
**2nd** J. H. Simpson/Norton
3hr 17m 7s/80.41 mph
**3rd** P. Hunt/Norton
3hr 17m 43s/80.16 mph
Fastest lap S. Woods/Norton
27m 22s/82.74 mph

**Junior 264¼ miles**
**1st** S. Woods/Norton
3hr 23m 0s/78.08 mph
**2nd** P. Hunt/Norton
3hr 23m 7s/78.03 mph
**3rd** A. J. Guthrie/Norton
3hr 26m 56s/76.59 mph
Fastest lap S. Woods/Norton
28m 35s/79.22mph

**Lightweight 264¼ miles**
**1st** S. Gleave/Excelsior
3hr 41m 23s/71.59mph
**2nd** C. J. P. Dodson/New Imperial
3hr 43m 43s/70.85 mph
**3rd** C. H. Manders/Rudge
3hr 49m 8s/69.17 mph
Fastest lap S. Gleave/Excelsior
31m 11s/72.62 mph

## 1934

**Senior 264¼ miles**
**1st** A. J. Guthrie/Norton
3hr 23m 10s/78.01 mph
**2nd** J. H. Simpson/Norton
3hr 30m 35s/75.27 mph
**3rd** W. F. Rusk/Velocette
3hr 36m 19s/73.27 mph
Fastest lap S. Woods/Husqvarna
28m 8s/80.49 mph

**Junior 264¼ miles**
**1st** A. J. Guthrie/Norton
3hr 20m 14s/79.16 mph
**2nd** J. H. Simpson/Norton
3hr 20m 23s/79.10 mph
**3rd** G. E. Nott/Husqvarna
3hr 26m 2s/76.93 mph
Fastest lap A. J. Guthrie/Norton
28m 16s/80.11 mph

**Lightweight 264¼ miles**
**1st** J. H. Simpson/Rudge
3hr 43m 50s/70.81 mph
**2nd** G. E. Nott/Rudge
3hr 47m 7s/69.76 mph
**3rd** G. W. Walker/Rudge
3hr 54m 13s/67.67 mph
**Fastest lap** J. H. Simpson/Rudge
30m 45s/73.64 mph

# 1935

**Senior 264¼ miles**
**1st** S. Woods/Guzzi
3hr 7m 10s/84.68 mph
**2nd** A. J. Guthrie/Norton
3hr 7m 14s/84.65 mph
**3rd** W. F. Rusk/Norton
3hr 9m 45s/83.53 mph
**Fastest lap** S. Woods/Guzzi
26m 10s/86.53 mph

**Junior 264¼ miles**
**1st** A. J. Guthrie/Norton
3hr 20m 16s/79.14 mph
**2nd** W. F. Rusk/Norton
3hr 21m 22s/78.71 mph
**3rd** J. H. White/Norton
3hr 22m 42s/78.19 mph
**Fastest lap** W. F. Rusk/Norton
28m 19s/79.96 mph

**Lightweight 264¼ miles**
**1st** S. Woods/Guzzi
3hr 41m 29s/71.56 mph
**2nd** H. G. Tyrell-Smith/Rudge
3hr 44m 17s/70.67 mph
**3rd** G. E. Nott/Rudge
3hr 48m 30s/69.37 mph
**Fastest lap** S. Woods/Guzzi
30m 31s/74.19 mph

# 1936

**Senior 264¼ miles**
**1st** A. J. Guthrie/Norton
3hr 4m 43s/85.80 mph
**2nd** S. Woods/Velocette
3hr 5m 1s/85.66 mph
**3rd** F. L. Frith/Norton
3hr 7m 35s/84.49 mph
**Fastest lap** S. Woods/Velocette
26m 2s/86.98 mph

**Junior 264¼ miles**
**1st** F. L. Frith/Norton
3hr 17m 46s/80.14 mph
**2nd** J. H. White/Norton
3hr 23m 16s/77.97 mph
**3rd** E. A. Mellors/Velocette
3hr 23m 25s/77.91 mph
**Fastest lap** F. L. Frith/Norton
27m 38s/81.94 mph

**Lightweight 264¼ miles**
**1st** A. R. Foster/New Imperial
3hr 33m 22s/74.28 mph
**2nd** H. G. Tyrell-Smith/Excelsior
3hr 38m 34s/72.51 mph
**3rd** A. Geiss/DKW
3hr 38m 37s/72.49 mph
**Fastest lap** S. Woods/DKW
29m 43s/76.20 mph

# 1937

**Senior 264¼ miles**
**1st** F. L. Frith/Norton
2hr 59m 41s/88.21 mph

**2nd** S. Woods/Velocette
2hr 59m 56s/88.09 mph
**3rd** J. H. White/Norton
3hr 8m 44s/83.97 mph
**Fastest lap** F. L. Frith/Norton
25m 5s/90.27 mph

**Junior 264¼ miles**
**1st** A. J. Guthrie/Norton
3hr 7m 42s/84.43 mph
**2nd** F. L. Frith/Norton
3hr 10m 17s/83.29 mph
**3rd** J. H. White/Norton
3hr 12m 0s/82.54 mph
**Fastest lap** F. L. Frith and
  A. J. Guthrie/Norton
26m 35s/85.18 mph

**Lightweight 264¼ miles**
**1st** O. Tenni/Guzzi
3hr 32m 6s/74.72 mph
**2nd** S. Wood/Excelsior
3hr 32m 43s/74.50 mph
**3rd** E. R. Thomas/DKW
3hr 36m 36s/73.17 mph
**Fastest lap** O. Tenni/Guzzi
29m 8s/77.72 mph

# 1938

**Senior 264¼ miles**
**1st** H. L. Daniell/Norton
2hr 57m 50.6s/89.11 mph
**2nd** S. Woods/Velocette
2hr 58m 5.8s/88.99 mph
**3rd** F. L. Frith/Norton
2hr 58m 7.4s/88.98 mph
**Fastest lap** H. L. Daniell/Norton
24m 52.6s/91.00 mph

**Junior 264¼ miles**
**1st** S. Woods/Velocette
3hr 8m 30s/84.08 mph
**2nd** E. A. Mellors/Velocette
3hr 12m 20s/82.40 mph
**3rd** F. L. Frith/Norton
3hr 12m 27s/82.35 mph
**Fastest lap** S. Woods/Velocette
26m 33s/85.30 mph

**Lightweight 264¼ miles**
**1st** E. Kluge/DKW
3hr 21m 56s/78.48 mph
**2nd** S. Wood/Excelsior
3hr 33m 5s/74.38 mph
**3rd** H. G. Tyrell-Smith/Excelsior
3hr 35m 16s/73.62 mph
**Fastest lap** E. Kluge/DKW
28m 11s/80.35 mph

# 1939

**Senior 264¼ miles**
**1st** G. Meier/BMW
2hr 57m 19s/89.38 mph
**2nd** J. M. West/BMW
2hr 59m 39s/88.22 mph
**3rd** F. L. Frith/Norton
3hr 0m 11s/87.96 mph
**Fastest lap** G. Meier/BMW
24m 57s/90.75 mph

**Junior 264¼ miles**
**1st** S. Woods/Velocette
3hr 10m 10s/83.19 mph
**2nd** H. L. Daniell/Norton
3hr 10m 38s/83.13 mph
**3rd** H. Fleischmann/DKW
3hr 12m 5s/82.51 mph

**Fastest lap** H. L. Daniell/Norton
26m 38s/85.05 mph

**Lightweight 264¼ miles**
**1st** E. A. Mellors/Benelli
3hr 33m 26s/74.25 mph
**2nd** E. Kluge/DKW
3hr 37m 11s/72.97 mph
**3rd** H. G. Tyrell-Smith/Excelsior
3hr 40m 23s/71.91 mph
**Fastest lap** S. Woods/Guzzi
28m 58s/78.16 mph

# 1947

**Senior 264¼ miles**
**1st** H. L. Daniell/Norton
3hr 11m 22.2s/82.81 mph
**2nd** A. J. Bell/Norton
3hr 11m 44.2s/82.66 mph
**3rd** P. J. Goodman/Velocette
3hr 12m 11s/82.46 mph
**Fastest lap** A. J. Bell/Norton and
  P. J. Goodman/Velocette
26m 56s/84.07 mph

**Junior 264¼ miles**
**1st** A. R. Foster/Velocette
3hr 17m 20s/80.31 mph
**2nd** M. D. Whitworth/Velocette
3hr 21m 26s/78.68 mph
**3rd** J. A. Weddell/Velocette
3hr 28m 7s/76.15 mph
**Fastest lap** M. D. Whitworth/Velocette
27m 45s/81.61 mph

**Lightweight 264¼ miles**
**1st** M. Barrington/Guzzi
3hr 36m 26.6s/73.22 mph
**2nd** M. Cann/Guzzi
3hr 37m 10.8s/72.97 mph
**3rd** B. Drinkwater/Excelsior
3hr 45m 57s/70.14 mph
**Fastest lap** M. Cann/Guzzi
30m 17s/74.78 mph

# 1948

**Senior 264¼ miles**
**1st** A. J. Bell/Norton
3hr 6m 31s/84.97 mph
**2nd** W. Doran/Norton
3hr 17m 16s/80.34 mph
**3rd** J. A. Weddell/Norton
3hr 19m 11.2s/79.56 mph
**Fastest lap** O. Tenni/Guzzi
25m 43s/88.06 mph

**Junior 264¼ miles**
**1st** F. L. Frith/Velocette
3hr 14m 33.6s/81.45 mph
**2nd** A. R. Foster/Velocette
3hr 19m 12.6s/79.55 mph
**3rd** A. J. Bell/Norton
3hr 20m 50.6s/78.91 mph
**Fastest lap** F. L. Frith/Velocette
27m 28s/82.45 mph

**Lightweight 264¼ miles**
**1st** M. Cann/Guzzi
3hr 30m 49s/75.18 mph
**2nd** R. H. Pike/Rudge
3hr 40m 33.4s/71.86 mph
**3rd** D. St J. Beasley/Excelsior
3hr 54m 9s/67.68 mph
**Fastest lap** M. Cann/Guzzi
29m 31s/76.72 mph

## 1949

**Senior 264¼ miles**
**1st** H. L. Daniell/Norton
3hr 2m 18.6s/86.93 mph
**2nd** R. St J. Lockett/Norton
3hr 3m 52.4s/86.19 mph
**3rd** E. Lyons/Velocette
3hr 5m 22s/85.50 mph
**Fastest lap** A. R. Foster/Guzzi
25m 14s/89.75 mph

**Junior 264¼ miles**
**1st** F. L. Frith/Velocette
3hr 10m 36s/83.15 mph
**2nd** E. Lyons/Velocette
3hr 11m 8s/82.92 mph
**3rd** A. J. Bell/Norton
3hr 11m 49s/82.62 mph
**Fastest lap** F. L. Frith/Velocette
26m 53s/84.23 mph

**Lightweight 264¼ miles**
**1st** M. Barrington/Guzzi
3hr 23m 13.2s/77.96 mph
**2nd** T. L. Wood/Guzzi
3hr 23m 25.8s/77.91 mph
**3rd** R. H. Pike/Rudge
3hr 37m 42.6s/72.79 mph
**Fastest lap** R. H. Dale and T. L. Wood/Guzzi
28m 9s/80.44 mph

## 1950

**Senior 264¼ miles**
**1st** G. E. Duke/Norton
2hr 51m 45.6s/92.27 mph
**2nd** A. J. Bell/Norton
2hr 54m 25.6s/90.86 mph
**3rd** R. St J. Lockett/Norton
2hr 55m 22.4s/90.37 mph
**Fastest lap** G. E. Duke/Norton
24m 16s/93.33 mph

**Junior 264¼ miles**
**1st** A. J. Bell/Norton
3hr 3m 35s/86.33 mph
**2nd** G. E. Duke/Norton
3hr 4m 52s/85.73 mph
**3rd** H. L. Daniell/Norton
3hr 7m 56s/84.33 mph
**Fastest lap** A. J. Bell/Norton
25m 56s/86.49 mph

**Lightweight 264¼ miles**
**1st** D. Ambrosini/Benelli
3hr 22m 58s/78.08 mph
**2nd** M. Cann/Guzzi
3hr 22m 58.2s/78.07 mph
**3rd** R. A. Mead/Velocette
3hr 29m 38s/75.60 mph
**Fastest lap** D. Ambrosini/Benelli
27m 59s/80.91 mph

## 1951

**Senior 264¼ miles**
**1st** G. E. Duke/Norton
2hr 48m 56.8s/93.83 mph
**2nd** W. Doran/AJS
2hr 53m 19.2s/91.44 mph
**3rd** W. McCandless/Norton
2hr 55m 27s/90.33 mph
**Fastest lap** G. E. Duke/Norton
23m 47s/95.22 mph

**Junior 264¼ miles**
**1st** G. E. Duke/Norton
2hr 56m 17.6s/89.90 mph
**2nd** R. St J. Lockett/Norton
2hr 59m 35s/88.25 mph
**3rd** J. Brett/Norton
3hr 0m 22.4s/87.87 mph
**Fastest lap** G. E. Duke/Norton
24m 47s/91.38 mph

**Lightweight 250 cc 151 miles**
**1st** T. L. Wood/Guzzi
1hr 51m 15.8s/81.39 mph
**2nd** D. Ambrosini/Benelli
1hr 51m 24.2/81.29 mph
**3rd** E. Lorenzetti/Guzzi
1hr 55m 0s/78.75 mph
**Fastest lap** F. K. Anderson/Guzzi
27m 3s/83.70 mph

**Lightweight 125 cc 75½ miles**
**1st** W. McCandless/Mondial
1hr 0m 30s/74.85 mph
**2nd** C. Ubbiali/Mondial
1hr 0m 52.4s/74.38 mph
**3rd** G. Leoni/Mondial
1hr 3m 19.8s/71.52 mph
**Fastest lap** W. McCandless/Mondial
30m 3s/75.34 mph

## 1952

**Senior 264¼ miles**
**1st** H. R. Armstrong/Norton
2hr 50m 28.4s/92.97 mph
**2nd** R. L. Graham/MV
2hr 50m 55s/92.72 mph
**3rd** W. R. Amm/Norton
2hr 51m 31.2s/92.40 mph
**Fastest lap** G. E. Duke/Norton
23m 52s/94.88 mph

**Junior 264¼ miles**
**1st** G. E. Duke/Norton
2hr 55m 30.6s/90.29 mph
**2nd** H. R. Armstrong/Norton
2hr 56m 57.8s/89.55 mph
**3rd** R. W. Coleman/AJS
2hr 58m 12.4s/88.93 mph
**Fastest lap** G. E. Duke/Norton
24m 53s/91.00 mph

**Lightweight 250 cc 151 miles**
**1st** F. K. Anderson/Guzzi
1hr 48m 8.6s/83.82 mph
**2nd** E. Lorenzetti/Guzzi
1hr 48m 40.8s/83.36 mph
**3rd** S. Lawton/Guzzi
1hr 49m 43.2s/82.54 mph
**Fastest lap** B. Ruffo/Guzzi
26m 42s/84.82 mph

**Lightweight 125 cc 113¼ miles**
**1st** C. C. Sandford/MV
1hr 29m 54.8s/75.54 mph
**2nd** C. Ubbiali/Mondial
1hr 31m 35s/74.16 mph
**3rd** A. L. Parry/Mondial
1hr 34m 2.6s/72.22 mph
**Fastest lap** C. C. Sandford/MV
29m 46s/76.07 mph

## 1953

**Senior 264¼ miles**
**1st** W. R. Amm/Norton
2hr 48m 51.8s/93.85 mph
**2nd** J. Brett/Norton
2hr 49m 3.8s/93.74 mph
**3rd** H. R. Armstrong/Gilera
2hr 49m 16.8s/93.62 mph
**Fastest lap** W. R. Amm/Norton
23m 15s/97.41 mph

**Junior 264¼ miles**
**1st** W. R. Amm/Norton
2hr 55m 5s/90.52 mph
**2nd** K. T. Kavanagh/Norton
2hr 55m 14.6s/90.44 mph
**3rd** F. K. Anderson/Guzzi
2hr 57m 40.6s/89.41 mph
**Fastest lap** W. R. Amm/Norton
24m 40s/91.82 mph

**Lightweight 250 cc 151 miles**
**1st** F. K. Anderson/Guzzi
1hr 46m 53s/84.73 mph
**2nd** W. Haas/NSU
1hr 47m 10s/84.52 mph
**3rd** S. Wunsche/DKW
1hr 51m 20s/81.34 mph
**Fastest lap** F. K. Anderson/Guzzi
26m 29s/85.52 mph

**Lightweight 125 cc 113¼ miles**
**1st** R. L. Graham/MV
1hr 27m 19s/77.79 mph
**2nd** W. Haas/NSU
1hr 28m 0s/77.18 mph
**3rd** C. C. Sandford/MV
1hr 28m 2s/77.15 mph
**Fastest lap** R. L. Graham/MV
28m 57s/78.21 mph

## 1954

**Senior 151 miles**
**1st** W. R. Amm/Norton
1hr 42m 46.8s/88.12 mph
**2nd** G. E. Duke/Gilera
1hr 43m 52.6s/87.19 mph
**3rd** J. Brett/Norton
1hr 45m 15.2s/86.04 mph
**Fastest lap** W. R. Amm/Norton
25m 12.8s/89.82 mph

**Junior 188¾ miles**
**1st** R. Coleman/AJS
2hr 3m 41.8s/91.51 mph
**2nd** D. Farrant/AJS
2hr 5m 34s/90.15 mph
**3rd** R. D. Keeler/Norton
2hr 5m 43.6s/90.03 mph
**Fastest lap** W. R. Amm/Norton
23m 56s/94.61 mph

**Lightweight 250 cc 113¼ miles**
**1st** W. Haas/NSU
1hr 14m 44.4s/90.88 mph
**2nd** R. Hollaus/NSU
1hr 15m 28.6s/89.99 mph
**3rd** H. R. Armstrong/NSU
1hr 15m 31.8s/89.92 mph
**Fastest lap** W. Haas/NSU
24m 49.4s/91.22 mph

**Lightweight 125 cc 114 miles**
**1st** R. Hollaus/NSU
1hr 33m 3.4s/69.57 mph
**2nd** C. Ubbiali/MV
1hr 33m 7.4s/69.52 mph
**3rd** C. C. Sandford/MV
1hr 37m 35.8s/66.35 mph
**Fastest lap** R. Hollaus/NSU
9m 3.4s/71.53 mph

**Sidecar 114 miles**
**1st** E. Oliver/Norton
1hr 34m 0.2s/68.87 mph
**2nd** F. Hillebrand/BMW

1hr 35m 56.2s/67.48 mph
3rd W. Noll/BMW
1hr 39m 16.4s/65.22 mph
Fastest lap E. Oliver/Norton
9m 9s/70.85 mph

## 1955

**Senior 264¼ miles**
1st G. E. Duke/Gilera
2hr 41m 49.8s/97.93 mph
2nd H. R. Armstrong/Gilera
2hr 43m 49s/96.74 mph
3rd K. T. Kavanagh/Guzzi
2hr 46m 32.8s/95.16 mph
Fastest lap G. E. Duke/Gilera
22m 39s/99.97 mph

**Junior 264¼ miles**
1st W. A. Lomas/Guzzi
2hr 51m 38.2s/92.33 mph
2nd R. McIntyre/Norton
2hr 52m 38.2s/91.79 mph
3rd C. C. Sandford/Guzzi
2hr 53m 2.2s/91.59 mph
Fastest lap W. A. Lomas/Guzzi
24m 3.2s/94.13 mph

**Lightweight 250 cc 97 miles**
1st W. A. Lomas/MV
1hr 21m 38.2s/71.37 mph
2nd C. C. Sandford/Guzzi
1hr 22m 29.4s/70.63 mph
3rd H. P. Muller/NSU
1hr 26m 21.6s/67.47 mph
Fastest lap W. A. Lomas/MV
8m 52s/73.13 mph

**Lightweight 125 cc 97 miles**
1st C. Ubbiali/MV
1hr 23m 38.2s/69.67 mph
2nd L. Taveri/MV
1hr 23m 40.2s/69.64 mph
3rd G. Lattanzi/Mondial
1hr 25m 53s/67.84 mph
Fastest lap C. Ubbiali/MV
9m 2.2s/71.65 mph

**Sidecar 97 miles**
1st W. Schneider/BMW
1hr 23m 14s/70.01 mph
2nd W. G. Boddice/Norton
1hr 26m 58.6s/66.99 mph
3rd P. V. Harris/Matchless
1hr 28m 22s/65.94 mph
Fastest lap W. Noll/BMW
9m 0s/71.93 mph

## 1956

**Senior 264¼ miles**
1st J. Surtees/MV
2hr 44m 5.8s/96.57 mph
2nd J. Hartle/Norton
2hr 45m 36.6s/95.69 mph
3rd J. Brett/Norton
2hr 46m 54.2s/94.96 mph
Fastest lap J. Surtees/MV
23m 9.4s/97.79 mph

**Junior 264¼ miles**
1st K. T. Kavanagh/Guzzi
2hr 57m 29.4s/89.29 mph
2nd D. Ennett/AJS
3hr 2m 7.4s/87.02 mph
3rd J. Hartle/Norton
3hr 4m 48.6s/85.75 mph
Fastest lap K. T. Kavanagh/Guzzi
24m 18.8s/93.15 mph

**Lightweight 250 cc 97 miles**
1st C. Ubbiali/MV
1hr 26m 54s/67.05 mph
2nd R. Colombo/MV
1hr 29m 2.6s/65.43 mph
3rd H. Baltisberger/NSU
1hr 29m 24.6s/65.17 mph
Fastest lap H. Baltisberger/NSU
9m 21.6s/69.17 mph

**Lightweight 125 cc 97 miles**
1st C. Ubbiali/MV
1hr 24m 16.8s/69.13 mph
2nd M. Cama/Montesa
1hr 29m 19.2s/65.24 mph
3rd F. Gonzalez/Montesa
1hr 35m 18.8s/61.13 mph
Fastest lap C. Ubbiali/MV
9m 9.8s/70.65 mph

**Sidecar 97 miles**
1st F. Hillebrand/BMW
1hr 23m 12.2s/70.03 mph
2nd P. V. Harris/Norton
1hr 24m 47.8s/68.71 mph
3rd W. Boddice/Norton
1hr 26m 19.2s/67.50 mph
Fastest lap W. Noll/BMW
9m 1.6s/71.12 mph

## 1957

**Senior 302 miles**
1st R. McIntyre/Gilera
3hr 2m 57s/98.99 mph
2nd J. Surtees/MV
3hr 5m 4.2s/97.86 mph
3rd R. N. Brown/Gilera
3hr 9m 2s/95.81 mph
Fastest lap R. McIntyre/Gilera
22m 23.2s/101.12 mph

**Junior 264¼ miles**
1st R. McIntyre/Gilera
2hr 46m 50.2s/94.99 mph
2nd K. Campbell/Guzzi
2hr 50m 29.8s/92.95 mph
3rd R. N. Brown/Gilera
2hr 51m 38.2s/92.34 mph
Fastest lap R. McIntyre/Gilera
23m 14.2s/97.42 mph

**Lightweight 250 cc 107¼ miles**
1st C. C. Sandford/Mondial
1hr 25m 25.4s/75.80 mph
2nd L. Taveri/MV
1hr 27m 12.4s/74.24 mph
3rd R. Colombo/MV
1hr 27m 21.8s/74.10 mph
Fastest lap T. Provini/Mondial
8m 18s/78 mph

**Lightweight 125 cc 107¼ miles**
1st T. Provini/Mondial
1hr 27m 51s/73.69 mph
2nd C. Ubbiali/MV
1hr 28m 25s/73.22 mph
3rd L. Taveri/MV
1hr 30m 37.8s/71.44 mph
Fastest lap T. Provini/Mondial
8m 41.8s/74.44 mph

**Sidecar 107¼ miles**
1st F. Hillebrand/BMW
1hr 30m 3.4s/71.89 mph
2nd W. Schneider/BMW
1hr 30m 54.8s/71.21 mph
3rd F. Camathias/BMW
1hr 32m 18.2s/70.14 mph

Fastest lap F. Hillebrand/BMW
8m 55.4s/72.55 mph

## 1958

**Senior 264¼ miles**
1st J. Surtees/MV
2hr 40m 39.8s/98.63 mph
2nd R. H. F. Anderson/Norton
2hr 46m 6s/95.40 mph
3rd R. N. Brown/Norton
2hr 46m 22.2s/95.25 mph
Fastest lap J. Surtees/MV
22m 30.4s/100.58 mph

**Junior 264¼ miles**
1st J. Surtees/MV
2hr 48m 38.4s/93.97 mph
2nd D. V. Chadwick/Norton
2hr 52m 50.6s/91.68 mph
3rd G. B. Tanner/Norton
2hr 53m 6.4s/91.54 mph
Fastest lap J. Surtees/MV
23m 43.4s/95.42 mph

**Lightweight 250 cc 107¼ miles**
1st T. Provini/MV
1hr 24m 12s/76.89 mph
2nd C. Ubbiali/MV
1hr 24m 20.2s/76.77 mph
3rd S. M. B. Hailwood/NSU
1hr 27m 7.8s/74.30 mph
Fastest lap T. Provini/MV
8m 6.2s/79.90 mph

**Lightweight 125 cc 107¼ miles**
1st C. Ubbiali/MV
1hr 28m 51.2s/72.86 mph
2nd R. Ferri/Ducati
1hr 29m 4.4s/72.68 mph
3rd D. V. Chadwick/Ducati
1hr 30m 27.8s/71.56 mph
Fastest lap C. Ubbiali/MV
8m 44s/74.13 mph

**Sidecar 107¼ miles**
1st W. Schneider/BMW
1hr 28m 40s/73.01 mph
2nd F. Camathias/BMW
1hr 29m 47.2s/72.11 mph
3rd J. Beeton/Norton
1hr 35m 34.8s/67.73 mph
Fastest lap W. Schneider/BMW
8m 44.4s/74.07 mph

## 1959

**Senior 264¼ miles**
1st J. Surtees/MV
3hr 0m 13.4s/87.94 mph
2nd A. King/Norton
3hr 5m 21s/85.50 mph
3rd R. Brown/Norton
3hr 10m 56.4s/83 mph
Fastest lap J. Surtees/MV
22m 22.4s/101.18 mph

**Junior 264¼ miles**
1st J. Surtees/MV
2hr 46m 8s/95.38 mph
2nd J. Hartle/MV
2hr 49m 12.2s/93.65 mph
3rd A. King/Norton
2hr 49m 22.6s/93.56 mph
Fastest lap J. Surtees/MV
23m 19.2s/97.08 mph

**Lightweight 250 cc 107¼ miles**
1st T. Provini/MV

1hr 23m 15.8s/77.77 mph
**2nd** C. Ubbiali/MV
1hr 23m 16.2s/77.76 mph
**3rd** D. Chadwick/MV
1hr 26m 52.4s/74.52 mph
**Fastest lap** T. Provini/MV
8m 4.2s/80.22 mph

**Lightweight 125 cc 107½ miles**
**1st** T. Provini/MV
1hr 27m 25.2s/74.06 mph
**2nd** L. Taveri/MZ
1hr 27m 32.6s/73.95 mph
**3rd** S. M. B. Hailwood/Ducati
1hr 29m 44s/72.15 mph
**Fastest lap** L. Taveri/MZ
8m 38s/74.99 mph

**Sidecar 107½ miles**
**1st** W. Schneider/BMW
1hr 29m 3.8s/72.69 mph
**2nd** F. Camathias/BMW
1hr 31m 6.8s/71.05 mph
**3rd** F. Scheidegger/BMW
1hr 33m 16.2s/69.42 mph
**Fastest lap** W. Schneider/BMW
8m 49.8s/73.32 mph

**Formula 1, 500 cc 113¼ miles**
**1st** R. McIntyre/Norton
1hr 9m 28.4s/97.77 mph
**2nd** R. N. Brown/Norton
1hr 10m 39s/96.14 mph
**3rd** T. Shepherd/Norton
1hr 10m 54.4s/95.79 mph
**Fastest lap** R. McIntyre/Norton
23m 1s/98.35 mph

**Formula 1, 350 cc 113¼ miles**
**1st** A. King/AJS
1hr 11m 45.4s/94.66 mph
**2nd** R. H. F. Anderson/Norton
1hr 12m 5.2s/94.23 mph
**3rd** S. M. B. Hailwood/Norton
1hr 12m 27.8s/93.73 mph
**Fastest lap** A. King/AJS
23m 45.6s/95.27 mph

## 1960

**Senior 226½ miles**
**1st** J. Surtees/MV
2hr 12m 35.2s/102.44 mph
**2nd** J. Hartle/MV
2hr 15m 14.2s/100.44 mph
**3rd** S. M. B. Hailwood/Norton
2hr 18m 11.6s/98.29 mph
**Fastest lap** J. Surtees/MV
21m 45s/104.08 mph

**Junior 226½ miles**
**1st** J. Hartle/MV
2hr 20m 28.8s/96.70 mph
**2nd** J. Surtees/MV
2hr 22m 24.2s/95.39 mph
**3rd** R. McIntyre/AJS
2hr 22m 50.4s/95.11 mph
**Fastest lap** J. Surtees/MV
22m 49.4s/99.20 mph

**Lightweight 250 cc 188¾ miles**
**1st** G. Hocking/MV
2hr 0m 53s/93.64 mph
**2nd** C. Ubbiali/MV
2hr 1m 33.4s/93.13 mph
**3rd** T. Provini/Morini
2hr 1m 44.6/92.98 mph
**Fastest lap** C. Ubbiali/MV
23m 42.8s/95.47 mph

**Lightweight 125 cc 113¼ miles**
**1st** C. Ubbiali/MV
1hr 19m 21.2s/85.60 mph
**2nd** G. Hocking/MV
1hr 19m 41s/85.24 mph
**3rd** L. Taveri/MV
1hr 21m 7.6s/83.72 mph
**Fastest lap** C. Ubbiali/MV
26m 17.6s/86.10 mph

**Sidecar 113¼ miles**
**1st** H. Fath/BMW
1hr 20m 45.8s/84.10 mph
**2nd** P. V. Harris/BMW
1hr 22m 10.2s/82.66 mph
**3rd** C. Freeman/Norton
1hr 28m 7.2s/77.08 mph
**Fastest lap** H. Fath/BMW
26m 23.4s/85.79 mph

## 1961

**Senior 226½ miles**
**1st** S. M. B. Hailwood/Norton
2hr 15m 2s/100.60 mph
**2nd** R. McIntyre/Norton
2hr 16m 56.4s/99.20 mph
**3rd** T. E. Phillis/Norton
2hr 17m 31.2s/98.78 mph
**Fastest lap** G. Hocking/MV
22m 3.6s/102.62 mph

**Junior 226½ miles**
**1st** P. W. Read/Norton
2hr 2m 50s/95.10 mph
**2nd** G. Hocking/MV
2hr 24m 7.8s/94.25 mph
**3rd** R. B. Rensen/Norton
2hr 25m 3s/93.65 mph
**Fastest lap** G. Hocking/MV
22m 41s/99.80 mph

**Lightweight 250 cc 188¾ miles**
**1st** S. M. B. Hailwood/Honda
1hr 55m 3.6s/98.38 mph
**2nd** T. E. Phillis/Honda
1hr 57m 14.4s/96.56 mph
**3rd** J. A. Redman/Honda
2hr 1m 36.2s/93.09 mph
**Fastest lap** R. McIntyre/Honda
22m 44s/99.58 mph

**Lightweight 125 cc 113¼ miles**
**1st** S. M. B. Hailwood/Honda
1hr 16m 58.6s/88.23 mph
**2nd** L. Taveri/Honda
1hr 17m 6s/88.09 mph
**3rd** T. E. Phillis/Honda
1hr 17m 49s/87.28 mph
**Fastest lap** L. Taveri/Honda
25m 35.6s/88.45 mph

**Sidecar 113¼ miles**
**1st** M. Deubel/BMW
1hr 17m 29.8s/87.65 mph
**2nd** F. Scheidegger/BMW
1hr 18m 2.6s/87.03 mph
**3rd** P. V. Harris/BMW
1hr 19m 40.4s/85.26 mph
**Fastest lap** M. Deubel/BMW
25m 44s/87.97 mph

## 1962

**Senior 226½ miles**
**1st** G. Hocking/MV Agusta
2hr 11m 13.4s/103.51 mph
**2nd** E. Boyce/Norton
2hr 21m 6.2s/96.27 mph
**3rd** F. J. Stevens/Norton
2hr 21m 9.4s/96.24 mph
**Fastest lap** G. Hocking/MV Agusta
21m 24.4s/105.75 mph

**Junior 226½ miles**
**1st** S. M. B. Hailwood/MV Agusta
2hr 16m 24.2s/99.59 mph
**2nd** G. Hocking/MV Agusta
2hr 16m 29.8s/99.52 mph
**3rd** F. Stastny/Jawa
2hr 23m 23.4s/94.74 mph
**Fastest lap** S. M. B. Hailwood/ MV Agusta
22m 17.2s/101.58 mph

**Lightweight 250 cc 226½ miles**
**1st** D. W. Minter/Honda
2hr 20m 30s/96.68 mph
**2nd** J. Redman/Honda
2hr 22m 23.6s/95.40 mph
**3rd** T. Phillis/Honda
2hr 26m 15.6s/92.87 mph
**Fastest lap** R. McIntyre/Honda
22m 51.2s/99.06 mph

**Lightweight 125 cc 113¼ miles**
**1st** L. Taveri/Honda
1hr 15m 34.2s/89.88 mph
**2nd** T. Robb/Honda
1hr 16m 40.6s/88.58 mph
**3rd** T. Phillis/Honda
1hr 16m 55s/88.30 mph
**Fastest lap** L. Taveri/Honda
25m 7s/90.13 mph

**Ultra-lightweight 50 cc 75½ miles**
**1st** E. Degner/Suzuki
1hr 0m 16.4s/75.12 mph
**2nd** L. Taveri/Honda
1hr 0m 34.4s/74.75 mph
**3rd** T. Robb/Honda
1hr 0m 47.6s/74.48 mph
**Fastest lap** E. Degner/Suzuki
29m 58.6s/75.52 mph

**Sidecar 113¼ miles**
**1st** C. Vincent/BSA
1hr 21m 16.4s/83.57 mph
**2nd** O. Kolle/BMW
1hr 21m 53.8s/82.93 mph
**3rd** C. J. Seeley/Matchless
1hr 22m 1.8s/82.90 mph
**Fastest lap** M. Deubel/BMW
24m 57.6s/90.70 mph

## 1963

**Senior 226½ miles**
**1st** S. M. B. Hailwood/MV
2hr 9m 48.4s/104.64 mph
**2nd** J. Hartle/Gilera
2hr 11m 1.8s/103.67 mph
**3rd** P. W. Read/Gilera
2hr 15m 42.2s/100.10 mph
**Fastest lap** S. M. B. Hailwood/MV
21m 16.4s/106.41 mph

**Junior 226½ miles**
**1st** J. Redman/Honda
2hr 23m 8.2s/94.91 mph
**2nd** J. Hartle/Gilera
2hr 29m 58.2s/90.58 mph
**3rd** F. Stastny/Jawa
2hr 31m 20.6s/89.76 mph
**Fastest lap** J. Redman/Honda
22m 20.8s/101.30 mph

**Lightweight 250 cc 226½ miles**
**1st** J. Redman/Honda
2hr 23m 13.2s/94.85 mph
**2nd** F. Ito/Yamaha
2hr 23m 40.4s/94.55 mph
**3rd** W. A. Smith/Honda
2hr 29m 5.2s/91.12 mph
**Fastest lap** J. Redman/Honda
23m 17s/97.23 mph

**Lightweight 125 cc 113¼ miles**
**1st** H. R. Anderson/Suzuki
1hr 16m 5s/89.27 mph
**2nd** F. G. Perris/Suzuki
1hr 17m 25s/87.74 mph
**3rd** E. Degner/Suzuki
1hr 17m 31.6s/87.61 mph
**Fastest lap** H. R. Anderson/Suzuki
24m 47.4s/91.23 mph

**Ultra-lightweight 50 cc 113¼ miles**
**1st** M. Itoh/Suzuki
1hr 26m 10.6s/78.81 mph
**2nd** H. R. Anderson/Suzuki
1hr 26m 37.4s/78.40 mph
**3rd** H. G. Anscheidt/Kreidler
1hr 26m 42s/78.33 mph
**Fastest lap** E. Degner/Suzuki
28m 37.2s/79.10 mph

**Sidecar 113¼ miles**
**1st** F. Camathias/FCS
1hr 16m 51s/88.38 mph
**2nd** F. Scheidegger/BMW
1hr 17m 29.2s/87.66 mph
**3rd** A. Birch/BMW
1hr 21m 17.6s/83.52 mph
**Fastest lap** F. Camathias/FCS
25m 19s/89.42 mph

## 1964

**Senior 226½ miles**
**1st** S. M. B. Hailwood/MV
2hr 14m 33.8s/100.95 mph
**2nd** D. Minter/Norton
2hr 17m 56.6s/98.47 mph
**3rd** F. Stevens/Matchless
2hr 20m 54.6s/96.40 mph
**Fastest lap** S. M. B. Hailwood/MV
22m 5s/102.51 mph

**Junior 226½ miles**
**1st** J. Redman/Honda
2hr 17m 55.4s/98.50 mph
**2nd** P.W. Read/AJS
2hr 25m 9.6s/93.58 mph
**3rd** M. A. Duff/AJS
2hr 25m 21.4s/93.46 mph
**Fastest lap** J. Redman/Honda
22m 28s/100.76 mph

**Lightweight 250 cc 226½ miles**
**1st** J. Redman/Honda
2hr 19m 23.6s/97.45 mph
**2nd** A. Shepherd/MZ
2hr 20m 4.6s/96.67 mph
**3rd** A. Pagani/Paton
2hr 37m 35.8s/86.20 mph
**Fastest lap** P. W. Read/Yamaha
22m 46.2s/99.42 mph

**Lightweight 125 cc 113¼ miles**
**1st** L. Taveri/Honda
1hr 13m 43s/92.14 mph
**2nd** J. Redman/Honda
1hr 13m 46s/92.08 mph
**3rd** R. Bryans/Honda
1hr 14m 28.2s/91.22 mph
**Fastest lap** L. Taveri/Honda
24m 12.2s/93.53 mph

**Ultra-lightweight 50 cc 113¼ miles**
**1st** H. R. Anderson/Suzuki
1hr 24m 13.4s/80.64 mph
**2nd** R. Bryans/Honda
1hr 25m 14.8s/79.68 mph
**3rd** I. Morishita/Suzuki
1hr 25m 15.4s/79.67 mph
**Fastest lap** H. R. Anderson/Suzuki
27m 54.2s/81.13 mph

**Sidecar 113¼ miles**
**1st** M. Deubel/BMW
1hr 16m 13s/89.12 mph
**2nd** C. Seeley/FCSB
1hr 18m 17.6s/86.76 mph
**3rd** G. Auerbacher/BMW
1hr 20m 26.2s/84.45 mph
**Fastest lap** M. Deubel/BMW
25m 15.4s/89.63 mph

## 1965

**Senior 226½ miles**
**1st** S. M. B. Hailwood/MV
2hr 28m 9s/91.69 mph
**2nd** J. Dunphy/Norton
2hr 30m 28.8s/90.28 mph
**3rd** M. Duff/Matchless
2hr 34m 12s/88.09 mph
**Fastest lap** S. M. B. Hailwood/MV
23m 48.2s/95.11 mph

**Junior 226½ miles**
**1st** J. Redman/Honda
2hr 14m 52.2s/100.72 mph
**2nd** P. W. Read/Yamaha
2hr 16m 44.4s/99.35 mph
**3rd** G. Agostini/MV
2hr 17m 53.4s/98.52 mph
**Fastest lap** S. M. B. Hailwood/MV
22m 0.6s/102.85 mph

**Lightweight 250 cc 226½ miles**
**1st** J. Redman/Honda
2hr 19m 45.8s/97.19 mph
**2nd** M. Duff/Yamaha
2hr 23m 26.4s/94.71 mph
**3rd** F. Perris/Suzuki
2hr 24m 32s/93.99 mph
**Fastest lap** J. Redman/Honda
22m 37s/100.09 mph

**Lightweight 125 cc 113¼ miles**
**1st** P. W. Read/Yamaha
1hr 12m 2.6s/94.28 mph
**2nd** L. Taveri/Honda
1hr 12m 8.4s/94.15 mph
**3rd** M. Duff/Yamaha
1hr 12m 23.6s/93.83 mph
**Fastest lap** H. R. Anderson/Suzuki
23m 34.6s/96.02 mph

**Ultra-lightweight 50 cc 113¼ miles**
**1st** L. Taveri/Honda
1hr 25m 15.6s/79.66 mph
**2nd** H. R. Anderson/Suzuki
1hr 26m 8.8s/78.85 mph
**3rd** E. Degner/Suzuki
1hr 28m 10s/77.04 mph
**Fastest lap** L. Taveri/Honda
28m 0.4s/80.83 mph

**Sidecar 113¼ miles**
**1st** M. Deubel/BMW
1hr 14m 59.8s/90.57 mph
**2nd** F. Scheidegger/BMW
1hr 15m 13.8s/89.11 mph
**3rd** G. Auerbacher/BMW
1hr 20m 26.2s/84.45 mph
**Fastest lap** M. Deubel/BMW
24m 39.6s/91.80 mph

## 1966

**Senior 226½ miles**
**1st** S. M. B. Hailwood/Honda
2hr 11m 44.8s/103.11 mph
**2nd** G. Agostini/MV
2hr 14m 22.6s/101.09 mph
**3rd** C. R. Conn/Norton
2hr 22m 26.8s/95.37 mph
**Fastest lap** S. M. B. Hailwood/Honda
21m 8.6s/107.07 mph

**Junior 226½ miles**
**1st** G. Agostini/MV
2hr 14m 40.4s/100.87 mph
**2nd** P. J. Williams/AJS
2hr 24m 46.6s/93.83 mph
**3rd** C. R. Conn/Norton
2hr 26m 45.4s/92.56 mph
**Fastest lap** G. Agostini/MV
21m 57.6s/103.09 mph

**Lightweight 250 cc 226½ miles**
**1st** S. M. B. Hailwood/Honda
2hr 13m 26s/101.79 mph
**2nd** L. S. Graham/Honda
2hr 19m 20s/97.49 mph
**3rd** P. G. Inchley/Villiers
2hr 28m 34.4s/91.43 mph
**Fastest lap** S. M. B. Hailwood/Honda
21m 42.4s/104.29 mph

**Lightweight 125 cc 113¼ miles**
**1st** W. Ivy/Yamaha
1hr 9m 32.8s/97.66 mph
**2nd** P. W. Read/Yamaha
1hr 10m 3.2s/96.96 mph
**3rd** H. R. Anderson/Suzuki
1hr 10m 9.2s/96.82 mph
**Fastest lap** W. Ivy/Yamaha
22m 58.2s/98.55 mph

**Ultra-lightweight 50 cc 113¼ miles**
**1st** R. Bryans/Honda
1hr 19m 17.2s/85.66 mph
**2nd** L. Taveri/Honda
1hr 20m 8.4s/84.74 mph
**3rd** H. R. Anderson/Suzuki
1hr 21m 41s/83.14 mph
**Fastest lap** R. Bryans/Honda
26m 10.2s/85.66 mph

**Sidecar 113¼ miles**
**1st** F. Scheidegger/BMW
1hr 14m 50s/90.76 mph
**2nd** M. Deubel/BMW
1hr 14m 50.8s/90.75 mph
**3rd** G. Auerbacher/BMW
1hr 16m 52.4s/88.35 mph
**Fastest lap** M. Deubel/BMW
24m 42.4s/91.63 mph

## 1967

**Senior 226½ miles**
**1st** S. M. B. Hailwood/Honda
2hr 8m 36.2s/105.62 mph
**2nd** P. J. Williams/Arter-Matchless
2hr 16m 20s/99.64 mph
**3rd** S. Spencer/Lancefield-Norton
2hr 17m 47.2s/98.59 mph
**Fastest lap** S. M. B. Hailwood/Honda
20m 48.8s/108.77 mph

**Junior 226½ miles**
**1st** S. M. B. Hailwood/Honda
2hr 9m 45.6s/104.68 mph
**2nd** G. Agostini/MV
2hr 12m 48.8s/102.28 mph
**3rd** D. Woodman/MZ
2hr 20m 53.6s/96.41 mph
**Fastest lap** S. M. B. Hailwood/Honda
21m 0.8s/107.73 mph

**Lightweight 250 cc 226½ miles**
**1st** S. M. B. Hailwood/Honda
2hr 11m 47.6s/103.07 mph
**2nd** P. W. Read/Yamaha
2hr 13m 6.4s/102.05 mph
**3rd** R. Bryans/Honda
2hr 16m 27s/99.55 mph
**Fastest lap** S. M. B. Hailwood/Honda
21m 39.8s/104.50 mph

**Lightweight 125 cc 113¼ miles**
**1st** P. W. Read/Yamaha
1hr 9m 40.8s/97.48 mph
**2nd** S. Graham/Suzuki
1hr 9m 44.2s/97.40 mph
**3rd** A. Motohashi/Yamaha
1hr 11m 49.6s/94.56 mph
**Fastest lap** P. W. Read/Yamaha
23m 0.8s/98.36 mph

**Ultra-lightweight 50 cc 113¼ miles**
**1st** S. Graham/Suzuki
1hr 21m 56.8s/82.89 mph
**2nd** H. G. Anscheidt/Suzuki
1hr 22m 58s/81.86 mph
**3rd** T. Robb/Suzuki
1hr 38m 2s/69.28 mph
**Fastest lap** S. Graham/Suzuki
26m 34.4s/85.19 mph

**Sidecar 113¼ miles**
**1st** S. Schauzu/BMW
1hr 14m 40.6s/90.96 mph
**2nd** K. Enders/BMW
1hr 14m 59.2s/90.58 mph
**3rd** C. Seeley/BMW
1hr 17m 15.6s/87.92 mph
**Fastest lap** G. Auerbacher/BMW
24m 41.2s/91.70 mph

**Production Machine Race
750 cc 113¼ miles**
**1st** J. Hartle/Triumph
1hr 9m 56.8s/97.10 mph
**2nd** P. Smart/Dunstall-Norton
1hr 11m 48s/94.60 mph
**3rd** A. J. Smith/BSA
1hr 15m 42s/89.73 mph
**Fastest lap** J. Hartle/Triumph
23m 7.8s/97.87 mph

**Production Machine Race
500 cc 113¼ miles**
**1st** N. Kelly/Velocette
1hr 15m 33.8s/89.89 mph
**2nd** K. Heckles/Velocette
1hr 16m 11.6s/89.15 mph
**3rd** D. J. Nixon/Triumph
1hr 19m 48s/85.11 mph
**Fastest lap** N. Kelly/Velocette
24m 52.6s/91.01 mph

**Production Machine Race
250 cc 113¼ miles**
**1st** W. A. Smith/Bultaco
1hr 16m 38.2s/88.63 mph
**2nd** T. Robb/Bultaco
1hr 16m 38.6s/88.62 mph
**3rd** B. Smith/Suzuki

1hr 18m 43.2s/86.29 mph
**Fastest lap** W. A. Smith/Bultaco
25m 19.4s/89.41 mph

# 1968

**Senior 226½ miles**
**1st** G. Agostini/MV
2hr 13m 39.4s/101.63 mph
**2nd** B. A. Ball/Seeley
2hr 22m 8.4s/95.57 mph
**3rd** B. J. Randle/Petty-Norton
2hr 22m 8.8s/95.56 mph
**Fastest lap** G. Agostini/MV
21m 34.8s/104.91 mph

**Junior 226½ miles**
**1st** G. Agostini/MV
2hr 9m 38.6s/104.78 mph
**2nd** R. Pasolini/Benelli
2hr 12m 19.6s/102.65 mph
**3rd** W. A. Smith/Honda
2hr 22m 58.6s/95.02 mph
**Fastest lap** G. Agostini/MV
21m 12.2s/106.77 mph

**Lightweight 250 cc 226½ miles**
**1st** W. D. Ivy/Yamaha
2hr 16m 24.8s/99.58 mph
**2nd** R. Pasolini/Benelli
2hr 18m 36.8s/98.00 mph
**3rd** H. Rosner/MZ
2hr 22m 56.4s/95.04 mph
**Fastest lap** W. D. Ivy/Yamaha
21m 27.4s/105.51 mph

**Lightweight 125 cc 113¼ miles**
**1st** P. W. Read/Yamaha
1hr 8m 31.4s/99.12 mph
**2nd** W. D. Ivy/Yamaha
1hr 9m 27.8s/97.78 mph
**3rd** K. Carruthers/Gates-Honda
1hr 18m 21.2s/86.69 mph
**Fastest lap** W. D. Ivy/Yamaha
22m 34s/100.32 mph

**Ultra-lightweight 50 cc 113¼ miles**
**1st** B. Smith/Derbi
1hr 33m 10.4s/72.90 mph
**2nd** C. M. Walpole/Honda
1hr 40m 59.6s/67.26 mph
**3rd** E. L. Griffiths/Honda
1hr 42m 36s/66.20 mph
**Fastest lap** B. Smith/Derbi
30m 46s/73.44 mph

**Sidecar 500 cc 113¼ miles**
**1st** S. Schauzu/BMW
1hr 14m 34.2s/91.09 mph
**2nd** J. Attenberger/BMW
1hr 15m 55.2s/89.47 mph
**3rd** H. Luthringshauser/BMW
1hr 17m 32.6s/87.60 mph
**Fastest lap** K. Enders/BMW
24m 0s/94.32 mph

**Sidecar 750 cc 113¼ miles**
**1st** T. Vinicombe/Kirby-BSA
1hr 19m 7.4s/85.85 mph
**2nd** N. Hanks/BSA
1hr 21m 44s/83.10 mph
**3rd** P. Brown/BSA
1hr 21m 48s/83.03 mph
**Fastest lap** C. Vincent/BSA
25m 25s/89.11 mph

**Production Machine Race
750 cc 113¼ miles**
**1st** R. Pickrell/Dunstall Norton

1hr 9m 13.2s/98.13 mph
**2nd** B. Nelson/Norton Atlas
1hr 11m 47.2s/94.62 mph
**3rd** A. J. Smith/BSA
1hr 12m 23.8s/93.82 mph
**Fastest lap** R. Pickrell/Dunstall Norton
22m 46.6s/99.39 mph

**Production Machine Race
500 cc 113¼ miles**
**1st** R. Knight/Triumph
1hr 15m 23.6s/90.09 mph
**2nd** J. Blanchard/Velocette
1hr 16m 41.2s/88.58 mph
**3rd** D. J. Nixon/Triumph
1hr 16m 44.4s/88.52 mph
**Fastest lap** R. Knight/Triumph
24m 52.2s/91.03 mph

**Production Machine Race
250 cc 113¼ miles**
**1st** T. E. Burgess/Ossa
1hr 17m 53.4s/87.21 mph
**2nd** G. E. Leigh/Bultaco
1hr 19m 41.8s/85.23 mph
**3rd** B. Smith/Thompson-Suzuki
1hr 19m 45s/85.17 mph
**Fastest lap** T. E. Burgess/Ossa
25m 45.4s/87.89 mph

# 1969

**Senior 226½ miles**
**1st** G. Agostini/MV
2hr 9m 40.2s/104.75 mph
**2nd** A. J. Barnett/Kirby-Metisse
2hr 18m 12.6s/98.28 mph
**3rd** T. Dickie/Kuhn-Seeley
2hr 18m 44.2s/97.92 mph
**Fastest lap** G. Agostini/MV
21m 18.4s/106.25 mph

**Junior 226½ miles**
**1st** G. Agostini/MV
2hr 13m 25.4s/101.81 mph
**2nd** B. Steenson/Aermacchi
2hr 23m 36.4s/94.60 mph
**3rd** J. Findlay/Beart-Aermacchi
2hr 24m 41.2s/93.89 mph
**Fastest lap** G. Agostini/MV
21m 46s/104 mph

**Lightweight 250 cc 226½ miles**
**1st** K. Carruthers/Benelli
2hr 21m 35.2s/95.95 mph
**2nd** F. Perris/Crooks-Suzuki
2hr 24m 59.4s/93.69 mph
**3rd** S. Herrero/Ossa
2hr 26m 21s/92.82 mph
**Fastest lap** K. Carruthers/Benelli
22m 51.8s/99.01 mph

**Lightweight 125 cc 113¼ miles**
**1st** D. A. Simmonds/Kawasaki
1hr 14m 34.6s/91.08 mph
**2nd** K. Carruthers/Aermacchi
1hr 20m 27.2s/84.43 mph
**3rd** R. J. Dickinson/Honda
1hr 21m 10.6s/83.67 mph
**Fastest lap** D. A. Simmonds/Kawasaki
24m 29s/92.46 mph

**Sidecar 500 cc 113¼ miles**
**1st** K. Enders/BMW
1hr 13m 27s/92.48 mph
**2nd** S. Schauzu/BMW
1hr 14m 39.4s/90.99 mph
**3rd** H. Fath/URS

149

1hr 15m 0s/90.56 mph
**Fastest lap** K. Enders/BMW
24m 27.8s/92.54 mph

**Sidecar 750 cc 113¼ miles**
**1st** S. Schauzu/BMW
1hr 15m 36.8s/89.83 mph
**2nd** P. Brown/BSA
1hr 19m 18.2s/85.65 mph
**3rd** L. W. Currie/LWC
1hr 23m 7.4s/81.72 mph
**Fastest lap** S. Schauzu/BMW
24m 35.4s/92.06 mph

**Production Machine Race
750 cc 113¼ miles**
**1st** M. Uphill/Triumph
1hr 7m 55.4s/99.99 mph
**2nd** P. Smart/Norton
1hr 8m 21.2s/99.37 mph
**3rd** D. Pendlebury/Triumph
1hr 10m 16.2s/96.66 mph
**Fastest lap** M. Uphill/Triumph
22m 33.2s/100.37 mph

**Production Machine Race
500 cc 113¼ miles**
**1st** W. G. Penny/Honda
1hr 17m 1.6s/88.18 mph
**2nd** R. L. Knight/Triumph
1hr 17m 30.4s/87.64 mph
**3rd** R. W. Baylie/Triumph
1hr 19m 4s/85.90 mph
**Fastest lap** T. Dunnell/Kawasaki
24m 55.2s/90.84 mph

**Production Machine Race
250 cc 113¼ miles**
**1st** A. M. Roger/Ducati
1hr 21m 3.8s/83.79 mph
**2nd** F. Whiteway/Suzuki
1hr 21m 33.4s/83.29 mph
**3rd** C. S. Mortimer/Ducati
1hr 22m 49.6s/82.01 mph
**Fastest lap** C. S. Mortimer/Ducati
26m 35.6s/85.13 mph

# 1970

**Senior 226½ miles**
**1st** G. Agostini/MV
2hr 13m 47.6s/101.52 mph
**2nd** P. J. Williams/Arter-Matchless
2hr 18m 57s/97.76 mph
**3rd** W. A. Smith/Kawasaki
2hr 21m 7.6s/96.26 mph
**Fastest lap** G. Agostini/MV
21m 30s/105.29 mph

**Junior 226½ miles**
**1st** G. Agostini/MV
2hr 13m 28.6s/101.77 mph
**2nd** A. Barnett/Aermacchi
2hr 18m 23.8s/98.16 mph
**3rd** P. Smart/Padgett-Yamaha
2hr 20m 8.8s/96.93 mph
**Fastest lap** G. Agostini/MV
21m 39s/104.56 mph

**Lightweight 250 cc 226½ miles**
**1st** K. Carruthers/Yamaha
2hr 21m 19.2s/96.13 mph
**2nd** R. Gould/Yamaha
2hr 24m 54s/93.75 mph
**3rd** G. Bartusch/MZ
2hr 26m 58.4s/92.43 mph
**Fastest lap** K. Carruthers/Yamaha
23m 5.4s/98.04 mph

**Lightweight 125 cc 113¼ miles**
**1st** D. Braun/Suzuki
1hr 16m 5s/89.27 mph
**2nd** B. Jansson/Maico
1hr 18m 28.4s/86.56 mph
**3rd** G. Bartusch/MZ
1hr 19m 2.8s/85.93 mph
**Fastest lap** D. Simmonds/Kawasaki
24m 52.2s/90.90 mph

**Sidecar 500 cc 113¼ miles**
**1st** K. Enders/BMW
1hr 13m 5.6s/92.93 mph
**2nd** S. Schauzu/BMW
1hr 14m 56.4s/90.64 mph
**3rd** H. Luthringshauser/BMW
1hr 16m 58s/88.25 mph
**Fastest lap** K. Enders/BMW
24m 8.2s/93.79 mph

**Sidecar 750 cc 113¼ miles**
**1st** S. Schauzu/BMW
1hr 15m 18s/90.20 mph
**2nd** P. Brown/BSA
1hr 19m 0.4s/85.97 mph
**3rd** E. Leece/LMS
1hr 23m 50.2s/81.02 mph
**Fastest lap** K. Enders/BMW
24m 30.6s/92.37 mph

**Production Machine Race
750 cc 188¾ miles**
**1st** M. Uphill/Triumph
1hr 55m 51s/97.71 mph
**2nd** P. J. Williams/Norton
1hr 55m 52.6s/97.69 mph
**3rd** R. Pickrell/Norton
1hr 58m 5.2s/95.86 mph
**Fastest lap** P. J. Williams/Norton
22m 38.4s/99.99 mph

**Production Machine Race
500 cc 188¾ miles**
**1st** F. Whiteway/Suzuki
2hr 5m 52s/89.94 mph
**2nd** G. Pantall/Triumph
2hr 7m 20s/88.90 mph
**3rd** R. Knight/Triumph
2hr 7m 20.4s/88.89 mph
**Fastest lap** F. Whiteway/Suzuki
24m 57s/90.75 mph

**Production Machine Race
250 cc 188¾ miles**
**1st** C. Mortimer/Ducati
2hr 13m 23.4s/84.87 mph
**2nd** J. Williams/Honda
2hr 13m 29s/84.80 mph
**3rd** S. Woods/Suzuki
2hr 14m 40.6s/84.06 mph
**Fastest lap** C. Mortimer/Ducati
26m 25.6s/86.71 mph

# 1971

**Senior 226½ miles**
**1st** G. Agostini/MV
2hr 12m 24.4s/102.59 mph
**2nd** P. J. Williams/Arter-Matchless
2hr 18m 3s/98.40 mph
**3rd** F. Perris/Suzuki
2hr 20m 45.4s/96.51 mph
**Fastest lap** G. Agostini/MV
21m 35.4s/104.86 mph

**Junior 188¾ miles**
**1st** A. Jefferies/Yamsel
2hr 5m 48.6s/89.98 mph
**2nd** G. Pantall/Padgett-Yamaha

2hr 6m 25s/89.55 mph
**3rd** W. Smith/Honda
2hr 7m 4.8s/89.09 mph
**Fastest lap** P. W. Read/Yamaha
22m 33.2s/100.37 mph

**Lightweight 250 cc 151 miles**
**1st** P. W. Read/Yamaha
1hr 32m 23.6s/98.02 mph
**2nd** B. Randle/Yamaha
1hr 34m 27.6s/95.87 mph
**3rd** A. Barnett/Yamaha
1hr 35m 2s/95.29 mph
**Fastest lap** P. W. Read/Yamaha
22m 37.2s/100.08 mph

**Lightweight 125 cc 113¼ miles**
**1st** C. Mortimer/Yamaha
1hr 20m 54s/83.96 mph
**2nd** B. Jansson/Maico
1hr 23m 43.6s/81.13 mph
**3rd** J. Kiddie/Honda
1hr 29m 12.2s/77.14 mph
**Fastest lap** C. Mortimer/Yamaha
26m 0.2s/87.05 mph

**Sidecar 500 cc 113¼ miles**
**1st** S. Schauzu/BMW
1hr 18m 47.8s/86.21 mph
**2nd** G. Auerbacher/BMW
1hr 18m 53.2s/86.10 mph
**3rd** A. Butscher/BMW
1hr 23m 32.6s/81.31 mph
**Fastest lap** G. Auerbacher/BMW
25m 56.2s/87.27 mph

**Sidecar 750 cc 113¼ miles**
**1st** G. Auerbacher/BMW
1hr 18m 12s/86.86 mph
**2nd** A. Sansum/Triumph
1hr 22m 20.2s/82.50 mph
**3rd** R. Williamson/WHB Weslake
1hr 22m 35s/82.25 mph
**Fastest lap** S. Schauzu/BMW
24m 13.6s/93.44 mph

**Production Machine Race
750 cc 151 miles**
**1st** R. Pickrell/Triumph
1hr 30m 30.2s/100.07 mph
**2nd** A. Jefferies/Triumph
1hr 32m 3s/98.38 mph
**3rd** R. Heath/BSA
1hr 33m 17.4s/97.08 mph
**Fastest lap** P. J. Williams/Norton
22m 24s/101.06 mph

**Production Machine Race
500 cc 151 miles**
**1st** J. Williams/Honda
1hr 39m 28.8s/91.04 mph
**2nd** G. Penny/Honda
1hr 41m 39.6s/89.09 mph
**3rd** A. Cooper/Suzuki
1hr 44m 32.8s/86.63 mph
**Fastest lap** J. Williams/Honda
24m 45.4s/91.45 mph

**Production Machine Race
250 cc 151 miles**
**1st** W. Smith/Honda
1hr 47m 43.6s/84.14 mph
**2nd** C. Williams/Yamaha
1hr 47m 52s/84.04 mph
**3rd** T. Robb/Honda
1hr 49m 47.6s/82.49 mph
**Fastest lap** C. Williams/Yamaha
26m 44.8s/84.64 mph

**Formula 750 113¼ miles**
**1st** A. Jefferies/Triumph
1hr 6m 2s/102.85 mph
**2nd** R. Pickrell/Triumph
1hr 6m 28s/102.18 mph
**3rd** P. J. Williams/Norton
1hr 7m 6.2s/101.22 mph
**Fastest lap** A. Jefferies/Triumph
21m 56s/103.21 mph

## 1972

**Senior 226½ miles**
**1st** G. Agostini/MV
2hr 10m 34.4s/104.02 mph
**2nd** A. Pagani/MV
2hr 18m 25.8s/98.13 mph
**3rd** M. Grant/Padgett-Kawasaki
2hr 20m 0s/97.03 mph
**Fastest lap** G. Agostini/MV
21m 28.8s/105.39 mph

**Junior 188¾ miles**
**1st** G. Agostini/MV
1hr 50m 56.8s/102.03 mph
**2nd** T. Rutter/Yamaha
1hr 55m 21.4s/98.13 mph
**3rd** M. Grant/Padgett-Yamaha
1hr 56m 1s/97.57 mph
**Fastest lap** G. Agostini/MV
21m 54.4s/103.34 mph

**Lightweight 250 cc 151 miles**
**1st** P. W. Read/Yamaha
1hr 30m 51.2s/99.68 mph
**2nd** R. Gould/Yamaha
1hr 32m 19.6s/98.09 mph
**3rd** J. Williams/Yamaha
1hr 33m 16.4s/97.09 mph
**Fastest lap** P. W. Read/Yamaha
22m 30s/100.61 mph

**Lightweight 125 cc 113¼ miles**
**1st** C. Mortimer/Yamaha
1hr 17m 38.2s/87.49 mph
**2nd** C. Williams/Yamaha
1hr 24m 23s/80.49 mph
**3rd** B. Rae/Maico
1hr 25m 39.8s/79.29 mph
**Fastest lap** C. Mortimer/Yamaha
24m 59.6s/90.58 mph

**Sidecar 500 cc 113¼ miles**
**1st** S. Schauzu/BMW
1hr 13m 57.2s/91.85 mph
**2nd** H. Luthringshauser/BMW
1hr 14m 4.6s/91.70 mph
**3rd** G. Boret/Renwick-Konig
1hr 20m 27.4s/84.43 mph
**Fastest lap** H. Luthringshauser/BMW
24m 28s/92.53 mph

**Sidecar 750 cc 113¼ miles**
**1st** S. Schauzu/BMW
1hr 14m 40s/90.97 mph
**2nd** A. J. Sansum/Quaife-Triumph
1hr 17m 24s/87.76 mph
**3rd** J. L. Barker/Devimead-BSA
1hr 18m 41.6s/86.32 mph
**Fastest lap** S. Schauzu/BMW
24m 47.2s/91.33 mph

**Production Machine Race**
**750 cc 151 miles**
**1st** R. Pickrell/Triumph
1hr 30m 34s/100 mph
**2nd** P. J. Williams/Norton
1hr 33m 48.8s/96.53 mph
**3rd** D. Nixon/Triumph
1hr 36m 18.4s/94.04 mph
**Fastest lap** R. Pickrell/Triumph
22m 16.8s/101.61 mph

**Production Machine Race**
**500 cc 151 miles**
**1st** S. Woods/Suzuki
1hr 38m 13.8s/92.20 mph
**2nd** R. Bowler/Triumph
1hr 38m 20.6s/92.09 mph
**3rd** W. A. Smith/Honda
1hr 46m 8s/91.16 mph
**Fastest lap** S. Woods/Suzuki
24m 11s/93.61 mph

**Production Machine Race**
**250 cc 151 miles**
**1st** J. Williams/Honda
1hr 46m 8.8s/85.32 mph
**2nd** C. Williams/Yamaha
1hr 47m 50.2s/84.06 mph
**3rd** E. Roberts/Suzuki
1hr 48m 56.4s/83.14 mph
**Fastest lap** J. Williams/Honda
26m 24.4s/85.73 mph

**Formula 750 188¾ miles**
**1st** R. Pickrell/Triumph
1hr 48m 36s/104.23 mph
**2nd** A. Jefferies/Triumph
1hr 49m 24.8s/103.46 mph
**3rd** J. Findlay/Suzuki
1hr 55m 7.4s/98.33 mph
**Fastest lap** R. Pickrell/Triumph
21m 25.2s/105.68 mph

## 1973

**Senior 226½ miles**
**1st** J. Findlay/Suzuki
2hr 13m 45.2s/101.55 mph
**2nd** P. J. Williams/Arter-Matchless
2hr 14m 59.4s/100.62 mph
**3rd** C. Sanby/Hi-Tac-Suzuki
2hr 15m 27.6s/100.27 mph
**Fastest lap** M. Grant/Yamaha
21m 40.8s/104.41 mph

**Junior 188¾ miles**
**1st** T. Rutter/Yamaha
1hr 50m 58.8s/101.99 mph
**2nd** K. Huggett/Dugdale-Yamaha
1hr 52m 31.6s/100.58 mph
**3rd** J. Williams/Yamaha
1hr 52m 49.4s/100.32 mph
**Fastest lap** T. Rutter/Yamaha
21m 43.2s/104.22 mph

**Lightweight 250 cc 151 miles**
**1st** C. Williams/Johnson-Yamaha
1hr 30m 30s/100.05 mph
**2nd** J. Williams/Yamaha
1hr 30m 54.6s/99.60 mph
**3rd** W. Rae/Padgett-Yamaha
1hr 31m 35.4s/98.86 mph
**Fastest lap** C. Williams/
Johnson-Yamaha
22m 8.4s/102.24 mph

**Lightweight 125 cc 113¼ miles**
**1st** T. Robb/Danfay-Yamaha
1hr 16m 23.6s/88.90 mph
**2nd** J. Kostwinder/Yamaha
1hr 17m 21.6s/87.79 mph
**3rd** N. Tuxworth/Yamaha
1hr 18m 27.2s/86.56 mph
**Fastest lap** T. Robb/Danfay-Yamaha
25m 22s/89.24 mph

**Sidecar 500 cc 113¼ miles**
**1st** K. Enders/BMW
1hr 11m 32.4s/94.93 mph
**2nd** S. Schauzu/BMW
1hr 14m 18.2s/91.40 mph
**3rd** R. Steinhausen/Konig
1hr 15m 35.4s/89.94 mph
**Fastest lap** K. Enders/BMW
23m 46.4s/95.25 mph

**Sidecar 750 cc 113¼miles**
**1st** K. Enders/BMW
1hr 13m 1s/93.01 mph
**2nd** S. Schauzu/BMW
1hr 14m 2.4s/91.72 mph
**3rd** J. Brandon/JCLS-Honda
1hr 20m 8s/84.75 mph
**Fastest lap** K. Enders/BMW
23m 22.2s/96.86 mph

**Production Machine Race**
**750 cc 151 miles**
**1st** A. Jefferies/Triumph
1hr 34m 41.6s/95.62 mph
**2nd** J. Williams/Triumph
1hr 35m 24.8s/94.90 mph
**3rd** D. Nixon/Triumph
1hr 38m 53.6s/91.56 mph
**Fastest lap** P. J. Williams/Norton
22m 31.2s/100.52 mph

**Production Machine Race**
**500 cc 151 miles**
**1st** W. Smith/Honda
1hr 42m 47s/88.10 mph
**2nd** S. Woods/Suzuki
1hr 42m 55.2s/87.98 mph
**3rd** K. Martin/Kawasaki
1hr 43m 2.8s/87.87 mph
**Fastest lap** S. Woods/Suzuki
23m 58.2s/94.44 mph

**Production Machine Race**
**250 cc 151 miles**
**1st** C. Williams/Yamaha
1hr 50m 45s/81.76 mph
**2nd** E. Roberts/Yamaha
1hr 51m 27s/81.24 mph
**3rd** T. Robb/Honda
1hr 53m 5.8s/80.06 mph
**Fastest lap** E. Roberts/Yamaha
26m 55.8s/84.06 mph

**Formula 750 188¾ miles**
**1st** P. J. Williams/Norton
1hr 47m 19.2s/105.47 mph
**2nd** M. Grant/Norton
1hr 50m 21.6s/102.56 mph
**3rd** A. Jefferies/Triumph
1hr 50m 55.2s/102.04 mph
**Fastest lap** P. J. Williams/Norton
21m 6.2s/107.27 mph

## 1974

**Senior 188¾ miles**
**1st** P. Carpenter/Yamaha
1hr 56m 41.6s/96.99 mph
**2nd** C. Williams/Dugdale-Yamaha
1hr 57m 31.6s/96.31 mph
**3rd** T. Rutter/Yamaha
1hr 59m 57.4s/94.35 mph
**Fastest lap** C. Williams/
Dugdale-Yamaha
22m 12.6s/101.92 mph

**Junior 188¾ miles**
**1st** T. Rutter/Yamaha
1hr 48m 22.2s/104.44 mph
**2nd** M. Grant/Yamaha

1hr 50m 6.2s/102.80 mph
**3rd** P. Cott/Yamaha
1hr 51m 47s/101.25 mph
**Fastest lap** C. Mortimer/Yamaha
21m 16.6s/106.39 mph

**Lightweight 250 cc 151 miles**
**1st** C. Williams/Dugdale-Yamaha
1hr 36m 9.8s/94.16 mph
**2nd** M. Grant/Yamaha
1hr 37m 9.2s/93.20 mph
**3rd** C. Mortimer/Danfay-Yamaha
1hr 37m 31.2s/92.85 mph
**Fastest lap** M. Grant/Yamaha
23m 8s/97.85 mph

**Lightweight 125 cc 113¼ miles**
**1st** C. Horton/Yamaha
1hr 16m 47s/88.44 mph
**2nd** I. Hodgkinson/Granby-Yamaha
1hr 17m 27s/87.68 mph
**3rd** T. Herron/Yamaha
1hr 18m 8.6s/86.91 mph
**Fastest lap** A. Hockley/
   Granby-Yamaha
25m 29.8s/88.78 mph

**Sidecar 500 113¼ miles**
**1st** H. Luthringshauser/BMW
1hr 13m 36.2s/92.27 mph

**2nd** G. O'Dell/Konig
1hr 18m 46.4s/86.21 mph
**3rd** M. Hobson/Hamilton-Yamaha
1hr 19m 35s/85.33 mph
**Fastest lap** J. Gawley/Konig
24m 14.8s/93.36 mph

**Sidecar 750 cc 113¼ miles**
**1st** S. Schauzu/BMW
1hr 10m 18.4s/96.59 mph
**2nd** H. Luthringshauser/BMW
1hr 13m 52.2s/91.93 mph
**3rd** M. Horspole/Bingham-Weslake
1hr 16m 30.6s/88.76 mph
**Fastest lap** R. Steinhausen/Konig
23m 3.4s/98.18 mph

**Production Machine Race
1,000 cc 151 miles**
**1st** M. Grant/Triumph
1hr 30m 48s/99.72 mph
**2nd** H. O. Butenuth/BMW
1hr 32m 41s/97.70 mph
**3rd** H. Dahne/BMW
1hr 33m 20.6s/97.01 mph
**Fastest lap** M. Grant/Triumph
22m 28.2s/100.74 mph

**Production Machine Race
500 cc 151 miles**
**1st** K. Martin/Kawasaki

1hr 36m 28.6s/93.85 mph
**2nd** A. Rogers/Triumph
1hr 36m 58s/93.38 mph
**3rd** P. Tickle/Ducati
1hr 38m 14.4s/92.17 mph
**Fastest lap** K. Martin/Kawasaki
23m 46.6s/95.21 mph

**Production Machine Race
250 cc 151 miles**
**1st** M. Sharpe/Yamaha
1hr 44m 9.2s/86.94 mph
**2nd** E. Roberts/Yamaha
1hr 44m 11.6s/86.90 mph
**3rd** B. Rae/Suzuki
1hr 45m 22.6s/85.93 mph
**Fastest lap** E. Roberts/Yamaha
25m 35s/88.48 mph

**Formula 750 262½ miles**
**1st** C. Mortimer/Yamaha
2hr 15m 7.2s/100.52 mph
**2nd** C. Williams/Dugdale-Yamaha
2hr 15m 15.8s/100.41 mph
**3rd** T. Rutter/Yamaha
2hr 15m 42.6s/100.08 mph
**Fastest lap** C. Williams/
   Dugdale-Yamaha
21m 14s/106.61 mph